D1156600

INFANTRY WEAPONS
OF WORLD WAR II

COBBATON COMBAT COLLECTION

Telephone: 01769 540740
Fax: 01769 540141
Website: www.cobbatoncombat.co.uk
Email: info@cobbatoncombat.co.uk

Set in the North Devon countryside seven miles southeast of Barnstaple, the Cobbaton Combat Collection is a unique collection of wartime material from World War I to the Gulf. This private museum is the result of one man's lifetime of collecting anything military. It has vehicles—tanks, trucks, and artillery—plus thousands of smaller items, from mess tins to machine guns. The civilian aspects of war are also covered: the Home Front section has National Fire Service and Bomb Disposal vehicles, Home Guard weaponry, Air Raid warning instructions, ration books, and gas masks.

A sizeable shop sells militaria, new and used combat clothing and uniforms, badges, deactivated guns, toys, souvenirs, and more. A NAAFI canteen truck provides hot and cold drinks and snacks during the main season.

Late production Smith & Wesson .38/200 revolver
(see pages 48-49).

INFANTRY WEAPONS OF WORLD WAR II

Jan Suermondt

This edition published in 2012 by
CHARTWELL BOOKS, INC.
A division of Book Sales, Inc.
276 Fifth Avenue, Suite 206
New York, NY 10001
USA

© 2004 Greene Media

All rights reserved. No part of this book may be reproduced or transmitted in any form or by any means electronic or mechanical, including photo-copying, recording or by any information storage and retrieval system, without permission in writing from the publishers, except by the reviewer who may quote brief passages in a critical article or review to be printed in a magazine or newspaper, or electronically transmitted on radio or television.

ISBN: 978-0-7858-2931-7

Printed in China

Cover design by Tom Nelsen
Edited by Don Gulbrandsen

Achnowledgments
I'd like to thank the following for their major contributions: Preston and Tim Isaacs at the Cobbaton Collection in Devon; Simon Forty, Rob Miller, and Otis Clay for their help during the photo shoots; Simon Clay for the professional photography.

Photographs
All the photographs in this book were taken by Simon Clay for Greene Media Publishing except the following by Jeremy Flack—pages 8 (below), 9 (below left), 12, 28 (below left), 32, 37 (top), 41 (bottom), 42, 44 (left), 45 (bottom), 58 (right), 59, 65, 66 (both), 67 (center), 71 (both), 74, 75, 82 (bottom), 83 (top), 93 (top), 109 (top), 121, 243 (top). The photographs on pages 15 (below right), 73 (all), 154 and the artwork on pages 31, 33, 81, 233, 243 (bottom center and right), 245 (right), 246, 247 are by the author.

A Note on Collector Values

Values are provided only to give collectors a rough idea of what these weapons might command on the secondary market. The ranges refer to commonly encountered, original World War II-era manufactured or used items, with all parts intact but no accessories, and in good to excellent condition. Establishing authenticity and values for these items can be quite complicated. Some of the firearms have numerous variations, while other models have been the target of knock-off artists that have manufactured cheap replicas sold to unwitting buyers as the real thing. Collectors are urged to work with only reputable dealers and to consult with a certified appraiser before entering into any transaction.

The pricing is based on information first published in the *Standard Catalog of Military Firearms 2nd Edition* (Krause Publications 2003) and is only a guide and not as an absolute valuation. Market prices vary regularly and any publication becomes out of date quickly. Readers who want up to date prices are strongly encouraged to refer to the latest edition of this resource, which covers many more variations of weapons and offers pricing for several conditions.

The realm of Class III (NFA) weapons is extremely complicated. The values provided refer to pre-1968 weapons manufactured or used during the WWII era and possessing the appropriate legal paperwork. In effect, the buyer is obtaining both the weapon and the grandfathered paperwork, which has considerable value on the secondary market. For more information on Class III weapons, and pricing for different variants, collectors are again referred to the *Standard Catalog of Military Firearrms*. And, more than ever, buyers and sellers are encouraged to work only with reputable, knowledgeable dealers able to provide a reference list of satisfied customers.

Contents

Introduction

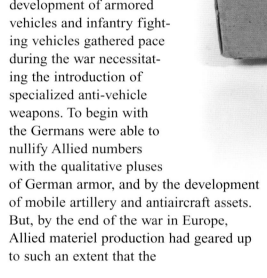

The development of the infantry weapons used at the start of World War II often dates back as far as the 1880s. However, the changes in the use of weapons in the five years of war saw huge transformations—particularly to antitank and assault weapons—and laid the foundations for most of the weapons in service around the world today.

The most serious threat likely to have been encountered by an infantryman in the 1880s was concentrated volley fire from well-drilled troops, armed with bolt-action rifles. World War I saw the first large-scale use of machine guns in the fire-support role and World War II saw the widespread tactical use of automatic weapons in the offensive role: first at squad level with light machine guns and then, increasingly, by individual soldiers with the proliferation of submachine guns and, later, more sophisticated assault rifles.

Technologically, too, this was a period of dramatic change, not only to infantry weapons themselves but also other areas of warfare. Advances in radio equipment enabled the execution of the closely integrated combined-arms operations that were first demonstrated by the Germans with their *Blitzkrieg* tactics and later adopted by all sides. The development of armored vehicles and infantry fighting vehicles gathered pace during the war necessitating the introduction of specialized anti-vehicle weapons. To begin with the Germans were able to nullify Allied numbers with the qualitative pluses of German armor, and by the development of mobile artillery and antiaircraft assets. But, by the end of the war in Europe, Allied materiel production had geared up to such an extent that the

battlefield was dominated by its airpower and German vehicles were all too often knocked out by Allied fighter-bombers before they reached the front. This hastened the development of German infantry antitank weapons such as the *Panzerschreck* and *Panzerfaust* that had been initiated by the Allied PIAT and Bazooka—but only the Germans succeeded in trialing a shoulder-fired antiaircraft weapon. Called the *Fliegerfaust*, it was a multibarreled device that fired a salvo of rockets into the path of a low-flying aircraft. Each warhead was equipped with a proximity fuse and was sufficient to bring down a fighter-bomber. How successful the weapon would have been remains unknown because the end of the war prevented its introduction, but it does, nonetheless, represent a milestone as the first shoulder-fired surface-to-air missile.

World War II was, like no other, a war of industry. The development of many weapons during the war follows a path of simplification as complex shapes and mechanisms were adapted to speed up production when it became apparent that far more weapons would be needed than any of the combatants realized when the war began. This race for production shows quite clearly in many of the weapons used during the war. Compare, for example, the prewar Thompson submachine gun with the later M3. The Thompson's shaped wooden stock and handgrip and expensive mechanism had to be machined from solid metal—a time-consuming and expensive task. The M3, however, was designed for wartime production and constructed largely from steel pressings, stamped out by the thousand in car factories.

Of all the main combatants, Japan was at a disadvantage from the start because the industrialization of what had been a feudal agrarian economy began only at the end of the nineteenth century. The lack of experience showed in the poor design and low quality of many Japanese weapons, and their inability to produce weapons in anything near the quantity required. Germany possessed a large well-established industrial base and was the technological equal, if not better, of any country but in the end was swamped by the vast combined industrial output of Soviet Russia and the United States.

This book traces the developments outlined in this introduction, showing how infantry weapons changed over the period. The photographs are of weapons from the extensive Cobbaton Collection and have been chosen to show the wide variety that were used during World War II.

HANDGUNS

In purely military terms, the handgun is a surprisingly ineffective weapon. It requires a great deal of training and practice to use accurately—even at short range—and even if used accurately, it does not offer the stopping power of a high-velocity round. Handguns are also costly and time-consuming to produce in comparison to other, often more effective, weapons. On the positive side, however, it is compact and easily carried and because of this fulfills a number of significant roles: personal protection, clandestine operations, signaling, and as a symbol of authority.

PERSONAL PROTECTION

For a great many service personnel, especially artillery troops, vehicle crews, and support personnel, it was simply impractical to carry a weapon as bulky as a rifle. While many of these troops spent much of their time either under armor protection or behind their own lines, nevertheless they often came under attack—from special forces, partisans, resistance fighters, or the main enemy troops if the front were fluid enough. In these situations handguns were the only real option. Purely defensive, often never actually fired in anger, the handguns provided a degree of confidence in a hostile environment.

SPECIAL FORCES

The one arena where the pistol was used as an offensive weapon was special operations. The very nature of the forces involved provided the opportunity for the amount of training and practice necessary to achieve a high level of proficiency and also required the use of compact weapons that could easily be concealed. The relatively small number of troops involved also meant that special equipment could be produced and used. Certainly the majority of instances where pistols were used successfully as offensive weapons involved commando units or resistance organizations.

SIGNALING

A specialized form of handgun, signaling or flare pistols were used by every combatant nation in many roles—from search and rescue through battlefield recognition aids. They were sturdily built and, in the main, were of at least a one-inch caliber.

SYMBOL OF AUTHORITY

It is no coincidence that officers carried pistols and, indeed, troops serving in occupation forces were rarely seen without sidearms. In both cases the pistol served largely as a symbol of authority without the overt threat of a larger-caliber weapon.

TOP Luger Artillery Model 1917. See page 40–41.

LEFT The standard British flare pistol of World War II, the Signal Pistol No. 1 Mk. V. Compare with the Mk. I version (see page 28).

LEFT Colt M1911A1 automatic. See pages 14–15.

BELOW LEFT Ceska Zbrojovka vz27 automatic pistol. See pages 18–19.

BELOW Typical mechanism of a solid-frame revolver where the cylinder is swung out for loading and reloading. The alternative—the top break—is well-illustrated on page 21.

Beretta Model 1934 pistol

Caliber: 9 mm short (.38 ACP)
Length: 6in (152mm)
Weight: 1lb 7.5oz (690gm) unloaded
Barrel: 3.75in (94mm) long, four grooves, right-hand twist
Feed system: Seven-round detachable box magazine
System of operation: Blowback
Manufacturer: P. Beretta, Gardone, Italy
Values: $200–$600

The firm of Pietro Beretta was founded as far back as 1680, and first entered the modern military pistol field with the production of a simple and reliable blowback pistol in 1915. In that year numbers of a new pistol design were produced to meet the requirements of the expanding Italian Army, and although the *Pistola Automatica Beretta modello 1915* (M1915) was widely used, it was never officially accepted as a service model. These original Berettas had a caliber of 7.65mm (0.301in), although a few were made in 9mm (0.38in). The 9mm cartridge fired by this weapon is not the universally accepted Parabellum but the 9mm short, known also as the 0.380 automatic cartridge, the cartridge that was to be the ammunition for the later 1934 model. This had a light bullet traveling at low velocity and delivered only about 160ft/lb of energy at the muzzle. While this is, of course, lethal, it lacked the shock value and knock-down ability of heavier or faster bullets.

After 1919 other Beretta pistols appeared, all of them following the basic Beretta design. By the time the M1934 appeared, the "classic" appearance had been well established with the snub outline and the front of the cutaway receiver wrapped around the forward part of the barrel to carry the fixed foresight. Only long enough to take seven rounds, the pistol grip was very short. To ensure a better grip the characteristic spur was carried over from a design introduced in 1919.

In operation the M1934 is a conventional blowback design without frills or anything unusual, although the receiver is held open once the magazine is empty—it moves forward again as soon as the magazine is removed for reloading. (Most pistols of this type were designed to keep the receiver slide open until the magazine had been replaced.) The M1934 has an exposed hammer which is not affected by the safety once applied, so although the trigger is locked when the safety was applied the hammer can be cocked either by hand or by accident—an unfortunate feature in an otherwise sound design.

The M1934 was immediately accepted into service by the Italian Army. The simplicity and robustness of this model, as well

ABOVE M1934 right side view. Note spur on heel of butt to give a longer grip.

FAR LEFT Typical M1934 holster with integral extra magazine pouch.

BELOW M1934 left side view, showing safety catch.

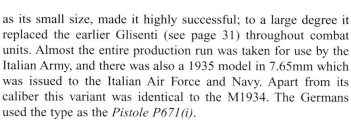

as its small size, made it highly successful; to a large degree it replaced the earlier Glisenti (see page 31) throughout combat units. Almost the entire production run was taken for use by the Italian Army, and there was also a 1935 model in 7.65mm which was issued to the Italian Air Force and Navy. Apart from its caliber this variant was identical to the M1934. The Germans used the type as the *Pistole P671(i)*.

The M1934 first saw action in 1935-36 during the Italian-Abyssinian War, and after that it was supplied in considerable numbers to Franco's forces in the Spanish Civil War. In both of these theaters it showed its reliability, and during World War II it was widely distributed throughout the Italian Army.

Despite its overall success the M1934 was technically underpowered; nevertheless, it is still one of the most famous of the handguns used during World War II.

Bodeo Model 1889 revolver

Caliber: 10.35mm

Length: 9.25in (235mm)

Weight: 2lb 1oz (930gm)

Barrel: 4.375in (11.1cm) long, four grooves, right-hand twist

Feed system: Six-chambered cylinder

System of operation: Revolver, double action, frame, rod ejection

Manufacturers:
Castelli, Brescia, Italy
Fabricca d'Armi, Brescia, Italy
Metallurgica Bresciana, Brescia, Italy
Siderugica Glisenti, Turin, Italy
Royal Fabrica d'Armi Glisenti, Brescia, Italy

Values: $150–$300

The Bodeo Model 1889 was named for the head of the Italian commission that recommended adoption of the weapon for service use. It is a thoroughly orthodox weapon. The lock mechanism is more or less the same as that used on the French M1892 revolver and seems to have been derived from some Belgian designs of 1875. The loading system uses a gate to allow single rounds to be loaded, and as this gate is opened the hammer is disconnected, both as a safety measure and to allow the cylinder to be rotated for loading the chambers. This feature, known as the "Abadie" system, was common among European weapons of the period. The only original feature seems to be the adoption of a hammer block, which moves in front of the hammer and prevents accidental firing of the weapon.

The original design incorporated an octagonal barrel and had no trigger guard. The trigger was folded forward under the frame when not in use and dropped into the firing position when the hammer was thumb-cocked. The design was later modified by the adoption of a rounded barrel and the provision of a conventional trigger and guard; this model is sometimes referred to as the Glisenti M1894.

Although largely superseded by Glisenti and Beretta automatic pistols, numbers of Bodeo revolvers remained in use during World War II as manufacture had continued well into the 1930s. The cartridge fired was among the last of the nineteenth-century low-velocity, large-caliber types to see military service. Originally using a plain lead bullet, final issues generally had a brass-jacketed bullet of unusual skirted shape; to the casual glance, it looks as if the whole round is made from one piece of brass. But due to the low muzzle velocity (827ft (252m)/sec) the energy created is poor for a weapon of this size and caliber. Despite this the Bodeo was a simple and robust weapon and remained in service for over 50 years.

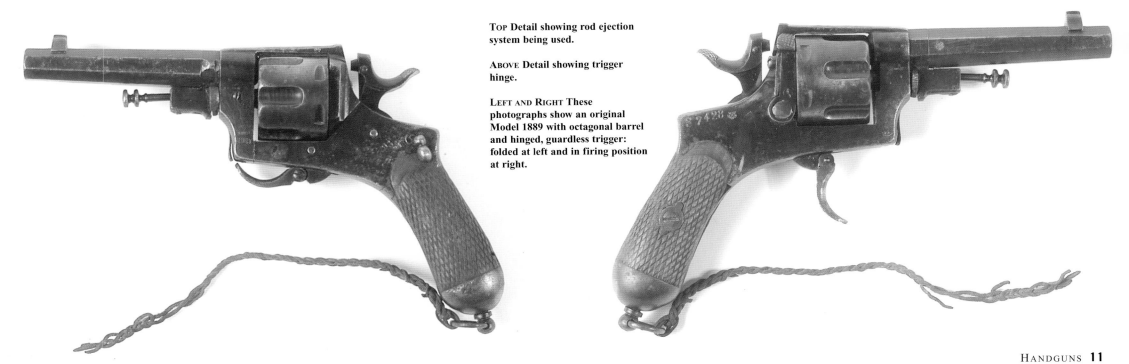

TOP Detail showing rod ejection system being used.

ABOVE Detail showing trigger hinge.

LEFT AND RIGHT These photographs show an original Model 1889 with octagonal barrel and hinged, guardless trigger: folded at left and in firing position at right.

Browning (FN) High Power No. 1 pistol

Caliber: 9mm

Length: 7.75in (197mm)

Weight: 2lb 3oz (990gm)

Barrel: 4.65in (116mm) long, four grooves, right-hand twist

Feed system: 13-round detachable box magazine

System of operation: recoil, Browning link

Manufacturer: John Inglis & Co., Toronto, Canada

Values: $500–$1,000 (Many variations)

This pistol was one of the last guns designed by John Moses Browning before his death in 1925. The design was developed by Fabrique National d'Armes de Guerre of Herstal, Belgium, and introduced into production in 1935 as the *Pistole Automatique Browning GP35 (Grand Puissance Modèle 1935)*. It was adopted by the Belgian Army and was also in service with Denmark, Lithuania, and Romania in small numbers prior to the outbreak of war. With the outbreak of hostilities in 1939 the drawings were brought to Britain, but there was no particular need for the weapon at that time, nor any spare manufacturing capacity available. In Belgium the FN factory was taken over by the Germans and the pistols were continued in production as the *Pistole Modell 35(b)*; most of them were supplied to German SS and Fallschirmjäger units.

The drawings had also been sent to Canada and the pistol was put into production there by the John Inglis Co. of Toronto as the Browning FN 9mm High Power No. 1. Large quantities were supplied to the Chinese Nationalist Army, and the pistol was also supplied to the Canadian and Australian armies. Numbers were sent to Britain where they were issued to commandos, airborne troops and special forces.

As originally designed, the pistol was supplied with an optimistic tangent back-sight graduated to 500 yards and a wooden holster-stock which could be clipped to the butt. The weapons supplied to China were of this pattern, such exotic fittings being popular in Chinese military circles. The models supplied to Britain and her allies substituted a more business-like fixed back sight and dispensed with the stock-butt.

The Browning was a highly popular weapon, firing the standard 9mm Parabellum cartridge as used in the Sten gun and freely obtainable throughout Europe; however, it was unusual in its magazine capacity of 13 rounds, far more than any other handgun. The Browning's main advantage, however, was that of excellent reliability. The weapon proved itself during the war and pro-

duction was resumed at Herstal in 1945. The Browning remains in use today with many western forces and is still in use with the British Army as the Pistol, Automatic, L9A1.

BELOW This view shows off well the businesslike appearance of the Browning High Power.

Browning (FN) Modèle 1910 pistol

Modèle 1910 pistol

Caliber: 7.65mm (.32 ACP)
Length: 6in (152 mm)
Weight: 1Lb 5oz (560gm)
Barrel: 3.5in (89 mm), six grooves, right-hand twist
Feed system: Seven-round detachable box magazine
System of operation: Blowback
Manufacturers: Fabrique National d'Armes de Guerre of Herstal, Belgium
Values: $250-$400

Modèle 1922 pistol

Caliber: 9mm short (.38 ACP)
Length: 7in (178mm)
Weight: 1lb 9oz (710gm)
Barrel: 4.5in (89mm), four grooves, left-hand twist
Feed system: Nine-round detachable box magazine
System of operation: Blowback
Manufacturers: Fabrique National d'Armes de Guerre of Herstal, Belgium
Values: $150-$300

The *Pistole Automatique Browning Modèle 1910* is unusual among pistol designs for although it has remained in production almost continuously since 1910, it has never been officially adopted as a service weapon. Despite this it has been used by many armed forces at one time or another and the basic design has been widely copied. The Modèle 1910 was developed by FN engineers and differed from the earlier Browning-designed FN products in the location of the recoil spring, which is wrapped around the barrel instead of being situated under or over the barrel. This resulted in a clean design in which the forward part of the receiver slides around a barrel that has a tubular appearance.

As is the case with all other FN products, the standard of manufacture and finish are excellent, and these were maintained even with the large-scale production run that occurred after 1940, when the German forces occupying Belgium required large numbers of pistols. The Modèle 1910 was kept in production to meet this demand, the bulk of the new output being allocated to Luftwaffe air crew who knew the type as the *Pistole P621(b)*. Before that the Modèle 1910 had been issued in small numbers to the Belgian armed forces, and many other nations obtained the type for limited use for their own military or police services

Modèle 1922 pistol

In 1922 the Modèle 1910 was modified to improve its accuracy. This involved fitting a lengthened nose cap that effectively increased the barrel length without any need to change the slide. Shortly after the development of this model, another change was introduced, when the Modèle 1922 was developed to fire the 9mm short cartridge (.38 ACP—automatic pistol chambering).

ABOVE Right-hand side view of the cocked Model 1910 with magazine extracted.

LEFT AND BELOW Left and right-hand side views of the Modèle 1910.

Colt M1911A1 pistol

Caliber: .45

Length: 8.5in (216mm)

Weight: 2lb 7.5oz (1.13kg)

Barrel: 5in (127mm) long, six grooves, left-hand twist

Feed system: Seven-round detachable box

System of operation: Recoil, Browning link

Manufacturers:
Colts Patent Firearms Mfg. Co., Hartford, Conn., U.S.

Remington Arms, UMC CO., Bridgeport, Conn., U.S.

Springfield Arsenal, Springfield, Mass., U.S.

Union Switch & Signal Co., Swissvale, Pa., U.S.

Ithaca Gun Co., Ithaca, N.Y., U.S.

Remington-Rand Inc., Syracuse, N.Y., U.S.

Values: $1,000–$2,500 (Many variations)

RIGHT AND FAR RIGHT Both sides of the standard issue leather holster.

BELOW The M1911 with receiver open and magazine removed. Note the holes in the magazine to show how many rounds it contains.

The M1911 was a development of the earlier Colt Browning Model 1900 and was designed to fire a new .45 caliber cartridge as the U.S. Army had decided that the .38 did not have sufficient knock-down power. Originally designed by John Browning as early as 1908 for trials by the U.S. Army to determine their future service pistol, this weapon was one of several models submitted, of which the Colt, Savage, and Parabellum (Luger) were the most promising. As a result of these trials the Colt was eventually selected to become the U.S. Army standard issue pistol as the Model 1911. In addition, a quantity of M1911 pistols, chambered for the .455 Webley & Scott automatic pistol cartridge, were made in 1915-16 for the British Royal Navy and Royal Flying Corps.

The Model 1911 served well during World War I, but user experience indicated the need for some small changes. The contour of the butt was altered to fit the hand better; the trigger was shortened; the front edge of the butt was cut away to allow the trigger finger a better grip; and the hammer spur was shortened. With these changes it became the M1911A1, entering service in 1922. During World War II it was manufactured by a number of companies in order to provide the quantities required.

For many years the M1911A1 was, together with the .455 Webley revolver, the most powerful military pistol in service. It was guaranteed to stop anyone it hit in their tracks, but this power also meant that a good deal of practice was required to fire the weapon effectively.

The M1911 was widely issued in the U.S. Army. As well as being an officer's weapon, it was carried by NCOs and was the personal arm for many operators of crew-served weapons such as heavy machine guns and mortars. Due to its limitations as a long-range weapon, it was largely replaced by the M1 carbine or M3 submachine gun after 1942, particularly among weapon crews.

There is no doubt that it was the most widely used of all combat pistols and ranks as one of the most successful designs ever produced. It has been manufactured in the millions and is still in service all over the world, almost a century after it was first produced.

Left, Far Left, and Below
Side views of the M1911A1.

Below Left and Right
Details showing barrel markings
including patent information.

Colt New Service revolver

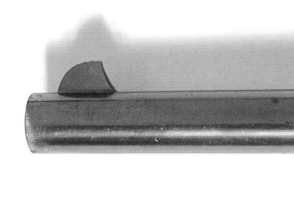

Caliber: .455

Length: 10.75in (273mm)

Weight: 2lb 8oz (1.13kg)

Barrel: 5.5in (140mm), six grooves, right-hand twist

Feed system: Six-chambered cylinder

System of operation: Revolver, single or double action

Manufacturer:
Colts Patent Firearms Mfg. Co., Hartford, Conn., U.S.

Values: $500–$1,200

The Colt New Service revolver was one of a group of designs produced by Colt in the last decade of the nineteenth century. It was made in six barrel lengths 4in (102mm); 4.5in (114mm); 5in (127mm); 5.5in (140mm); 6in (152mm); and 7.5in (190mm), and was used as a U.S. service arm from 1907 onward, until it was at last superseded by a self-loading pistol. Even after that, however, many continued to be carried privately.

With the advent of World War I the Colt New Service took on a new importance. By 1916, the British and Commonwealth Army was desperate for new sources of munitions. Demand was far outstripping Britain's domestic production capacity, and so large orders were placed with American manufacturers for all types of weapons. When it came to handguns, it was decided to adapt existing American designs to accept the British .455 cartridge, in order to speed production. Orders were placed with Colt and Smith & Wesson for .455-chambered revolvers and large numbers of these were subsequently delivered to the Western Front. When America entered the war the U.S. Army found itself in a very similar position and again large orders were placed with Colt and Smith & Wesson, this time for guns chambered for American .45 rounds. These guns were officially designated Revolver, Caliber .45, Smith & Wesson Hand Ejector, M1917, and Revolver, Caliber .45, Colt New Service, M1917—although both were more commonly known as M1917s. The two guns were almost identical in performance and design and to all intents and purposes interchangeable. The change from British to U.S. ammunition did bring one problem: the U.S. round was rimless and if loaded into the cylinder in the usual way would fall right through. To overcome this, ammunition was supplied in pressed-steel, crescent-shaped, three-round clips; the M1917 had a recess cut into the rear face of the cylinder to accommodate two clips. This system proved to be an improvement since it speeded loading and ejection of spent cases. Both the Colt and the Smith & Wesson went on to see front-line service in World War II although mostly in British hands. The Colt was, however, retained for use by the U.S. Army Military Police.

LEFT AND THIS PAGE The weapon shown in these photographs is of the usual solid-frame type and has a round, 5.5in (140mm) long barrel. The cylinder is released by pulling back a thumb-catch on the left side of the frame; this allows the cylinder to be swung out side-ways, to the left, on a separate yoke. The empty cases are ejected with the manual extractor. The butt is large, providing a comfortable grip, and has chequered plates bearing the word COLT. The well-known trademark of the rearing horse is shown on the left side of the frame, below the hammer.

This revolver is chambered for the British .455 Eley cartridge. It bears the additional stamps of the Royal Small Arms Factory, Enfield showing that it was one of the revolvers imported for use by the British Army in World War I.

Ceska Zbrojovka vz27 pistol

Caliber: 7.65mm (.32 ACP)
Length: 6.25in (159mm)
Weight: 1lb 9oz (710gm)
Barrel: 3.82in (97mm), six
   grooves, right-hand twist
Feed system: Eight-round
   detachable box magazine

System of operation: Blowback
Manufacturers:
   Ceska Zbrojovka Brno
   Ceska Zbrojovka Prague
     (Böhmische Waffen Fabric
     AG during occupation)
Values: $300–$500

The famous Ceska Zbrojovka factory was set up just after World War I, and was to develop some of the the most successful weapons in the world. The Czech-made self-loading pistols were no exception, and a series of excellent designs were produced starting with the CZ vz22.

The vz22 was designed by Josef Nickl of Mauser. This was a 9mm locking-breech model that utilized a rotating barrel. In 1924 production of pistols was switched from Brno to a facility in Prague. This necessitated a change in design of the vz22 to suit the new production facilities; at the same time the opportunity was taken to add a magazine safety. This model was known as the vz24.

The final prewar model in this series was the vz27. The design team realized that the added complexity of a locking breech was not really necessary in a pistol firing a 7.65mm cartridge, and so the vz24 was redesigned as a 7.65mm with a blowback mechanism. The pistol suffered no detrimental effects as a result, and was quicker and easier to produce—a factor that no doubt played a part in the German Army's decision to continue production of the vz27 after the occupation. Externally there is little to differentiate between these three models. Those produced under occupation are marked *Pistole Modell 27 Kal. 7.65* on one side (see detail photograph at right) and *Böhmische Waffen Fabric AG in Prag* on the other.

The vz27 continued in production after the war under communist auspices and became the most extensively produced of the prewar Czech models, remaining in production until 1951.

ABOVE AND ABOVE RIGHT Left and right-hand side views of the CZ vz27.

LEFT The markings on this weapon show it to be an example produced during World War II while the country was under German occupation.

RIGHT Side view of CZ vz27 with eight-round detachable box magazine separated.

Enfield No. 2 Mks. I, I*, and I** revolvers

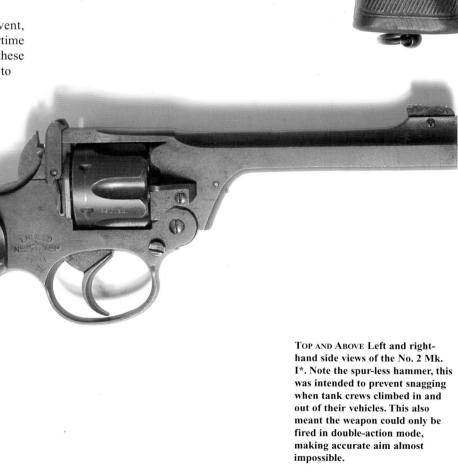

Caliber: .352 (nominally .38)

Length: 10.25in (260mm)

Weight: 1lb 11.5oz (780gm)

Barrel: 5in (127mm) long, seven grooves, right-hand twist

Feed system: Six-chambered cylinder

System of operation: Revolver, single or double action, top-break

Manufacturers:
Royal Small Arms Factory Enfield Lock, Middlesex, England

Singer Sewing Machine Co., Clydebank, Scotland

Albion Motor Co., Glasgow, Scotland

Values: $150–$275

Although the British Army had long favored large caliber pistols for their stopping power, the situation was reviewed in the 1920s. After extensive tests it was decided that a pistol of .38 caliber would have sufficient power and would be easier to fire accurately because of the lighter recoil.

The new weapon was to be based very closely on the Webley & Scott Mk. VI, although scaled down. The Royal Small Arms Factory designers developed their own model with a slightly different lock and trigger mechanism, and this was eventually accepted for service on June 2, 1932.

The Mk. I was capable of operation as a single or double-action revolver. However, one of the principal users was the Royal Tank Regiment, and there were complaints from the "tankies" that the hammer spur tended to catch on various parts of the tanks as the crews scrambled in and out—a potentially disastrous situation when the pistol was loaded. As a result, the Mk. I* was introduced in 1938. This model had the spur removed, which prevented the hammer from being thumb-cocked. Converted pistols could only be fired in double-action mode, and in an attempt to preserve some degree of accuracy the mainspring was lightened to reduce the trigger pull. In order to ensure that tank crews always got Mk. I* pistols, it was decided to convert all Mk. Is to Mk. I* standard.

The final change in design came with the introduction of the Mk. I** on July 29, 1942. This was a simplified Mk. I* with the hammer safety stop omitted and some other minor modifications, intended to speed up production. An unfortunate side effect was the tendency of the modified weapon to go off if dropped on the

hammer; this was deemed an unlikely event, however, and the design was accepted as a wartime concession. As soon as the war was over these models were all recalled and modified back to Mk. I* standards of safety.

The Enfield pistol was not often used in action. It was unpopular, since the fact that it could only be fired in double-action mode made accurate shooting almost impossible. The excessive trigger pull required invariably ruined the aim. As a result the Enfield was seldom used as anything more than an emergency weapon.

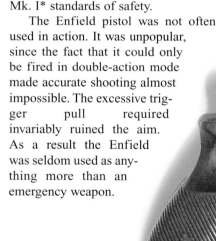

TOP AND ABOVE Left and right-hand side views of the No. 2 Mk. I*. Note the spur-less hammer, this was intended to prevent snagging when tank crews climbed in and out of their vehicles. This also meant the weapon could only be fired in double-action mode, making accurate aim almost impossible.

RIGHT AND FAR RIGHT Two contrasting views of the Enfield No. 2 revolver. The first shows a sectionalized, broken, Mk. I illustrating the details of the mechanism. Note the hammer with spur. The second shows a similar view of the Mk. I* (with spurless hammer) but without sectionalization.

BELOW, RIGHT, AND BELOW RIGHT
Three views of a Mk. I** made by
Albion Motors Ltd. of Scotstoun
Glasgow. (Note comparison of makers' marks below right.)

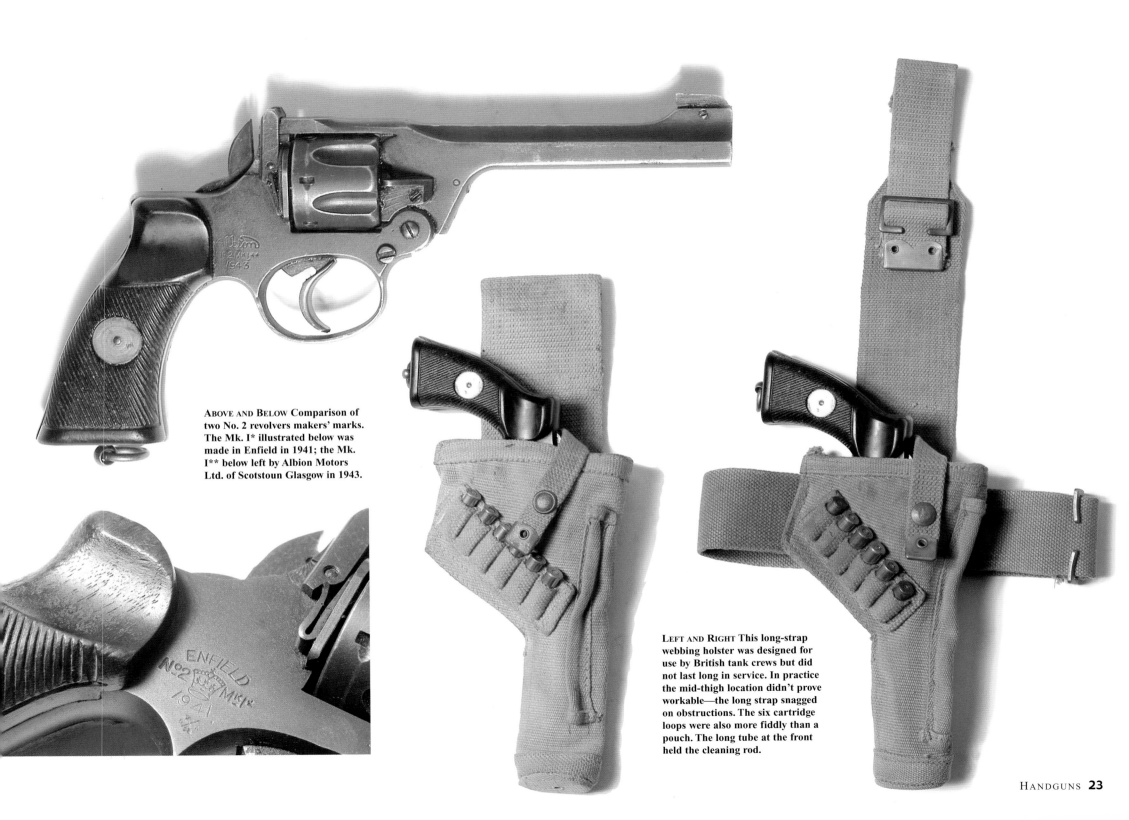

ABOVE AND BELOW Comparison of two No. 2 revolvers makers' marks. The Mk. 1* illustrated below was made in Enfield in 1941; the Mk. I** below left by Albion Motors Ltd. of Scotstoun Glasgow in 1943.

LEFT AND RIGHT This long-strap webbing holster was designed for use by British tank crews but did not last long in service. In practice the mid-thigh location didn't prove workable—the long strap snagged on obstructions. The six cartridge loops were also more fiddly than a pouch. The long tube at the front held the cleaning rod.

Femaru-Fegyver Model 37 pistol

Caliber: 9mm short (.38) and 7.65mm (.32 ACP)

Length: 7.175in (182mm)

Weight: 1lb 11oz (770gm)

Barrel: 4.33in (110mm) long, six grooves, right-hand twist

Feed system: Seven-round detachable box

System of operation: Blowback

Manufacturer: Femaru-Fegyver es Gepgyar, Budapest, Hungary

Values: $200–$300

The Pisztoly 37M was manufactured by Femaru-Fegyver es Gepgyar (FEG—Metal Products, Weapon and Machinery Factory Co.) in Budapest. FEG had been founded in 1919 out of the earlier Fegyver es Gepgyar Reszvenytarsasag, whose main designer was the remarkable Hungarian, Rudolf Frommer. Born in 1868, he joined the company in 1896 after qualifying as an engineer. He became factory manager in 1900 and controlled the company's designs until retirement in 1935, a year before he died. The 37M was an improved version of Frommer's final design, the Model 29, a straightforward, robust 9mm short (.38 ACP) chambered automatic. The main differences were that the pinned-in cocking grips at the rear of the slide of the 27 were abandoned for conventional grooving in the 37M, which had a smaller hammer and an additional finger-rest on the toe of the butt. Markings on this version were 37M on the bottom of the magazine and FEMARU FEGYVER — ES GEPGYAR RT 37M on the slide.

Hungary was firmly on the side of the Nazis in World War II until the final months of the war when it was occupied by German forces. No obstacles stopped, therefore, the German procurement of a contract for some 50,000 7.65mm pistols (most would be used by the Luftwaffe). Other than the caliber change, there were initially no differences between the weapons produced for the Germans and the original 37M. However, a manual safety catch was added to the left rear of the frame at the request of the Luftwaffe, and this led to a change in the lettering on the slide marking to P. MOD. 37 KAL 7,65 (as visible on the left-hand side view below) and German Waffenamt acceptance stamps. The German code "jvh" identified the manufacturer. Called the *Pistole 37 (ung)* (Ungar = Hungary in German) production finished in 1944, with over 85,000 units produced. A holster (see right and below) was also manufactured.

ABOVE AND RIGHT Left and right-hand side views of the 7.65mm-version of the Model 37 produced for the Luftwaffe.

LEFT AND FAR LEFT The holster manufactured for the German Model 37 with a detail of the lettering inside the flap.

RIGHT Detail of lettering on the slide: P. MOD. 37 KAL 7,65. Note the "jhv 43"—code for the manufacturer and year of manufacture.

BELOW The Model 37 with magazine separated and slide cocked.

Flare Pistols

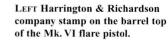

Hebel flare pistol

ABOVE Right and left-hand sides of a 27mm smooth-bore Hebel signal pistol. It is cocked by hand and opened for loading by pulling down the lever in front of the trigger guard.

An interesting German development during World War II was the *Kampfpistole*—an early hand-held antitank weapon that began life as a Walther 27mm *Leuchtpistole* (signal pistol). A rifled barrel liner with five grooves and a caliber of 23mm rifled was inserted into the otherwise unchanged *Leuchtpistole*. In this form it was also called the *Kampfpistole Z* because a white Z was painted on the side of the chamber to differentiate it from the *Leuchtpistole*. It fired the *Sprenggranate Leuchtpistole* (explosive round, signal pistol or Spgr.LP), a 125mm long grenade with a small, 30gm warhead— too small to be of any antitank significance.

Flare pistols are much used by all military units for a variety of battlefield signals, during search and rescue operations, for illumination at night, and are available in quantities to firearm and weapon collectors. The selection of pistols shown here is not intended to be exhaustive but to give a taste of a specialist subject.

The term "Very pistol" (sometimes seen misspelled as "Verey") is often used as a synonym for flare pistols for the very simple reason that it was the American naval officer Edward Wilson Very (1847–1910) who created the Very pistol in 1877. Looking similar to an ordinary pistol, usually with a short barrel and a large caliber, Very pistols quickly became standard issue to military units, and were used extensively in both world wars.

Harrington & Richardson Mk. VI flare pistol

LEFT AND ABOVE Based in Worcester, Mass., the company has long and proud antecedents. It was started by Frank Wesson and his nephew, Gilbert Harrington in 1871. Four years later, in 1875, Frank Wesson sold his interest to William Richardson, so creating the Harrington & Richardson Arms Co., that would become one of the most prolific American manufacturers of firearms, including flare pistols, until 1986 when they ceased production. The name is now used by another company.

No. 2 Mk. I flare pistol

THIS PAGE The standard British flare pistol of World War II, the one-inch (2.54mm) Signal Pistol No. 1 came in various forms—the Mk. I and Mk. V (below) are illustrated here. The Mk. V was 9.5in (241mm) long, weighed just under 2lb (880gm), and was manufactured by I.L. Berridge.

No. 4 Mk. I flare pistol

THIS PAGE Originally designed for use in British aircraft, the four lugs on the front end of the barrel and the brass catch on the top of the body are the means of securing this 1.5in pistol to the aircraft mounting.

Webley and Scott No. I Mk. III★ flare pistol

THIS PAGE Webley & Scott is based in Birmingham, England, and has been active since the 1790s. Founded by William Davies, in 1834 Philip Webley, Davies' son-in-law, took over, concentrating on the manufacture of guns, particularly revolvers. The company amalgamated in 1897 with shotgun manufacturers W. & C. Scott and Sons, becoming The Webley and Scott Revolver and Arms Company Ltd. of Birmingham. The name was shortened in 1906 to Webley & Scott Ltd. It continued to produce firearms until 1979 when it ceased production to concentrate on air rifles.

The photographs show a Webley & Scott one-inch caliber World War I vintage flare pistol that continued in use during World War II. Note the close-up of the frame showing the "Webley & Scott London & Birmingham Ltd" markings, the military acceptance mark and proof marks, and the year mark of 1916. The pistol is made of brass with walnut grips, and the 5.75in barrel is flared on the muzzle. Note also the lanyard ring at the bottom of the grip.

RIGHT The Mk. III broken open for loading.

BELOW RIGHT Typical ammunition tin and cartridge cases for the Mk. III.

Glisenti Model 1910 pistol

Caliber: 9mm

Length: 8.25in (210mm)

Weight: 1lb 14.5oz (865gm)

Barrel: 3.5in (89mm) long, six grooves, right-hand twist

Feed system: Seven-round detachable box magazine

System of operation: Recoil, hinged block lock

Manufacturers:
Metallurgica Bresciana, Brescia, Italy
Siderugica Glisenti, Turin, Italy

Values: $375–$750

The M1910 started life as the Brixia, but the various relevant patents together with production of the weapon were taken over by Societa Siderugica Glisenti in the 1900s. In 1910 it was taken into Italian Army service as the *Pistola Automatica, Modello 1910 (Glisenti)*.

The Glisenti was a fragile weapon; the breech lock was not particularly strong and the construction of the weapon was mechanically and structurally weak. One aspect of the design, the ammunition, was potentially disastrous. In order to offset the inherent weakness of the design, the Model 1910 was provided with a special 9mm Glisenti cartridge. This cartridge was dimensionally the same as the 9mm Parabellum, but loaded less powerfully to give a muzzle velocity of 1,050ft/sec instead of the Parabellum's 1,300ft/sec. The Glisenti cartridge enabled the gun to be fired with a reasonable margin of safety, but when Parabellum rounds were used in error the gun could—and often did—explode on firing.

There is little record of the Glisenti in combat. It was officially an officer's weapon, but most officers appear to have preferred to use the Beretta Model 1934. Few Glisenti pistols were found in the fighting in North Africa in 1941–42, and it seems that the principal issue was to non-combatant elements such as quartermasters and clerks.

The intention had been to produce a pistol to replace the aging Bodeo revolver but the Glisenti only ever supplemented the earlier weapon and was actually dropped from production in the 1920s, ten years before the gun it was intended to replace.

LEFT Artwork by the author of the right-hand side of the Glisenti M1910.

Japanese handguns

Meiji 26 revolver

Caliber: 9mm
Length: 8.5in (216mm)
Weight: 2lb 4oz (1.02kg)
Barrel: 4.7in (120mm) long, six grooves, left-hand twist
Feed system: Six-chambered cylinder

System of operation: Revolver, hinged-frame, double-action only, self-ejecting
Manufacturer: State Arsenal, Nagoya, Japan
Values: $200-$400

The Meiji 26 revolver was adopted in 1893, the 26th year of the Meiji Era. Although a Japanese design, it was put together from a combination of features derived from various western weapons. The Japanese Navy had purchased a number of Smith & Wesson revolvers in 1879, and the barrel latch and cylinder lock were copied from this; the basic construction came from Belgian Nagant designs, and the lock mechanism leaned heavily on the contemporary Dutch service revolver. It also featured a hinged side plate which could be opened for cleaning or repair of the lock work, very similar to that found on the French Lebel M1892 service revolver. Japan was at this time only just emerging from three centuries of medieval seclusion, something that accounts for the way Japanese manufacturers tried to benefit from the experience of others. Her industry was correspondingly primitive, and the resultant weapon, perhaps inevitably, left a lot to be desired. It was muzzle-heavy, hard to fire (due to its double-action lock), and poorly made of inferior material. Its accuracy was equally poor, and the round of ammunition was a peculiar 9mm rimmed cartridge unknown outside Japan. This developed no more than 136 foot-pounds at the muzzle, and was one of the least effective rounds ever taken into military service. On the plus side the weapon was structurally strong and sufficiently serviceable to be used in two world wars.

Initial issues of the Model 26 revolver were, it seems, made to cavalry units, but after the general adoption of the Nambu automatic pistol, the revolver then found its way into the hands of other corps. During World War II it was principally issued to reserve and home defense units, but numbers of NCOs of infantry units in the South Pacific were found to be carrying the Meiji 26.

Taisho 04 pistol

Caliber: 8mm
Length: 9in (228mm)
Weight: 1lb 15.5oz (893gm)
Barrel: 4.7in (120mm) long, six grooves, right-hand twist
Feed system: Eight-round detachable box magazine

System of operation: recoil, hinged block lock
Manufacturer: Japan Special Steel Co. State Arsenal, Nagoya, Japan
Values: $700-$1,500

The Taisho 04 was the first self-loading pistol developed in Japan and was perfected and offered for sale in the fourth year of the Taisho reign, or 1915 in the Christian calendar. The name "Nambu" came from Colonel Kirijo Nambu, the designer. Although bearing a superficial resemblance to the Luger, internally the two guns are completely different. The breech-locking mechanism, a drop-down block beneath the bolt, is almost identical to that of the Glisenti, but an oddity of the Nambu design is that it was quite possible to assemble the pistol without the breech lock in place, something which made the pistol extremely dangerous to fire.

The cartridge was an unusual bottle-necked round carrying a 100-grain jacketed bullet of poor stopping power only used in the Taisho 04 and some Japanese submachine guns. The weapon's principal defects seem to have been a weak striker spring, which soon lost its resilience and gave light striker blows and misfires; together with a general weakness of construction, this made for poor reliability.

Widely used by Japanese officers, the Taisho 04 was often encountered in combat, but was never officially accepted for service with the Imperial Japanese forces. However, the sheer numbers purchased by Japanese officers prompted the provision of an official designation, and all subsequent pistols in the Japanese forces came to be known as Nambus. In spite of its faults the Taisho 04 remained in use throughout World War II, even though an improved model—the Taisho 14—was introduced in 1925.

LEFT The Type 94 automatic, one of the worst pistol designs ever to see military service.

Taisho 14 pistol

Caliber: 8mm
Length: 8.95in (227mm)
Weight: 1lb 15.75oz (900gm)
Barrel: 4.75in (121mm) long, six grooves, right-hand twist
Feed system: Eight-round detachable box magazine

System of operation: Recoil, hinged block lock
Manufacturers: Japanese state arsenals
Values: $200-$350

ABOVE Author's artwork of the Taisho, or Type, 14 Nambu, Kiska Model.

RIGHT The Baby Nambu with standard issue leather holster.

Although still called the Nambu and similar in appearance to the Taisho 04, this version was not designed by Colonel Nambu. Its development appears to be the work of a government arsenal design office, probably Nagoya. The model number indicates its adoption in the fourteenth year of the Taisho reign, or 1925. The Taisho 14 was designed to be more suited to mass production than the 04, and was officially approved as a service issue. The changes from the 04 consisted of: adding a safety catch that could only be operated by the firer's free hand; replacement of the single offset recoil spring by two springs, one at each side of the frame; some minor internal changes to simplify manufacture. No attempt was made to improve the striker spring, the weak point of the Taisho 04. As with the 04, this model was widely used and found in combat throughout the Greater East Asian Co-Prosperity Sphere.

VARIANTS

Baby Nambu
Smaller model taking a special 7mm cartridge. Developed commercially, the entire run seems to have gone to the Air Force.

Kiska Model
Has an enlarged triggerguard allowing it to be fired while wearing gloves—a vital consideration when fighting in the hostile climate of Manchuria. Its (unofficial) name resulted from its discovery by Allied troops in the Aleutian Islands campaign.

Type 94 pistol

Caliber: 8mm
Length: 7.125in (181mm)
Weight: 1lb 12oz (794gm)
Barrel: 3.125in (79mm) long, six grooves, right-hand twist
Feed system: Six-round detachable box magazine

System of operation: Recoil, vertical sliding lock
Manufacturers: Japanese state arsenals
Values: $250-$350

The introduction of the Type 94 marked a break in self-loading pistol development in Japan, all previous models having been of the Nambu type. It appears to have been developed in the early 1930s in a further attempt to develop a weapon suitable for mass production. The Type 94 was originally produced commercially but the demands of the Sino-Japanese war led the Japanese government to purchase large quantities of the Type 94 for military use. It was first produced in 1934, or 2594 in the Japanese calendar, hence Type 94.

The Type 94 was, possibly, the worst military pistol ever issued. It fired the same ammunition as the Nambu pistols but from a shorter barrel, and so developed no more than 180 foot-pounds at the muzzle. The pistol itself, although generally made of sound materials, was poorly finished and possessed two major design defects: the disconnector and lock mechanism are so constructed that it is possible to release the striker and fire the pistol before the barrel and breech are locked together; and the sear that releases the striker is an exposed metal strip on the left-hand side of the frame. This can be depressed—and the weapon fired—simply by grasping it carelessly. Other defects include the exposure of the recoil spring, and the general vulnerability of the mechanism to dirt and dust.

The majority of these pistols were issued to airmen and tank crew, perhaps in the hope that they would not actually be used.

Lahti L35 pistol

Caliber: 9mm

Length: 9.4in (239mm)

Weight: 2lb 12oz (1.25kg)

Barrel: 4.7in (119mm), six grooves, right-hand twist

Feed system: Eight-round magazine

System of operation: Recoil, rising bolt block

Manufacturer: Valtion Kivaarithedas, State Rifle Factory, Jyvaskyla, Finland

Values: $800-$1,200

This pistol was invented by Aimo Lahti of Finland and was produced by Valtion, the Finnish state factory. It was originally intended to be made in two calibers, 7.65mm and 9mm Parabellum, but the former never got beyond the prototype stage. The arm was adopted as the official pistol of the Finnish armed forces in 1935; it gave good service in the Finnish campaign against the Russians in the early part of World War II when it was found to be particularly reliable in very low temperatures. Although, as maybe seen, it bears a general resemblance to the Luger, the two are quite different mechanically. The Lahti fires from a closed breech, the bolt being unlocked after a brief rearward travel and going on to complete the usual cycle. The mechanism incorporates a bolt accelerator—a curved arm that is so designed that it increases the rearward velocity of the bolt and so improves the reliability of the pistol in low temperatures. However, the drawback is that the weapon cannot be stripped and cleaned completely in the field.

A version of the Lahti was also used by Swedish forces, by whom it was called the M/40. The Swedes had originally settled for the German Walther P38 (see pages 56–57), but when war intervened they turned instead to Finland. The Finns supplied some Lahtis, but later they were made under license by the Swedish firm of Husqvarna Vapenfabrik. Although the Swedes make excellent weapons, their M/40 was generally considered inferior to the Finnish-produced weapons.

RIGHT Swedish-made version of the L35 Lahti. The Finnish version has a lozenge-shaped space on the grips for the Valtion monogram—VKT.

Luger Model 1908 (P08) pistol

Caliber: 9 mm

Length: 8.75in (223mm)

Weight: 1lb 14oz (850gm)

Barrel: 4in (102mm) long, eight grooves, right-hand twist

Feed system: Eight-round detachable box magazine

System of operation: Recoil, toggle joint

Manufacturers: Deutsche Waffen und Munitionsfabrik, Berlin, Germany

Royal Arsenal, Erfurt, Germany

Simson & Cie, Suhl, Germany

Mauserwerke AG, Oberndorf, Germany

Heinrich Krieghoff Waffenwerke, Suhl, Germany

Values: $600-$1,500 (Many variations)

The *Parabellum Pistole '08*—better known as the Luger—was perfected at the turn of the century by Georg Luger, using the earlier Borchardt pistol as his starting point. The Borchardt introduced the toggle-joint system of locking and other mechanical features in a pistol which, while a workable proposition, was at best a cumbersome device. Luger refined the mechanics, his principal change being in the arrangement of the mainspring, which had been a coiled clock-type spring and which now became a flat leaf spring in the rear edge of the butt. This changed the whole outline of the weapon and made it much better balanced. Further improvements followed: the main spring was changed to a coil and the original 7.65mm caliber was improved to 9mm in order to make the bullet rather more combat effective. In 1908 it became the standard pistol of the German Army, having already been accepted by the Swiss Army in 7.65mm caliber and the German Navy in 9mm.

It was widely tested in the years 1906–14 by almost every army in the world, and a .45 caliber came very close to being adopted by the U.S. Army in 1908. Although of distinctive appearance, it is not among the most reliable of weapons; the toggle lock is too dependent upon consistent ammunition quality and the multiplicity of exposed moving parts are prone to suffer from mud and sand. Nevertheless, it served the German Army well enough in 1914–18 to be retained after the war. By the middle 1930s, however, it was clear that a large and expanding army needed a pistol which could be mass-produced faster than the Parabellum, and in 1938 manufacture of a replacement—the Walther P38 (see pages 56–57)—began. In spite of this the P08 was continued in production until about 1942 for the German Army, and later than that for export; the last batch, in 7.65mm caliber, was sold to Portugal in 1944.

The Pistole 08 was issued throughout the German Army, and its infantry role was as an officer's sidearm and also by weapon crews, despatch riders, signalers, and NCOs. It saw wide combat use, though tales of individual feats of arms with the weapon are rare. It was, of course, highly prized as a souvenir by Allied troops, and many thousands must still be in private hands today.

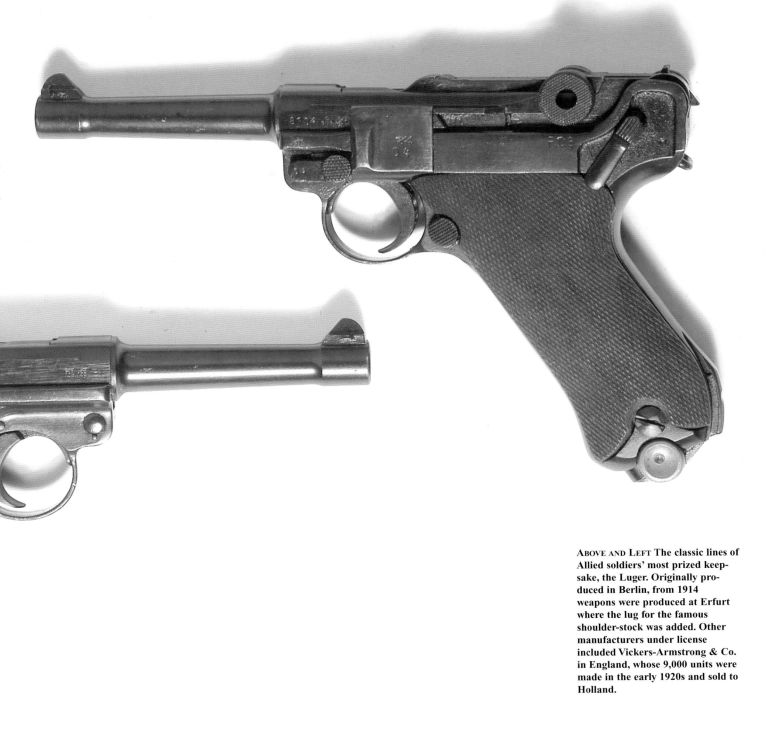

ABOVE AND LEFT The classic lines of Allied soldiers' most prized keepsake, the Luger. Originally produced in Berlin, from 1914 weapons were produced at Erfurt where the lug for the famous shoulder-stock was added. Other manufacturers under license included Vickers-Armstrong & Co. in England, whose 9,000 units were made in the early 1920s and sold to Holland.

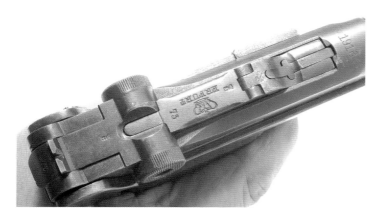

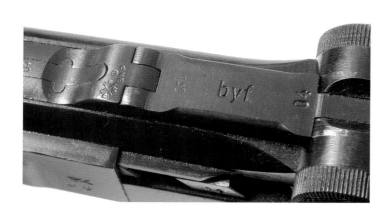

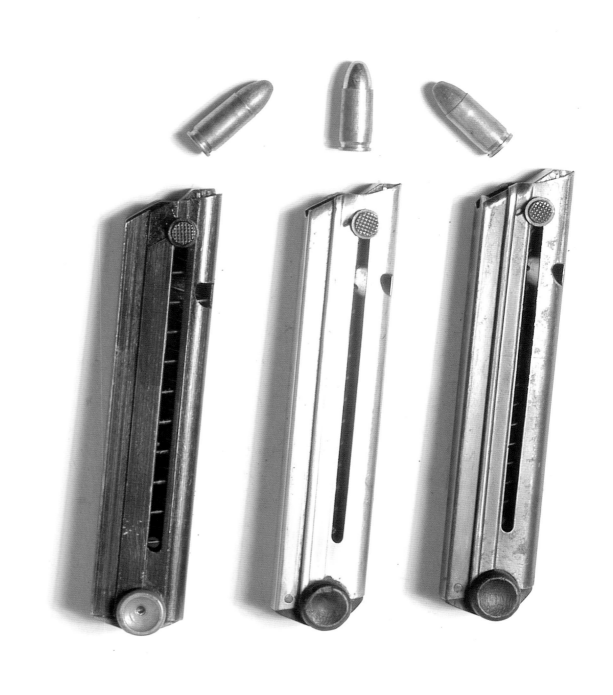

ABOVE P08 used by the British Special Operations Executive and photographed at the School of Infantry in Warminster. It is fitted with a Maxim silencer.

RIGHT AND FAR RIGHT The unusual toggle action is shown in these photographs.

FAR LEFT: Three top views of the P08 showing makers' marks. The top photograph shows a pistol manufactured at the Königlich Gewehrfabrik (Royal Arsenal) at Erfurt; the center photograph shows an example produced by Deutsche Waffen und Munitionsfabriken, Berlin; the final pistol is identified by the "byf" lettering as having been built by Mauser at Oberndorf.

LEFT: Three variations of magazine extracted by depressing the button at the bottom of the eight-round magazine.

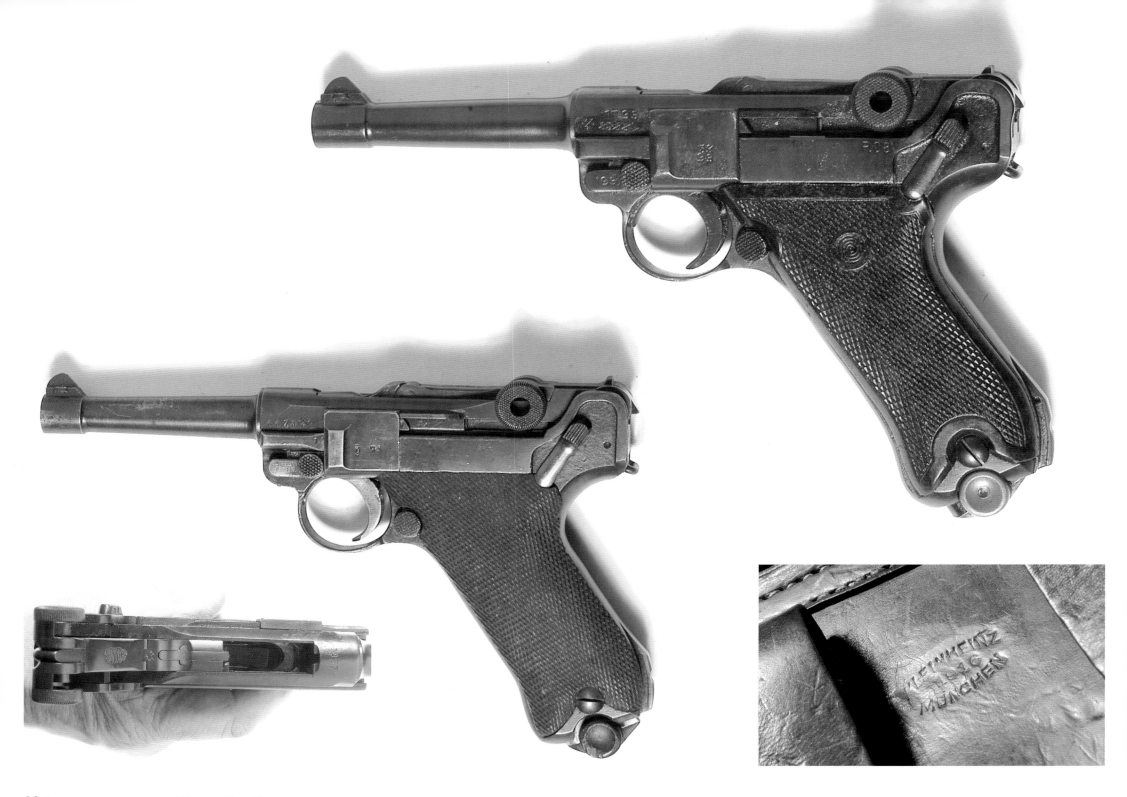

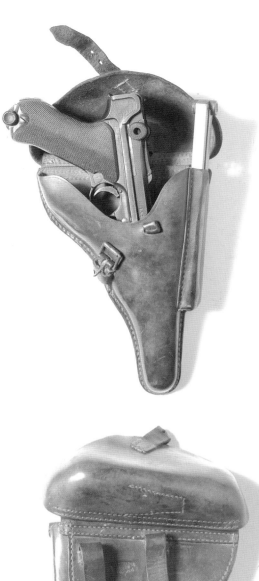

ABOVE AND ABOVE LEFT 1917 model P08 made by the Deutsche Waffen und Munitionsfabrik, Berlin.

RIGHT AND CENTER LEFT P08 made at the Royal Arsenal, Erfurt.

FAR RIGHT, ABOVE, AND BELOW Standard issue holster with spare magazine pocket.

LEFT Manufacturer's stamp on holster reads "Kleinheinz 1916 München."

FAR LEFT P08 made by Deutsche Waffen und Munitionsfabrik, Berlin (note maker's mark) in 1917. The toggle action has opened the chamber.

Luger Artillery Model 1917 pistol

Caliber: 9 mm

Length: 12.75in (324mm)

Weight: 2lb 5oz (1.06kg)

Barrel: 7.5in (192mm) long, eight grooves, right-hand twist

Feed system: Eight-round detachable box magazine, 32-round drum magazine

System of operation: Recoil, toggle joint

Manufacturers:
Deutsche Waffen und Munitionsfabrik, Berlin, Germany
Royal Arsenal, Erfurt, Germany
Simson & Cie, Suhl, Germany
Mauserwerke AG, Oberndorf, Germany
Heinrich Krieghoff Waffenwerke, Suhl, Germany

Values: $1,300–$2,400

In 1917 a long-barreled version of the Parabellum Pistole '08, that had been produced commercially in 1903–04 was adopted as the standard pistol of the German Navy and this was followed in turn by the Artillery Model. This introduced a longer barrel to improve its long-range performance and to this end it was provided with detachable stock. Although the standard Model 1917 shared the eight-round box magazine of the P08, an extension magazine was also produced that held 32 rounds in a drum and was known as the "snail drum." This was loaded using a special tool and was prone to jamming until a new, more pointed bullet was developed that cured the problem.

It was originally issued exclusively to machine gun crews and artillery observers in exposed forward positions, and proved to be a light and handy weapon for close in defense. As more were produced they were made available to NCOs and forward infantry units where they were found to be very handy in night raids and came to be used in a role that would later be filled by the submachine gun.

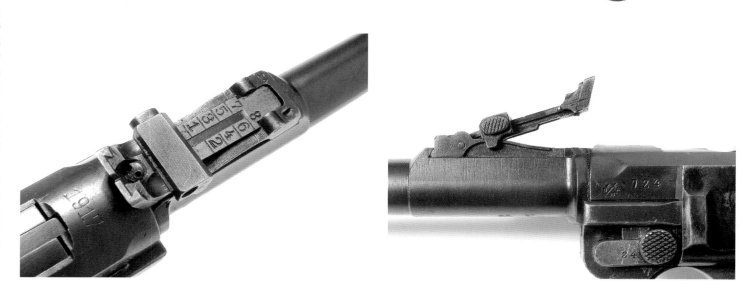

ABOVE LEFT, ABOVE, AND ABOVE RIGHT Left, right-hand side and top views of the *9mm Parabellum Artillerie-Pistole Modell 1917*.

LEFT AND FAR LEFT Two details of tangent-leaf rear sight, provided to take advantage of the longer range provided by the 7.5in barrel. Note that it is graduated to 800 meters (2,625 feet).

RIGHT The "Snail" magazine, designed by the Austro-Hungarian pair Tatarek and von Benkö, would go on to be used on the early Bergmann submachine guns. The shoulder stock was issued for use with the Artillery Luger.

M1935A and M1935S pistols

Caliber: 7.65mm

Length: 7.45in (189mm)

Weight: 1lb 10oz (760gm)

Barrel: 4.3in (109mm) long, four grooves, right-hand twist

Feed system: Eight-round detachable box magazine

System of operation: Recoil, Browning swinging link

Manufacturers:
Société Alsacienne de Construction Méchanique (SACM), France
Manufacture d'Armes de St. Étienne (MAS), France
Manufacture d'Armes de Tulle (MAT), France
Manufacture d'Armes de Chatellerault (MAC), France

Values: $125-$300

The Model 1935 pistol was designed by a Swiss, Charles G. Fetter, who worked for SACM in the 1920s and eventually took charge of its firearms department. During this period he worked on a pistol design which he patented in 1934; the principal feature of this was the construction of the lock mechanism as a separate unit. This is the same as the system used on the Russian Tokarev TT33 pistol (see page 55), but since at that time few TT33s had been made and the pistol was entirely unknown outside Soviet military circles, there seems little doubt that this coincidence is the result of two good designers thinking about the same problem and coming up with the same answer completely independently of each other.

In other respects Petter's design is basically Browning, using the usual system of locking the breech by a rib on the barrel mating with a recess on the undersurface of the slide top, and unlocked by a cam beneath the breech. The prototype was submitted to the French Army for trials and adopted for issue as the Model 1935. In about 1937 the design was reworked by the St. Étienne design staff with a view to making it easier to manufacture; after this the original model was known as the M1935A, while the new, simplified, model became the 1935S. The differences are immediately apparent; the 1935A is a much smoother product, with the butt shaped to fit the hand. The 1935S, on the other hand, has a straight butt, an angular and slab-sided appearance, and the finish is to a much lower standard.

There is little record of the use of the M1935 pistols by the French Army as very few weapons had been made and issued before the outbreak of war. What is even more remarkable is that there is no evidence of this weapon having been taken over by the German Army, who were generally quick to adopt good designs. This was probably because the M1935 was chambered for a very

odd cartridge, the 7.65mm *Longue*, or French Service Auto. This round, which fired an 85-grain bullet at 1,120ft/sec to give 240lb/ft of muzzle energy, was only marginally effective as a combat round, and had been developed specifically for this pistol.

BELOW Right-hand side of the M1935A. Note the butt shaped to fit the hand and the high degree of finish. The simplified M1935S had a straight-sided butt and coarser finish.

Mauser pistols

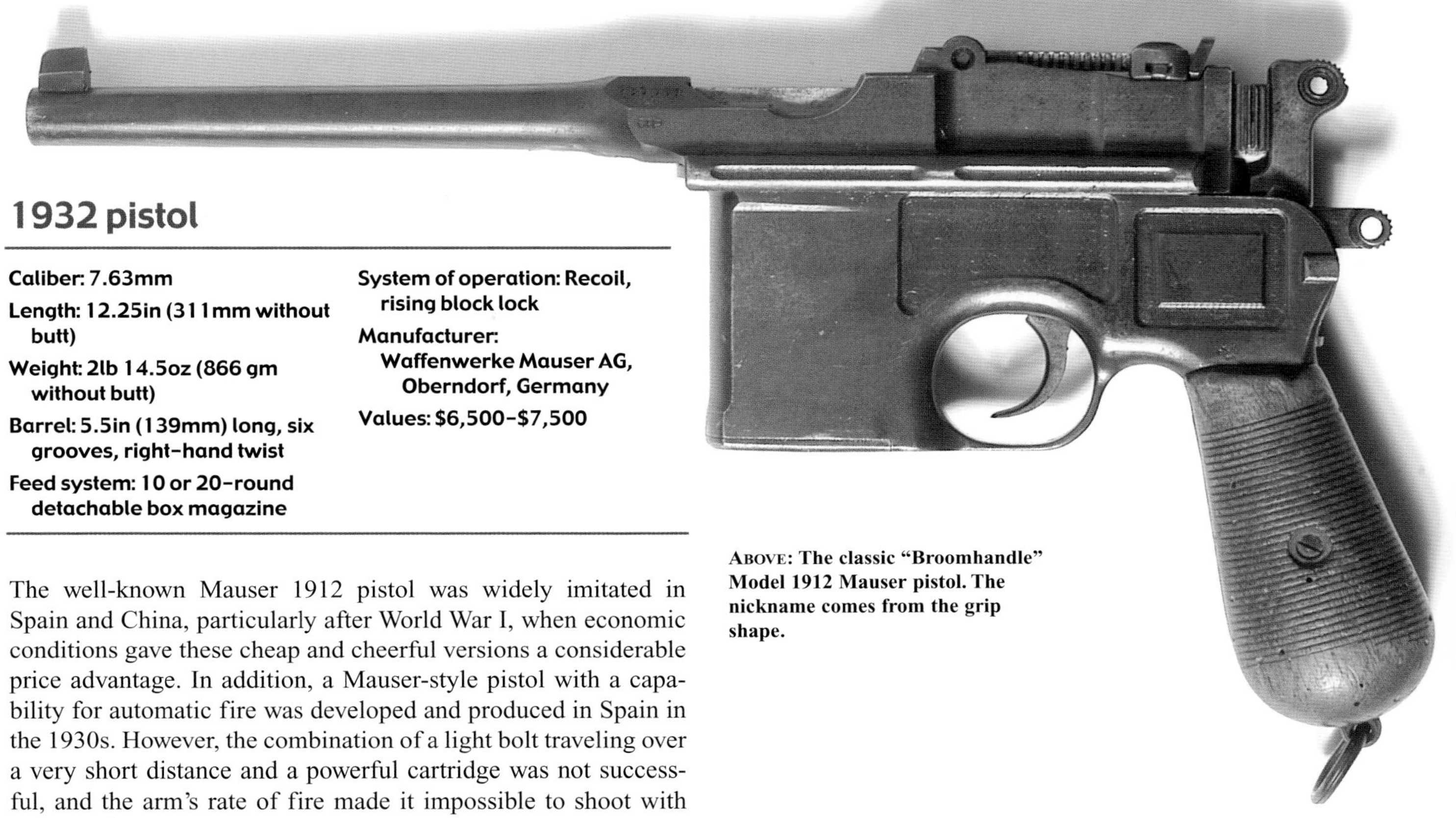

1912 pistol

Caliber: 7.63mm

Length: 11.75in (300mm without butt)

Weight: 2lb 12oz (1.25kg without butt)

Barrel: 5.5in (139mm) long, six grooves, right-hand twist

Feed system: Ten-round fixed box magazine

System of operation: Recoil, rising block lock

Manufacturer: Waffenwerke Mauser AG, Oberndorf, Germany

Values: $500–$2,500 (Many variations)

The origins of the "Broomhandle" Mauser date back to the design of the first Mauser self-loading pistol in 1896 which, with a few modifications, entered production two years later as the Model 1898. The Model 1898 was followed by others in 1903 and 1905; and at one time it seemed possible that these would be the last of the series, for Mauser had begun experimenting in other fields. However, his new project was abandoned, and another self-loading pistol, the Model 1912, shown here, duly appeared. It did not differ significantly from its predecessor of 14 years before, although it was issued with a wooden stock to facilitate its use as a light carbine.

In 1916 the German Army had a requirement for Mauser pistols to fire the straight-sided 9mm Parabellum cartridge, and it was quickly realized that conversion of the standard Model 1912 would be relatively simple. The arms thus altered were all distinguished by a large figure "9" cut into the butt-grips and painted red.

The Mauser pistol was widely used in World War I because, unlike other wars of the period, it involved a good deal of close-quarter fighting. The emphasis as far as the infantry was concerned was, of course, on the rifle, light machine gun, and medium machine gun; nevertheless, it was found that a Mauser pistol with its shoulder-stock attached was a handy weapon for raids, clearing trenches, and similar operations. It was used in very similar fashion to the submachine gun which the Germans finally adopted in 1918. The large number of Mauser Model 1912s made for use in World War I ensured that the weapon remained in widespread use throughout World War II.

1932 pistol

Caliber: 7.63mm

Length: 12.25in (311mm without butt)

Weight: 2lb 14.5oz (866 gm without butt)

Barrel: 5.5in (139mm) long, six grooves, right-hand twist

Feed system: 10 or 20-round detachable box magazine

System of operation: Recoil, rising block lock

Manufacturer: Waffenwerke Mauser AG, Oberndorf, Germany

Values: $6,500–$7,500

The well-known Mauser 1912 pistol was widely imitated in Spain and China, particularly after World War I, when economic conditions gave these cheap and cheerful versions a considerable price advantage. In addition, a Mauser-style pistol with a capability for automatic fire was developed and produced in Spain in the 1930s. However, the combination of a light bolt traveling over a very short distance and a powerful cartridge was not successful, and the arm's rate of fire made it impossible to shoot with very much accuracy.

Unwilling to be outmaneuvered by these competitors, Mauser proceeded to make its own version, using the 1926 Model pistol as a basis. As might be expected, the result was rather better engineered than the Spanish versions; two types appeared, differing only in the selector mechanism. The first model, produced in 1932, was designed by Josef Nickl and is identifiable by the diamond-shaped fire selector on the left side of the frame. In 1936 a second model appeared with a rectangular selector mechanism designed by Karl Westinger.

Like all such weapons the *Schnellfeuerpistole* (quick fire pistol) is a poor substitute for a submachine gun. The rate of fire—850rpm cyclic—is impossible to control in such a light weapon, with the result that the second and subsequent shots of a burst rarely land on the target; moreover, due to its automatic pistol origin it fires from a closed breech. When the trigger is released after firing a burst, the bolt closes, loading a fresh round, but the hammer does not fall. This means that the cartridge is sitting in a warm chamber, and if the gun has been heated up by firing several bursts, a "cook off"—the spontaneous ignition of the cartridge in the chamber due to heat absorption—is

ABOVE: The classic "Broomhandle" Model 1912 Mauser pistol. The nickname comes from the grip shape.

inevitable. Experiments have shown that three ten-round bursts are sufficient to make the chamber hot enough to guarantee the next round "cooking off" within seconds.

So far as can be ascertained, the few *Schnellfeuerpistolen* acquired by the German Army appear to have been issued to Waffen-SS units on the Eastern Front. Photographs showing them in use have been seen, but no details of their employment or effectiveness are known. They were also supplied to the Chinese and Yugoslavian armies in prewar days. The German government, both prior to and after Hitler's accession to power, supported Chiang Kai-shek's Chinese government, but ceased to do so after the Anti-Comintern Pact with Japan was signed. Hitler also supported Yugoslavia after 1934. A few Model 1932s seem to have turned up in the hands of Marshal Tito's men during the war. As a guerrilla weapon it was doubtless useful, being readily broken down and concealed, and when restricted to use as a self-loading single-shot carbine it was a highly effective weapon.

LEFT The elaborate leather holster with cleaning kit.

CENTER LEFT The Model 1912 with a charger of 7.63mm ammunition.

BELOW LEFT The wooden holster/stock.

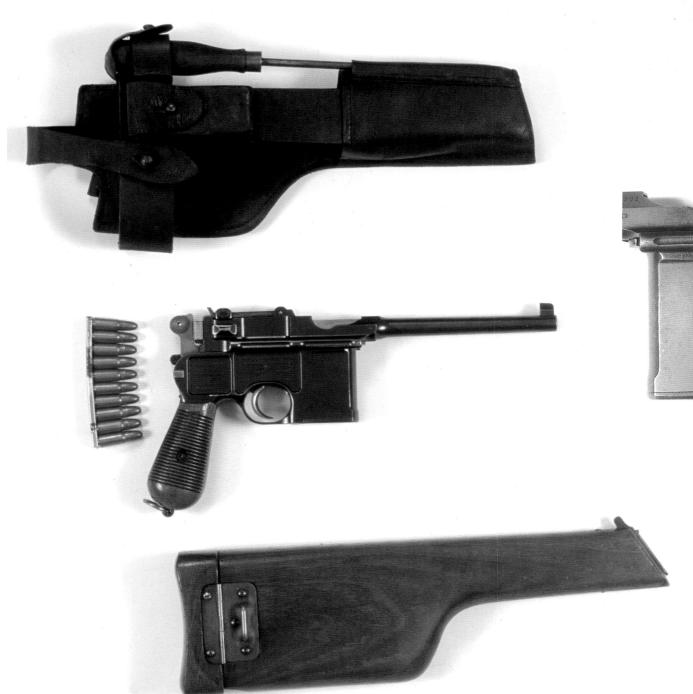

ABOVE The Broomhandles are fairly accurate and, with good ammunition, the addition of the stock allows decent ranges—but the tangent sights (seen here) are graduated to 1,000 meters (3,280ft): rather optimistic.

ABOVE The first successful semi-automatic fighting handgun, more than a million Mauser Broomhandles were made during more than 45 years of production in countries across the world. Today the Mauser is extremely collectible, particularly with stock.

BELOW With the wooden holster/stock attached, the length of the Broomhandle exceeds two feet. The first reported use of a Mauser Broomhandle was in 1898 when Winston Churchill, then a subaltern in the British cavalry, used his C96 at the battle of Omdurman in the Sudan rather than a saber.

Nagant Model 1895 revolver

Caliber: 7.62mm	**System of operation:** Revolver, single or double-action, solid-frame, gas-seal, with swing-out cylinder and hand ejector
Length: 9.06in (229mm)	
Weight: 1lb 12oz (820gm)	
Barrel: 4.33in (110mm)long, four grooves, right-hand twist	**Manufacturers:** Nagant Frères, Liège, Belgium State Arsenal, Tula, U.S.S.R.
Feed system: Seven-chambered cylinder	**Values:** $100–$200

The Nagant Model 1895 was designed at the Fabrique d'Armes Emile et Léon Nagant, founded by the two brothers in Liège in 1859. Having built up their reputation—for example by acting as a subcontractor for Remington—in 1888, they were contacted by Russian military officials to develop a new rifle, in 7.62mm caliber. The result, the Mosin-Nagant, was produced and adopted in 1891 (see pages 103 onward). The rifle proved successful, so it was unsurprising that the Russians returned to the Nagants when they decided to replace the Smith & Wesson revolvers in use in the Russian Army. The new revolver had to keep the same 7.62mm caliber used in the Mosin-Nagant rifle. The firm proposed a weapon with impressive, innovative, technical characteristics that was eventually adopted by the Russians in 1895—thus becoming the *Revolver Nagant Obrazets 1895* (Nagant revolver model of the year 1895).

The revolver was a weapon of unusual design that originated in Belgium in 1878. The inventor and patentee, Léon Nagant, took an idea attributed to another Belgian gunsmith, Pieper, and developed it into a workable pistol. The Nagant saw service with the armies of Belgium, Argentina, Brazil, Denmark, Norway, Portugal, Romania, Serbia, and Sweden and in a variety of calibers. By far the largest production, however, was undertaken in Russia, the Nagant Model 1895 being manufactured from 1895 to 1940.

The most innovative feature of the design was the system of moving the cylinder forward on cocking, so that the coned breech end of the barrel entered the mouth of the aligned chamber to create a near gas-tight seal. In addition, the cartridge case completely enclosed the bullet, the mouth of the case extending in front of the bullet nose, so that as the bullet left the case on firing, the case mouth was opened out into the barrel breech to complete the seal. The idea was to improve the efficiency of the cartridge by minimizing the loss of propellent gases through the small gap between cylinder and barrel, but it is arguable whether

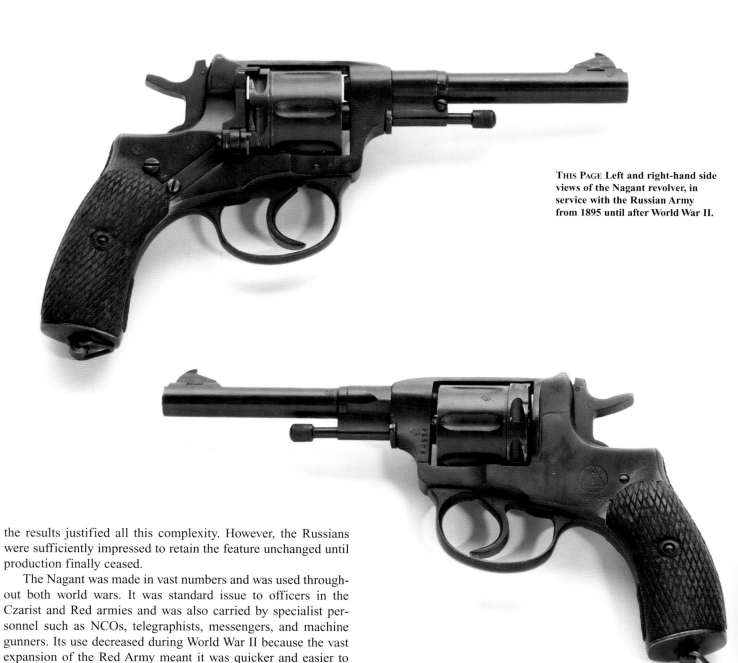

THIS PAGE Left and right-hand side views of the Nagant revolver, in service with the Russian Army from 1895 until after World War II.

the results justified all this complexity. However, the Russians were sufficiently impressed to retain the feature unchanged until production finally ceased.

The Nagant was made in vast numbers and was used throughout both world wars. It was standard issue to officers in the Czarist and Red armies and was also carried by specialist personnel such as NCOs, telegraphists, messengers, and machine gunners. Its use decreased during World War II because the vast expansion of the Red Army meant it was quicker and easier to provide troops with submachine guns that were, in any event, far more effective in relatively untrained hands.

Radom wz.35 pistol

Caliber: 9mm
Length: 8.31in (211mm)
Weight: 2lb 5oz (1.05kg)
Barrel: 4.53in (115mm) long, six grooves, right-hand twist
Feed system: Eight-round detachable box magazine

System of operation: Recoil, Browning link
Manufacturer: Polish State Arsenal, Radom, Poland
Values:
    Polish: $900–$1,700
    Nazi: $250–$500

In the 1930s the Polish Army, newly formed after World War I, was still trying to rationalize its equipment. Their issue pistols had been supplied as army surplus from several nations and included Parabellum, Mauser, Steyr, Mannlicher, Colt, Nagant, Webley, and Browning weapons among others, in every caliber from .32 to .455. As part of the standardization program, the Polish War Ministry held a trial early in 1935, from which it selected one pistol; contestants were to be chambered for the 9mm Parabellum. The design selected was developed by two Polish engineers, P. Wilniewczyc and I. Skrzypinski, and was largely based on Browning practice. The barrel was locked to the slide by grooves and unlocked by a cam working against a pin in the frame in a similar manner to the Browning HP Model 1935. The main addition was a large catch on the slide that allowed the hammer to be lowered safely onto a loaded chamber, so that the pistol could be carried fully loaded and brought to a state of readiness by simply cocking the hammer.

The pistol went into production at the Fabryka Broni w Radomiu, initially under the guidance of engineers from Fabrique Nationale. It was known as the *Pistolet ViS wz.35*, derived from the initials of the designers, or the *Pistolet Radom wz.35*, from its place of manufacture. After the German occupation in 1939 production continued for the German Army, post-occupation examples being recognizable by the marking "P Mod 35(p)" on the slide in place of the Polish Eagle engraved on prewar models. Because of the relatively small number manufactured and issued in Poland prior to 1939, Polish use appears to have been limited to the cavalry, with a few issued to infantry officers. It received wider use in the German Army, where it was particularly favored by parachute troops and Waffen-SS units. As a combat pistol, the Radom was among the best in the world. Strong and reliable, excellently made from first-class material (except for some made in 1943–44), it was on the heavy side for its caliber, which reduced the effects of recoil and made it accurate and easy to use.

TOP AND ABOVE Left and right-hand side views of the Radom wz.35 pistol. This example bears the markings of a weapon produced under German occupation.

TOP RIGHT Photo of the wz.35 with magazine extracted and weapon cocked.

Smith & Wesson .38/200 revolver

Caliber: .357 (nominally .38)

Length: 10.125in (258mm) with 6in (152mm) barrel

Weight: 1lb 8oz (680gm) with 6in (152mm) barrel

Barrel: 4in (102mm), 5in (127mm), or 6in (152mm) long, five grooves, right-hand twist

Feed system: Six-chambered cylinder

System of operation: Revolver, single or double action, solid frame, side-opening, hand ejector

Manufacturer: Smith & Wesson Arms Co., Springfield, Mass., U.S.

Values: $200–$350

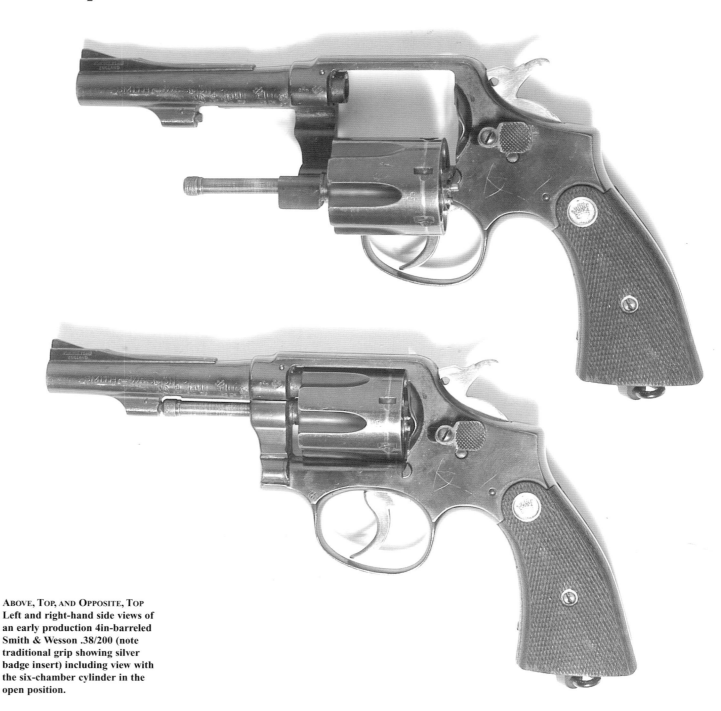

In 1940, after the losses at Dunkirk and with a rapidly expanding army to equip, the British government went to the United States to purchase of a variety of weapons. Among the items required was a revolver, and a contract was placed with Smith & Wesson to produce a model suited to the standard British Army .38 cartridge. The resulting weapon was the "British Military" or "38/200" Model. Basically it was no more than Smith & Wesson's standard Military and Police .38 that had been commercially available for several years, but the chambers were dimensioned to suit the British cartridge.

The weapon was extremely robust and made only of the highest quality materials. The first supplies were to Smith & Wesson's usual standard of excellent finish, blued, and polished steel with chequered walnut grips bearing the S & W medallion in silver. These early models were supplied in three barrel lengths as tabulated above, though the 4in and 5in lengths were not common. After April 1942, under the pressure of war production, the finish was changed to sandblasting and the grips were of smooth walnut without the medallion. From that time too, only the 6in barrel model was produced.

The S&W .38/200 was undoubtedly the most popular revolver ever issued to British troops. Light, well-balanced, accurate, and reliable, it was a better fighting weapon than either the Enfield or the Webley. It was supplied to all arms of the British forces, many Commonwealth forces, and was frequently carried by Commando and Airborne troops. More than 890,000 were produced between 1940 and 1946 and it remained in service long after the war.

ABOVE, TOP, AND OPPOSITE, TOP Left and right-hand side views of an early production 4in-barreled Smith & Wesson .38/200 (note traditional grip showing silver badge insert) including view with the six-chamber cylinder in the open position.

LEFT AND PAGE 50 Side views of a late production version with simplified grip to speed manufacture and a 5in barrel.

THIS PAGE AND PAGE 49 Side views
of a late production version with
simplified grip to speed
manufacture and a 5in barrel.

ABOVE Butt detail showing lanyard
ring and British War Department
marks.

THIS PAGE Side views of a late-production version. Note barrel lettering.

Smith & Wesson Triple Lock revolver

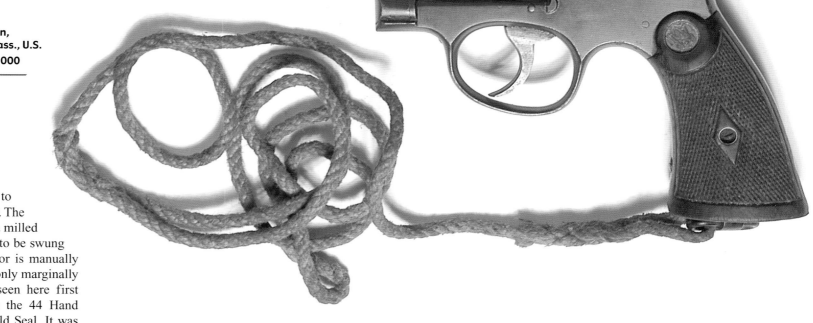

Caliber: .455

Length: 11.75in (298mm)

Weight: 2lb 6oz (1.08kg)

Barrel: 6.5in (165mm), six grooves, right-hand twist

Feed system: Six-chamber revolver

System of operation: Revolver, single or double action, solid frame, side-opening, hand ejector

Manufacturer: Smith & Wesson, Springfield, Mass., U.S.

Values: $400–$1,000

Although the Smith & Wesson No. 3 revolver was a reliable, well-made weapon, it never really became popular in the United States where there was an inherent distrust of large caliber, hinged-frame revolvers. By the end of the nineteenth century, Smith & Wesson had succumbed to market forces and produced a solid-frame revolver. The principle is simple and reliable: pushing forward a milled catch on the left of the frame allows the cylinder to be swung out to the left a separate yoke. Then the extractor is manually operated by means of the pin, a method which is only marginally slower than a hinged-frame type. The version seen here first appeared in 1908 and was variously known as the 44 Hand Ejector First Model, the New Century, or the Gold Seal. It was best known as the Triple Lock, from the fact that the cylinder locked not only at the rear, but also by means of a bolt into the front end of the rod and another in the casing below it. The lock was of rebounding, double-action type.

The standard production model was chambered for a special .44 cartridge, but versions were also made in various other calibers. A small number of original .44 caliber revolvers were converted to fire the British .455 Eley cartridge, mostly at the outbreak of World War I, but later large quantities of a .455 caliber model were made and sold to the British Army.

ABOVE AND ABOVE RIGHT Left and right-hand side views of the S&W Triple Lock .455 with typical British lanyard attached.

RIGHT Smith & Wesson identification mark.

FAR RIGHT Leather holster.

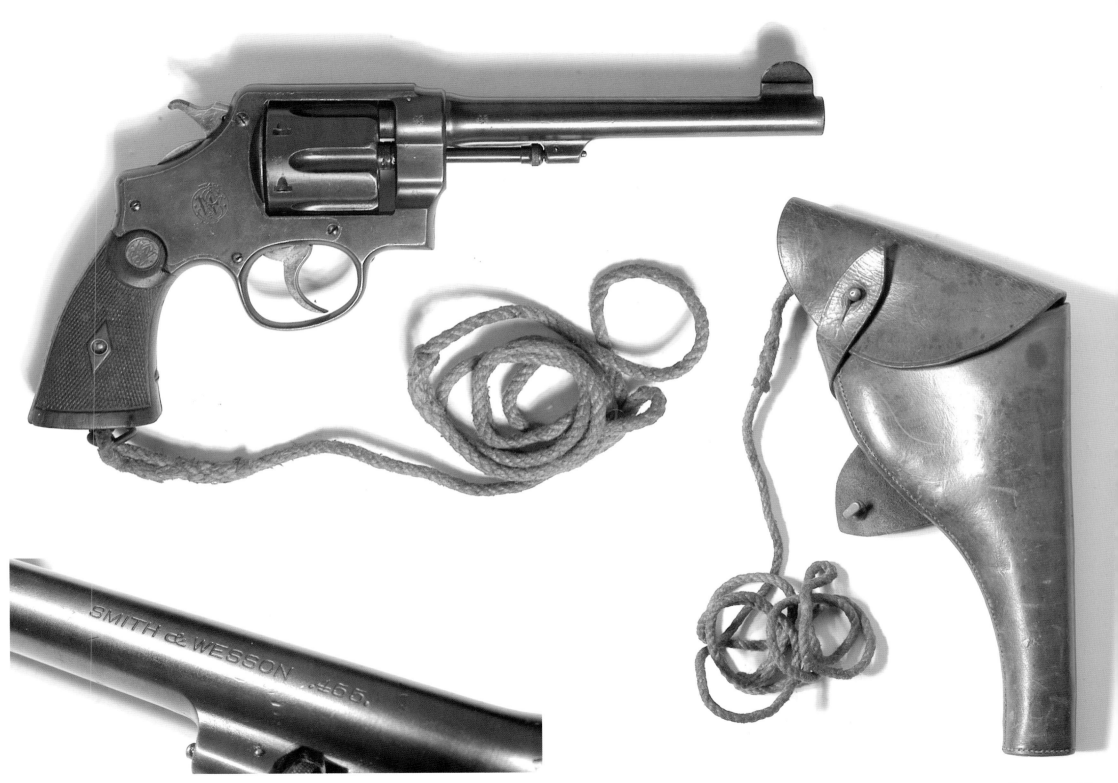

SMITH & WESSON .455

Smith & Wesson M1917 revolver

Caliber: .45

Length: 9.6in (244mm)

Weight: 2lb 2oz (9.6kg)

Barrel: 5.5in (140mm), six grooves, left-hand twist

Feed system: Six-chambered cylinder

System of operation: Revolver, single or double action, solid frame, side-opening, hand ejector

Manufacturer: Smith & Wesson Arms Co., Springfield, Mass., U.S.

Values: $300–$750

The S&W M1917 was, like the Colt equivalent, the product of the British need to find alternative sources of munitions in World War I. The requirements for all types of armaments far exceeded Britain's industrial capacity and so contracts were placed with U.S. manufacturers to meet the demand. Smith & Wesson agreed to supply the British Army with revolvers in .455 caliber and large numbers were delivered to the Western Front. When the U.S. entered World War I in 1917, the U.S. Army was not well equipped and all available suitable weapons had to be pressed into service. It was, however, considered essential to have uniformity of cartridge and as the standard service pistol was then the Model 1911 Colt self-loader, a considerable number of revolvers were manufactured to take the standard .45 ACP rimless round. These weapons were standardized as the Revolver, Caliber .45, Smith & Wesson Hand Ejector, M1917.

The change from British to U.S. ammunition did bring one problem, the U.S. round was rimless and if loaded into the cylinder in the usual way would fall right through. To overcome this ammunition was supplied in pressed steel, crescent-shaped, three-round clips. The M1917 had a recess cut in the rear face of the cylinder to accommodate two clips, this system proved to be an improvement since it speeded loading and ejection of spent cases. Both the Colt and the Smith & Wesson went on to see front-line service in World War II although mostly in British hands. The Smith & Wesson was, however, retained for use by American MPs up until 1945.

ABOVE Right-hand side view of the S&W M1917 revolver.

BELOW Left-hand side view of the S&W M1917 revolver with the cylinder open.

Tokarev Model TT33 pistol

Caliber: 7.62mm

Length: 7.68in (193mm)

Weight: 1lb 13oz (840gm)

Barrel: 4.57in (116mm) long, four grooves, right-hand twist

Feed system: Eight-round detachable box

System of operation: Recoil, Browning link

Manufacturer: State Arsenal, Tula, USSR

Values: $250–$350

The first automatic pistol adopted for general service use by the Soviet forces—the TT30—was designed by Feydor V. Tokarev and manufactured at Tula, which explains the use of the TT prefix in this weapon's designation. Standardized in 1930, not many examples of this early weapon had been produced before a modified design—the TT33—succeeded it in production during 1933. This TT33 pistol was then adopted as the standard, intended to succeed the Nagant revolver (see page 46). In the end, the TT33 did not wholly replace the reliable Nagant until after the end of World War II. This was largely as a result of the fact that the revolver, which had been produced in very large numbers, was still a completely reliable and sturdy weapon under the rough active service conditions.

The Tokarev pistol is based on the John Browning design as exemplified by the U.S. Colt M1911 pistol; it uses the same swinging link system of locking barrel and slide together. The only major change is the absence of a grip safety and the manufacture of the firing pin, hammer, and lock mechanism in a removable sub-unit; indeed the TT33 lacks any form of safety catch or device other than a half-cock notch on the hammer. A second notable feature is the machining of the feed lips, normally part of the magazine, into the frame of the pistol. As a result the magazine itself is a relatively simple box, and any rough handling is much less likely to result in misfeeds than with most of its contemporaries.

There is no external difference between the TT30 and TT33, the change being in the method of locking the barrel to the slide. The TT30 has two ribs formed on the upper surface of the barrel, that engage in two grooves on the underside of the slide top, in the usual Browning fashion. The TT33, on the other hand, has the ribs running completely around the barrel; this simplified and speeded up production because the ribs could be turned on a lathe while the rest of the barrel was being finished to correct dimensions instead of being milled out in a separate operation.

The exact distribution of these pistols is not known, but it can be assumed it was issued to infantry officers, it was not turned out in sufficient quantities to make its use widespread amongst the rank and file during World War II. Small numbers were first seen during the Russo-Finnish War, but the sub machine gun tended to become the individual weapon of the Red Army during the latter stages of the war against Germany.

The Tokarev is a powerful weapon, despite its small caliber; the cartridge is derived from the 7.63mm Mauser, and propels an 86 grain bullet at almost 1,400ft/sec, to give a striking energy of 365 foot-pounds, quite sufficient to cause considerable damage. The combination of power and lightness, makes this a rather violent weapon to shoot.

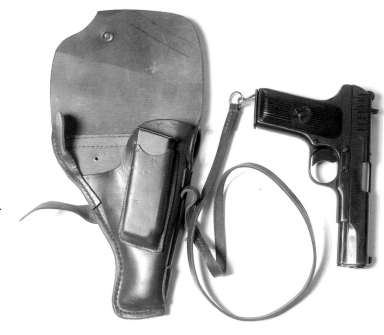

RIGHT Leather holster with spare magazine holder.

BELOW Right-hand side view of the TT33 with (detail) serial number, proof, and date stamps.

Walther Model 38 pistol

Caliber: 9mm

Length: 8.38in (213mm)

Weight: 2lb 1.2oz (960gm)

Barrel: 5in (127mm) long, six grooves, right-hand twist

Feed system: Eight-round detachable box magazine

System of operation: Recoil, wedge lock, double action firing lock

Manufacturers:
Carl Walther Waffenfabrik, Zella–Mehlis Spreewerke GmbH, Berlin, Germany
Mauserwerke AG, Oberndorf, Germany

Values: $300–$1,500 (Many variations)

During the early 1930s the company of Carl Walther of Zella-Mehlis, which had been making a series of pocket pistols of excellent quality for many years, began work on a military pistol in 9mm Parabellum caliber. The new weapon was designed from the outset as a military pistol, suitable for mass production to replace the P08. Unlike the company's earlier designs, the new pistol had a locked-breech mechanism and used an internal hammer.

This weapon was known as the *Modell AP* (*Armee-Pistole*) and a very few were made. Offered to the army, it was refused on the grounds that the hammer was enclosed; soldiers liked to see the hammer as a visible sign of the state of readiness of the weapon. Walther promptly redesigned it with an external hammer, and while it was being considered by the army, offered it commercially as the *Modell HP* (*Heeres-Pistole*). In 1938 it was adopted as the standard sidearm of the Wehrmacht and changed its name once more to Pistole 38, or P38. The P38 was also taken into use by the Swedish Army in 1939 as the Model 39, though it is doubtful if that many left Germany for Sweden.

The P38 had been designed with mass production in mind, and during the war three factories were devoted to its manufacture, as well as numerous subcontractors who made components for assembly at the major plants. It was this characteristic which led to its adoption, since the manufacture of the P38 demanded far less skilled labor than did the Parabellum 08. Production stopped after the war, but it was revived in 1957 by the new Carl Walther company at Ulm and the pistol was adopted by the Bundeswehr as the Pistole 1. As with the P08, the P38 was distributed to all ranks of the German Army. It was a remarkably robust weapon and performed particularly well on the Russian Front, where extreme cold conditions put many other weapons out of action. It was also accurate and easy to shoot well, attributes that accounted for its combat popularity and effectiveness.

RIGHT AND BELOW Left-hand side of the P38 with detail showing model and serial number.

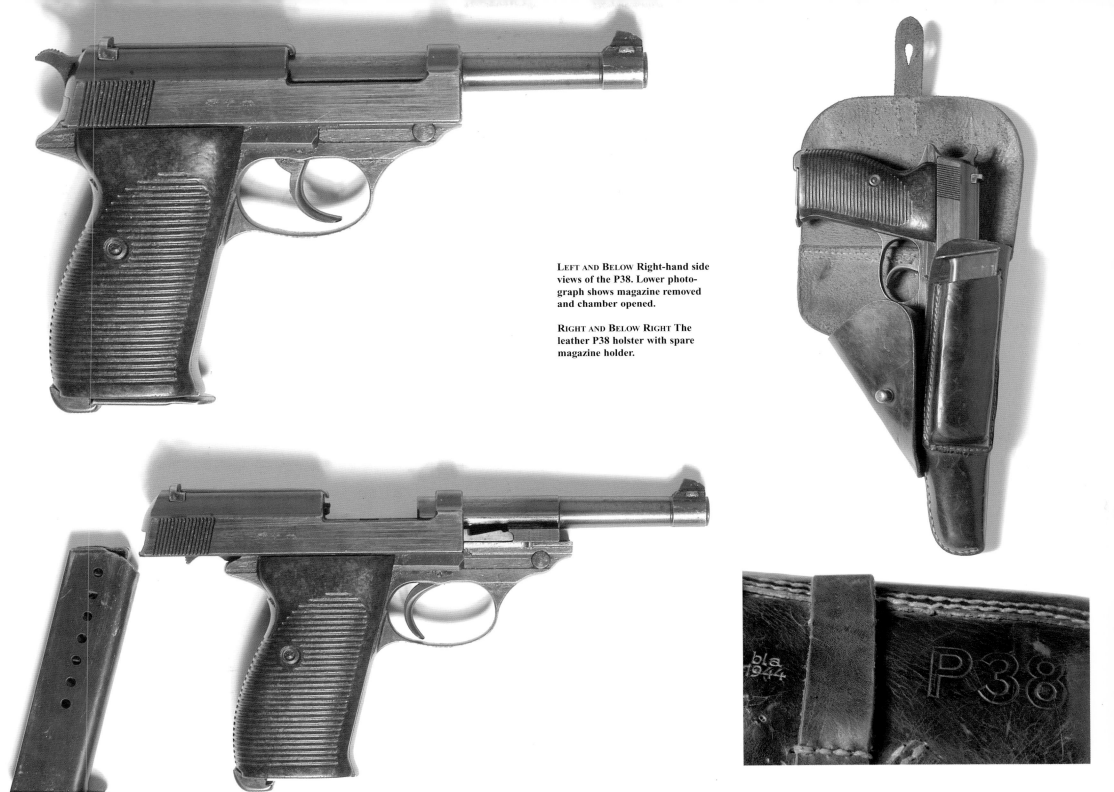

LEFT AND BELOW Right-hand side views of the P38. Lower photograph shows magazine removed and chamber opened.

RIGHT AND BELOW RIGHT The leather P38 holster with spare magazine holder.

Walther PP and PPK pistols

Walther PP pistol

Caliber: 7.65mm

Length: 6.4in (163mm)

Weight: 1lb 9oz (710gm)

Barrel: 3.8in (97mm), six grooves, right-hand twist

Feed system: Eight-round detachable magazine

System of operation: Blowback

Manufacturer
   Carl Walther Waffenfabrik AG, Zella-Mehlis, Germany

Values: $250-$1,000 (Many variations)

When first introduced in 1929 the Walther PP was of a new and, to some extent, revolutionary design, and it rapidly achieved popularity. It was made principally for police use—the designation PP stands for *Polizei Pistole*. It was very soon adopted as a holster arm by several European police forces, and later also became the standard pistol of the German Luftwaffe. Its main feature was its double-action lock, which was basically of revolver type and which involved the use of an external hammer. Carrying an automatic with a round in the chamber is normally dangerous, but with a Walther PP when the safety catch is applied, the action of the safety places a steel guard between the hammer and the firing pin preventing accidental discharge of the weapon. Various calibers were made including 9mm short. Postwar the PP has continued to be manufactured by many countries.

LEFT: Walther's maker's mark. Note also safety stud.

ABOVE Right-hand side view of the Walther PP.

RIGHT Walther mark and caliber information as the magazine is extracted from the butt.

FAR RIGHT Walther PPK. Note lack of plastic butt extension.

Walther PPK pistol

Caliber: 7.65mm
Length: 5.8in (147mm)
Weight: 1lb 4oz (570gm)
Barrel: 3.15in (80mm), six grooves, right-hand twist
Feed system: Seven-round detachable magazine

System of operation: blowback
Manufacturer
  Carl Walther Waffenfabrik AG, Zella-Mehlis, Germany
Values: $325-$1,000
  (Many variations)

Following the success of the PP, two years later, a smaller version was made for concealed use. It was intended for plain clothes police work and was known as the PPK. The Walther PPK pistol is of blowback type and, like the PP, has a double-action lock that allows the pistol to be carried safely with a round in the chamber and the hammer down. It also has an indicator pin which protrudes through the top of the slide when there is a cartridge in the chamber, although this was often omitted in wartime-manufactured examples to ease production. The earliest versions of this pistol had complete butt-frames with a pair of grips, but later examples had a front strap only, with a one-piece, molded, wrap around, plastic grip. Most also had a plastic extension on the bottom of the magazine, to make the weapon easier to hold. The PPK, like the PP, was widely used by Germany's armed forces and was also produced in France Hungary and Turkey.

LEFT Right-hand side view of the Walther PP with magazine extracted and chamber open.

Webley Mk. IV revolver

Caliber: .352 (nominally .38)

Length: 10.5in (266mm)

Weight: 1lb 11oz (810gm)

Barrel: 5in (127mm) long, seven grooves, right-hand twist

Feed system: Six-chambered cylinder

System of operation: Revolver, single or double action, top-break

Manufacturer Webley & Scott Ltd., Birmingham, England

Values: $225–$375

The Webley .455 revolver of World War I was admittedly an effective man-stopper, but it was a heavy and violent weapon that required extensive training and a good deal of practice to shoot accurately. As a result, after the war, the British Army did some research into revolver ballistics and decided that a .38 caliber weapon would offer sufficient power and would be easier to use. The Webley & Scott company was, at that time, developing a .38 revolver for possible military and police use and the company submitted this for trial. The army elected to develop its own design, the Enfield No.2 Mk. I, and the Webley model was turned down; it was subsequently perfected by the company and became a commercial pattern, widely adopted by police forces throughout the world.

In 1941, with the expansion of the British Army under way, the manufacturing capacity of the Royal Small Arms Factory at Enfield was insufficient to meet demand. In order to make up the shortfall Webley & Scott was asked to produce its .38 revolver for the armed forces, and it was officially introduced for service in 1942. Eventually, thousands of Webley Mk. IVs saw service throughout the war and for many years afterward. Because the Enfield revolver had been largely based on the Webley design, there was little difference between the two. However as the Webley retained the ability to be fired in single-action mode it was far easier to shoot accurately.

ABOVE Webley Mk. IV; note maker's mark on grip.

LEFT Gun broken open and extractor extended.

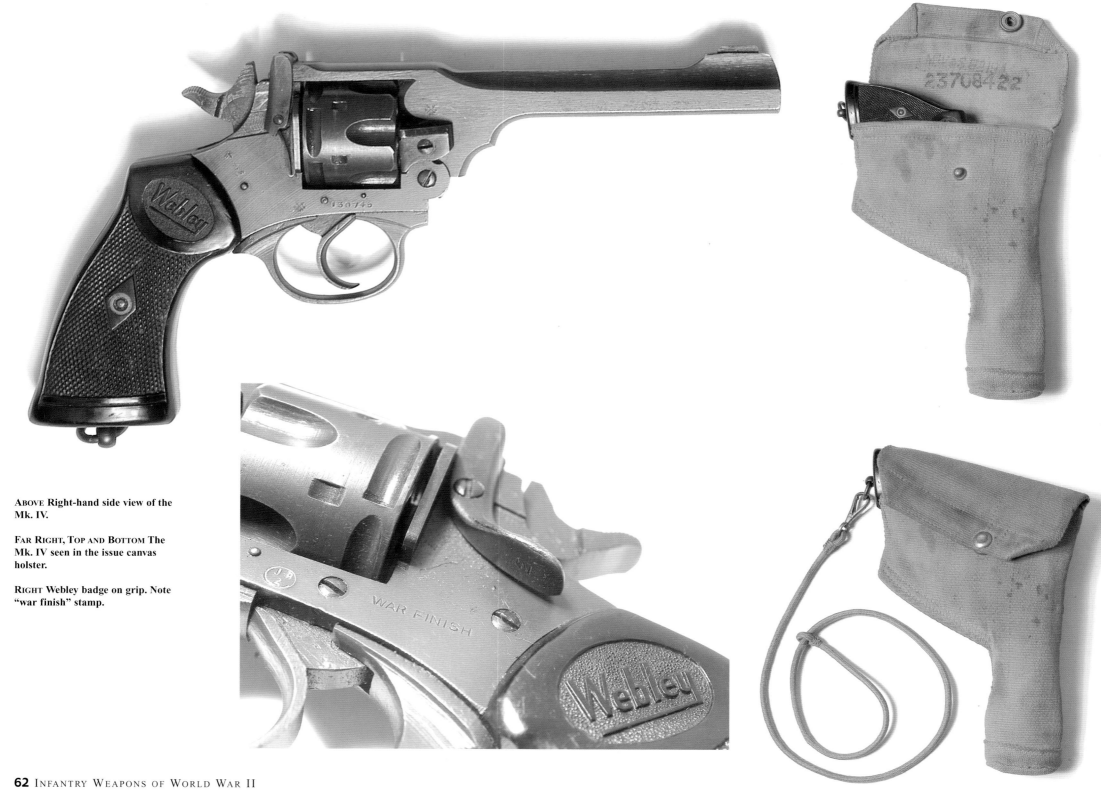

Above Right-hand side view of the Mk. IV.

Far Right, Top and Bottom The Mk. IV seen in the issue canvas holster.

Right Webley badge on grip. Note "war finish" stamp.

WAR FINISH

Webley & Scott Mk. VI revolver

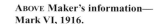

Caliber: .455

Length: 11in (279mm)

Weight: 2lb 5oz (1.05kg)

Barrel: 6in (152mm), seven grooves, right-hand twist

Feed system: Six-chambered cylinder

System of operation: Revolver, single or double action, top-break

Manufacturer Webley & Scott Ltd., Birmingham, England

Values: $250-$375

The famous Birmingham firm of P. Webley and Son (later Webley & Scott) had a virtual monopoly on the supply of British government revolvers for very many years. The company's last, and probably best-known, .455 service revolver was the Webley & Scott Mark VI. It was officially introduced in 1915 and did not differ very much from its predecessors except that the earlier bird-beak butt had been abandoned in favor of the more conventional squared-off style. It was of standard hinged-frame construction, with a stirrup-type barrel catch. The Mk. VI was robust and durable, and generally well suited to service use. It stood up remarkably well to the mud and dirt of trench warfare in the period 1914–18.

During World War I a short bayonet was designed for the revolver, although it was never officially adopted; it proved effective for trench raids and similar operations, and many officers bought one privately. A detachable butt, much like those available for the Mauser and Luger self-loading pistols, was also produced, but was not widely used. The Webley and Scott Mk. VI was officially abandoned in 1932 in favor of similar .38 revolvers but many reserve officers still carried Mk. VIs in .455 caliber when they were recalled in 1939.

ABOVE Maker's information— Mark VI, 1916.

LEFT AND BELOW LEFT The Webley and Scott Mk. VI, a stalwart of the fighting in the Great War was to see action again in World War II in the hands of reserve officers called up for active service. These left-hand side views show the revolver broken and ready for firing.

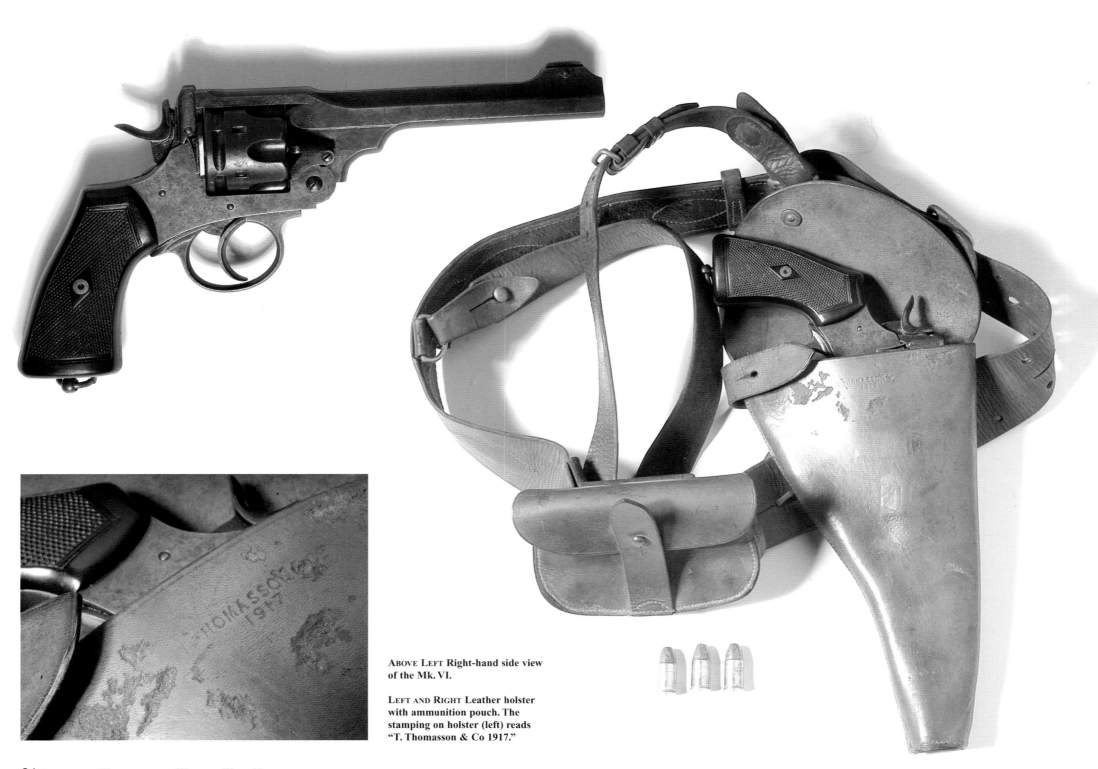

ABOVE LEFT Right-hand side view of the Mk. VI.

LEFT AND RIGHT Leather holster with ammunition pouch. The stamping on holster (left) reads "T. Thomasson & Co 1917."

Welrod Mk. I assassination pistol

Caliber: .32 (8.1mm)	**Feed System:** Single shot, six-round magazine
Length: 12.2in (312mm)	
Weight: 2lb (1.1kg)	**Manufacture:** BSA Ltd., England
Barrel: 4.37in (111mm), six grooves, right-hand twist	**Values:** n/a

The Welrod was a very efficient silent assassination pistol developed by the British Special Operations Executive at their workshops in Welwyn Garden City in 1942 and manufactured by BSA Ltd. Technically, it is not very difficult to silence a weapon; what is difficult is to make an effective silencer that is not so bulky as to make the weapon hopelessly clumsy in use. There are two problems involved: one is to suppress the noise of the explosion; the other is to conceal the sonic boom when the bullet breaks the sound barrier (assuming that it is of such velocity). In the case of the Welrod the sound of the propellant was muffled by an integral silencer in the forward part of the gun body. This was fitted with a series of self-sealing, oil-impregnated, leather washers. These close behind the passage of the bullet and trap the sound. The problem of sonic boom was avoided by selecting the 7.65mm Browning .32 ACP, a subsonic round.

The Welrod was a single-shot weapon, with a magazine in the butt. To operate it, the knurled cap at the rear end of the receiver was turned and drawn back, opening the bolt, and then pushed forward to load a cartridge and cock the striker, after which it was turned to lock. Grasping the pistol depressed the grip safety at the rear of the butt, and pulling the trigger fired the cartridge. There was also a Mk. II model, similar to the Mk. I shown here but without a trigger guard and with the magazine release at the back of the butt. The Welrod remained in production from 1942 to 1945

BELOW Welrod Mk. I assassination pistol. Crude but effective, the cylindrical body houses the silencer and the knurled knob at the rear retracts the bolt. The pistol grip houses the magazine.

RIFLES AND SHOTGUNS

The rifle has long been the traditional arm of the infantryman. Basic training required that every serviceman be trained in the use of the rifle and during World War II the vast majority of front-line troops were equipped with rifles, although the numbers using other weapons increased as the war progressed. The origins of most of the rifles with which the armies of the combatant nations were equipped at the start of hostilities can be traced back to the turn of the century, if not earlier. The armed forces of Britain, Japan, and Italy, all retained bolt-action rifles throughout the war. Only America had succeeded in completely rearming her troops with automatic rifles, and Germany was well on the way when the war ended. The Soviet Union, after a false start, was to partially reequip with automatics, the sheer numbers of bolt-action rifles in service and the policy of producing large numbers of submachine guns, tending to slow the process. Nevertheless, the war would end as it started, with most soldiers carrying rifles. However, in the hands of some German soldiers were the first of a new breed, a different type of rifle that would become the weapon of choice for most armies soon after World War II finished. The German MP44 (see page 107) was the first assault rifle that combined the features of the rifle, submachine gun, and light machine gun to provide the soldier with substantially greater firepower.

ABOVE RIGHT The classic British rifle of World War I, the SMLE (Short, Magazine, Lee-Enfield) was probably the finest bolt-action rifle to see wartime service. See page 78 onward.

RIGHT The American M1 Garand rifle. See pages 86–87.

Top The classic rifle of the nineteenth century, the Martini Henry was not in military service in 1939 but would see action in World War II in the hands of Home Guard and colonial police units.

Above The German Kar 98, this one carrying a rifle grenade. See page 77.

Right An oddity from the Cobbaton Military Collection is this Greener Mk. III of 1907. An Australian cadet's rifle that was not in military service in 1939, most had been deactivated in the 1920s for use in drill practice. This one came from a British Home Guard unit.

Berthier Modèle (Mle) 07/15 rifle

Caliber: 8 mm

Length: 51.24in (1,303mm)

Weight: 8lb 6oz (3.79kg)

Barrel: 31.4in (798mm), four grooves, left-hand twist

Feed system: Three-round clip-fed internal box magazine

Manufacturers:
Manufactures d'Armes, Chatellerault, St. Étienne, and Tulle, France

Manufacture d'Armes de Paris (components only), France

Etablissements Contin–Souza, Paris, France

Société Française Delaunay-Belleville, France

Remington Arms–Union Metallic Cartridge Co., Ilion, New York

Values: $150-$275

The Bethier Mle 1907 was one of a long line of weapons originating with the *Carabine de Cavallerie Modèle* (Mle) *1890* designed by Adolphe Berthier. His design was based on the Lebel but incorporated modifications to improve the locking and speed of the action, and replaced the tube magazine of the Lebel with an internal Mannlicher clip type. There followed a succession of models each modified in minor ways to suit their particular application—such as the 1890 cuirassiers' carbine, the 1890 gendarmerie carbine, and the 1892 artillery musketoon. These were followed, in turn, by the Mle 1902 colonial rifle that consisted of the Berthier carbine mechanism mounted in the body of a light rifle. This was the first Berthier rifle taken into French service and was used by colonial troops in Annam, Cambodia, and French Indochina. The Mle 1902 proved a great success, being lighter, easier to handle, and more effective than the standard Lebel Mle 86. Encouraged by this success the French authorities issued a full-size version for use by Senegalese sharpshooters, the Mle 1907. This had a turned-down bolt handle and was not provided with a cleaning rod because the Senegalese carried cleaning equipment separately.

With the outbreak of war in 1914 the French authorities realized that something better than the standard service rifle, the Lebel Mle 86, was going to be required for the forthcoming conflict. As a stopgap some Mle 1892 artillery musketoons were produced with extended barrels, but the long-term solution was the Mle1907/15 rifle. Based on the Mle 1902, the Mle 1907/15 differed only in that it was provided with a straight bolt handle and a cleaning rod was fitted. The mechanism was identical and retained the three-round clip-loaded internal magazine.

VARIANTS

Mle 07/15 T16

This was the Mle 07/15 modified to accept the five-round magazine of the Mle1916

Mle 1916

This was a development of the Mle 07/15 in which the three-round magazine was replaced with a five-round type. It entered service in 1917.

Mle 07/15 M34

With the introduction of the *7.5mm Balle 1929C* cartridge in 1929 it was decided to modify the Mle 07/15 to accept the new round pending development of the MAS 36. Many conversions were carried out between 1934 and 1939 by Manufactures d'Armes, St. Étienne.

ABOVE AND BELOW Left and right-hand side views of a Mle 07/15 M34, the version modified to take the 7.5mm Balle 1929C cartridge.

Browning Automatic Rifle M1918

Data: M1918A2	**Rate of fire:** Fully automatic, 450 or 650rpm
Caliber: .30	**Manufacturers:**
Length: 47.75in (1.22m)	**Colt Patent Firearms Manufacturing Co., U.S.**
Weight: 19lb 6oz (8.75kg)	**Winchester Repeating Arms Co., New Haven, Conn., U.S.**
Barrel: 24in (610mm) long, four grooves, right–hand twist	
Feed system: 20–round detachable box magazine	**Marlin-Rockwell Corp., U.S.**
System of operation: Gas, lifting bolt	**Values:** $15,000–$20,000 (Class III; many variations)

When the U.S. Army entered World War I in 1917 it was desperately short of all types of weapons. One of its most pressing needs was for light automatic weapons. John M. Browning offered two designs, one of which was this automatic rifle. Unfortunately, organizing production took time, and it was not until the summer of 1918 that issues began. From then until after World War II the Browning automatic rifle Model 1918A1 remained the squad light automatic of the U.S. Army.

Unfortunately the Browning was not one of the best of its kind. It was originally intended to be used during assault, its operator firing from the hip, a tactic that would become familiar in World War II with the widespread adoption of the submachine gun. But the action of the weapon was so violent that accurate fire under these conditions was almost impossible, and the gun was later provided with a bipod so that it could be used in the prone position associated with the light machine gun.

The mechanism used a tipping bolt operated by a gas piston, a system based on Browning's pump-action shotgun of 1904. However, the lightness of the weapon, 15.5lb in original form, led to light reciprocating parts, and to keep the rate of fire within reasonable bounds, a shock absorber was included in the return spring assembly. Despite this, the violent action led to rapid wear, and the rate of attrition in action was higher than for other light automatics. Another drawback was the bottom-mounted 20-round magazine, inconvenient to change in action and with a limited capacity for automatic fire. However, the BAR had the advantage of being designed with mass production in mind, and it was relatively easy to produce. As well as being standard in the U.S. Army, it was widely adopted by other countries as a light machine gun, and large numbers were supplied to Britain during the war when it was used to arm Home Guard detachments.

VARIANTS

M1918
The original model, no bipod, sights not adjustable for windage selective full-automatic or single-shot fire.

M1918Al
Hinged butt plate, bipod attached just ahead of the fore-end stock.

M1918A2
This model was introduced in 1940 with two fully automatic rates of fire. It had a bidpod (often removed in the field because it weighed more than 21lb) with skid feet and a monopod beneath the butt. The woooden forend was reduced in size to expose more of the barrel to improve cooling. The M1918A2 was manufactured by Colt, Marlin-Rockwell and Winchester, and was the standard U.S. squad weapon in World War II and the Korean War.

M1922
The M1918 with the barrel finned to improve cooling.

BELOW AND BELOW RIGHT M1918A2rear and fore sight details. The rear sight came from the Browning M1919A4 machine gun. Note bipod attachments to flash hider on this model.

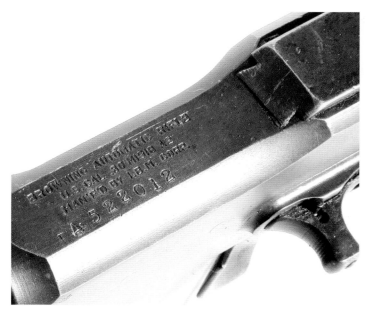

ABOVE Maker's mark and serial number on anM1918A2.

THIS PAGE The M1918A2 was the main service model in World War II. It had a bipod fitted with skis instead of spiked feet mounted on the flash muzzle of the barrel. It was fitted with a hinged shoulder rest, had a shorter shoulder stock, and smaller fore grip.

ABOVE The M1918, the original production version, had no provision for fitting a bipod.

BELOW The BAR was manufactured in Europe and saw use in many countries, particularly Belgium. This is an example rechambered to take 7.62mm ammunition (note curved magazine).

RIGHT AND FAR RIGHT **Magazine attachment details.**

BELOW **Hinged shoulder rest detail.**

BOTTOM **Bipod, mounting bracket, muzzle, and fore sight detail.**

Fallschirmjägergewehr (FG or FjG) 42 rifle

Caliber: 7.92mm

Length: 37in (940mm)

Weight: 9lb 15oz (4.53kg)

Barrel: 19.75in (502mm) long, four grooves, right hand twist

Feed system: 20-round detachable box magazine

System of operation: Gas, turning bolt

Rate of fire: cyclic, 750rpm

Manufacturers:
Rheinmetall–Borsig AG, Düsseldorf, Germany
Heinrich Krieghoff Waffenfabrik, Suhl, Germany

Values: $25,000–$45,000 (Class III)

When the MP43 development began, the German parachute troops took an interest in it. They felt that a selective-fire weapon would fill a void in their armory, because airborne operations always demand the maximum firepower in the smallest package. On further examination, however, they rejected the design on the grounds that the short cartridge, around which the new weapon was being developed, was insufficient for their particular needs, and they demanded a similar weapon taking the full-sized service round. This demand arose from experience in Crete, where they had been the targets for long-range rifle fire by British troops, and also from the fact that they considered that the standard 7.92mm round would be more easily available on any fighting front. The army was not interested in such a weapon so, because the parachute troops were part of the Luftwaffe, they re-submitted their demand through air force channels and had it approved.

The weapon was designed by Rheinmetall-Borsig of Sommerda, who received the specification late in 1940 and had a prototype ready for testing in mid-1942. The specification had, in fact, been put out to eight companies, but only the Rheinmetall design was considered worth pursuing. Although it was eventually put into production, there were numerous design changes and modifications, and the design was still not finalized when the war ended. A relatively small number were made—7,000 is generally quoted—because during the development priorities had changed; the airborne assault on Crete, while providing the paratroops with a useful case for having the weapon, had also shown that such operations were too expensive to be repeated, and the airborne forces spent the rest of the war fighting as conventional ground forces. Moreover, the production facilities were controlled by the Army Weapons Bureau, who were reluctant to allot factory capacity to a weapon that was considered superfluous.

The FG42 was a sound design, based on well-tried principles. It was gas-operated, and the bolt mechanism was so designed that when firing single-shot the bolt closed on the cartridge, after which pressing the trigger fired the weapon, which then automatically reloaded. On automatic fire, however, the bolt remained open when the trigger was released so as to allow the chamber and barrel to cool down between bursts. Much of the weapon was fabricated from steel pressings, while the furniture was of laminated wood or plastic. While it was an ingenious and effective weapon, it was difficult to shoot accurately because of the heavy recoil from the full-sized cartridge and the light and flimsy bipod, and it was hard to control in the automatic mode.

Reportedly, the first use of the FG42 was in the raid to release Mussolini in September 1943. The majority of weapons were issued to units on the Western Front; large numbers were captured by Allied troops in 1944, giving rise to the belief that the rifle was being produced in greater numbers than was the case.

RIGHT Right-hand side view of the FG42. An outstanding weapon, it had an integral bayonet and only one drawback—the 20-round box magazine attached to the left-hand side (much like the Sten) rather than from below. While produced in smallish numbers in World War II, it would influence many postwar designs.

Gewehr 41(W) and Gewehr 43 rifles

Gewehr 41(W) rifle

Caliber: 7.92mm
Length: 44.5in (1.13m)
Weight: 11lb (5kg)
Barrel: 21.5in (545mm) long, four grooves, right-hand twist
Feed system: 10-round integral box magazine

System of operation: Gas, locking flaps
Manufacturers: Carl Walther Waffenfabrik, Zella Mehlis, Thuringia, Germany
Values: $1,500-$3,000

Gewehr 43 with telescopic sight—it was an excellent sniper's rifle.

While numerous automatic rifle designs had been put forward in Germany since the turn of the century, and one or two of them actually tried in service, it was not until 1937 that the German Army really began to take an interest in the question of providing a self-loader to replace the bolt-action Mauser. It is possible that the action of the U.S. Army in standardizing the Garand in 1936 had something to do with the timing of this decision. As a result of the requirements, the first self-loading rifle to be produced in any quantity was the Gewehr 41, two versions of which were developed: the 41(M) built by Mauserwerke and the 41(W) built by Carl Walther.

Both these weapons used an unusual system of operation: a muzzle-expansion chamber that turned some of the emerging gases backward to actuate an annular piston surrounding the barrel. This, in turn, drove an operating rod to the rear to manipulate the bolt. The 41(M) had its operating rod beneath the barrel and used a rotating bolt opened and closed by cam surfaces. Although theoretically sound (as one might expect from Mauser) the design failed to stand up to trials and no more than a few were ever made. The 41(W) had its operating rod above the barrel and used a totally different bolt-locking system in which two flaps were pushed outward to lock the bolt to the receiver as the firing pin moved forward; this method was derived from the Frijberg-Kjellman machine gun of the early 1900s and had achieved prominence in the Russian Degtyarev designs of 1928. The Walther version was easier to make and much better suited to the rough and tumble of service use, and it was adopted in preference to the Mauser design.

Several thousand rifles were made, the vast majority of which were sent to the Eastern Front and eventually lost there. While the 41(W) worked, it could not be called popular; its muzzle cone design carried the penalty of considerable fouling, and thus demanded constant and meticulous maintenance. Moreover, the weapon was ill-balanced, with a pronounced muzzle preponderance, making it difficult to handle, and it was extremely heavy for an infantry rifle. As a result, when something better came along, the soldiers were not slow to discard the Gewehr 41, though it remained officially in service, throughout the war.

Gewehr 43 rifle

Caliber: 7.92mm
Length: 44in (1.17m)
Weight: 9lb 9oz (4.4kg)
Barrel: 22in (558mm) long, four grooves, right-hand twist
Feed system: 10-round detachable box magazine
System of operation: Gas, locking flaps

Manufacturers: Carl Walther Waffenfabrik, Zella-Mehlis, Germany
Berliner-Lübecker Maschinenfabrik AG, Lübeck
Gustloffwerke, Suhl, Germany
Values: $1,500-$3,000

Experience with the Gewehr 41(W) soon showed the areas in which improvement was desirable. The bolt-locking system was satisfactory, but the weight was excessive and the muzzle cone acted, in the words of one authority, as a "built-in fouling generator." As a result of these criticisms the gas operating system was changed to the more conventional piston type, the gas being tapped from the barrel about halfway between chamber and muzzle and directed into a gas channel above. Around this channel was a cup-like tubular piston, driving an operating rod which emerged above the chamber to drive a bolt carrier—a very similar layout to that of the Soviet Tokarev. This gives rise to the question of how many times the designer looked at the Tokarev during his designing.

The bolt locking system was the same as that used on the G41(W), pivoting flaps controlled by the movement of the firing-pin assembly, which in turn was controlled by the bolt carrier. The whole weapon was much lighter and better balanced than its predecessor, and moreover, had been designed with rapid production in mind so that it was an easier proposition to turn out in quantity.

One unusual feature (for a military rifle) was the inclusion in the design of a machined-out dovetail section on the receiver to act as a seating for a sighting telescope, and a large number of these rifles were issued for sniping, fitted with the Zundblickfernrohr 4 telescope.

The G43 was extensively used on the Eastern Front, being first issued in 1943, and was found in much lesser numbers on other fronts. An interesting comment on the increasing difficulty of production in Germany is the gradual change in the appearance of the weapon as produced in 1944 and 1945; originally finished to a reasonably high standard and with solid wooden furniture, the external finish gradually deteriorated until final versions exhibited numerous tool-marks, and the furniture was of resin-bonded plywood laminations or phenolic plastic compounds. Nevertheless, the internal quality was always to a satisfactory standard, and the weapon had a good reputation for accuracy and reliability.

It remained in production until the end of the war and was afterwards adopted by the Czech Army as its standard sniping rifle—something of a compliment when one considers the considerable expertise the Czechs themselves have shown with firearms. In addition, several thousand were disposed of commercially in postwar years.

Gewehr 98 rifle

Caliber: 7.92mm

Length: 49.2in (1.25m)

Weight: 9lb (4.14kg)

Barrel: 29.15in (740mm) long, four grooves, right-hand twist

Feed system: Five-round, integral box magazine

System of operation: Bolt operation

Manufacturers: Various German state and private concerns

including:

Bavarian state arsenal, Amberg

DWM, Berlin

Königlich Gewehrfabrik, Erfurt

Haenel Waffen und Fahrradfabrik AG, Suhl,

Mauserwerke AG, Oberndorf

Königlich Gewehr und Munitionsfabrik, Spandau

Values: $300-$500

The development of the Gewehr 98 is inextricably bound up with the story of the Mauser brothers, Peter Paul and Wilhelm. (See also Mauser rifles on pages 97–99.) The two brothers were both trained as gunsmiths and worked at the Royal Wurttemberg Arms Factory. It was Peter who developed the famous Mauser bolt action and the brothers designed a rifle around this new action which they offered to the Prussian authorities. It was not until some time later that their design was adopted for the new German Army as the Model 1871.

In 1872 the brothers set up a factory in Oberndorf to produce their new rifle. A succession of models followed over the next few years incorporating various improvements to the mechanism and innovations such as charger loading. 1898 saw the introduction of the Model 1898—or Gewehr 98 as it was later redesignated. This weapon was the culmination of more than twenty years of development and was one of the best rifles in the world.

The Gewehr 98 was developed from the Model 1888 and was the first German Army rifle to fire the the new 7.92mm cartridge. It was destined to become one of the most widely used and successful weapons of its type, and was produced in enormous quantities. Many Model 98s were also produced in Spain and both Spanish and German produced weapons were to be found in the armories of countries all over the world. These are covered under the entry Mauser rifles on pages 97–99.

The Gewehr 98 saw service throughout World War I and, in modified form, throughout World War II as well.

VARIANTS

Kar 98b

A Gewehr 98 rifle with its bolt handle turned down and with some improvements to the sights.

ABOVE AND BELOW LEFT The classic lines of the Gewehr 98, the long-lived Mauser bolt-action rifle that saw service in the German Army for some 50 years.

Karabiner Kar 98k carbine

Caliber: 7.92mm
Length: 43.6in (1.11m)
Weight: 8lb 9oz (3.9kg)
Barrel: 23.6in (600mm)long, four grooves, right-hand twist
Feed system: Five-round integral box magazine

System of operation: Mauser turn bolt
Manufacturers: Principally Mauserwerke AG, Germany, but many other subcontractors built rifles or components during the war
Values: $300-$500

The Karabiner Kar 98k (k for *kurz* = short) was the last of the long line of Mauser rifles used by the German Army that started with Model 1871, the first to be designed around the now-famous bolt action developed by Peter Mauser.

Before World War I the Germans—as did the British with the Short Lee-Enfield in 1903 and the Americans with their short Springfield—decided to produce a short version of the Gew 98, calling it the Karabiner 98. The main change was to reduce the length of the barrel by six inches, in addition the bolt handle was turned down and the wood of the stock was cut away to allow the bolt to be grasped more easily. The rear sight was also simplified. The weapon so created became the standard German infantry weapon of World War I and afterward completely replaced the Gew 98 rifle. Between the wars it was redesignated the Kar 98a.

In the early 1930s the design was simplified to facilitate mass production, and the resulting weapon was adopted as the standard rifle for the new Wehrmacht in 1935 as the Kar 98k. It was produced by the millions in a number of factories, and production continued until the end of the war in 1945, because there were never sufficient automatic weapons to replace bolt-action rifles completely.

VARIANTS

Kar 98k/42

This is a production variation of the 98k and is rarely encountered. The principal differences are that the foresight is enclosed in a tunnel, and the butt-plate is protected by a metal cup, which encloses the end of the butt for a depth of about half an inch.

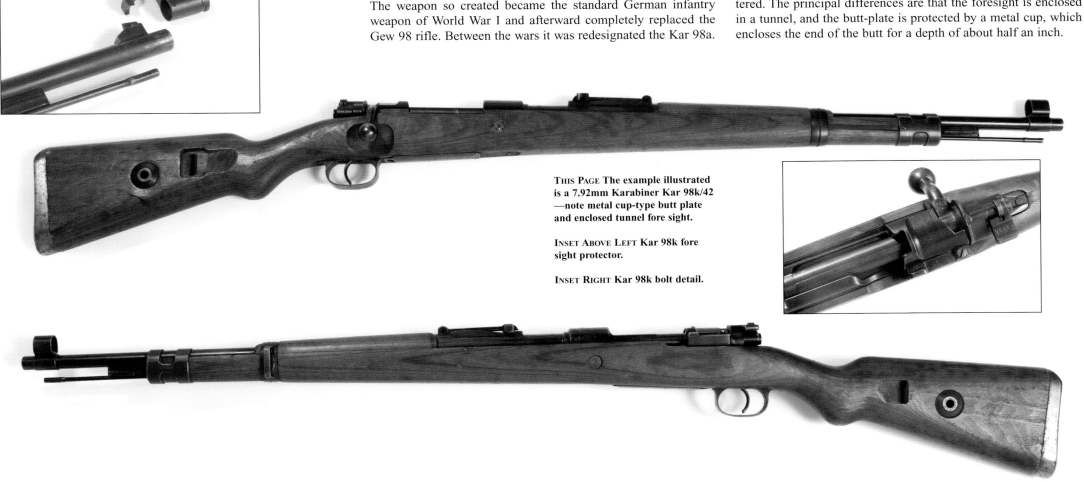

THIS PAGE The example illustrated is a 7.92mm Karabiner Kar 98k/42 —note metal cup-type butt plate and enclosed tunnel fore sight.

INSET ABOVE LEFT Kar 98k fore sight protector.

INSET RIGHT Kar 98k bolt detail.

Lee-Enfield rifles

SMLE No. 1 Mk. III & Mk. III* rifles

Data: Mk. III

Caliber: .303

Length: 44.57in (1.13m)

Weight: 8lb 10oz (3.93kg)

Barrel: 25.19in (640mm) long, five grooves, right-hand twist

Feed system: 10-round detachable box magazine

System of operation: Lee turn-bolt

Manufacturers:

Various British companies including—BSA, Enfield, LSA, NRFI, SSA

Values: $100–$200

Introduced in 1903 the SMLE No. 1 Mk. I was a new concept in military rifles. Conventional thinking at the time dictated the production of two versions of any service rifle, a full-length rifle for infantry use and a shorter carbine for cavalry and special purpose troops such as engineers and artillery. The SMLE, or Short Lee Enfield, dispensed with this practice by introducing a design that was midway between the two. This approach payed great dividends in terms of production and logistics since all branches of

the army were supplied with the same standardized rifle. The rifle itself was a development of the original Lee-Enfield Mk. I first introduced in 1895, which was, in turn, derived from the Lee-Metford of 1888. This was based on the magazine and bolt mechanism designed by the American engineer James Lee and developed at the Royal Small Arms Factory at Enfield Lock, Middlesex, England.

The SMLE Mk. I was not without its problems but after eleven years of development the SMLE Mk. III that the troops of the British Expeditionary Force took with them to France in 1914 was one of the best rifles in service with any army. It was a fully stocked weapon, fitted to accommodate a long bayonet. The action was of the turnbolt variety and used rear-locking lugs as opposed to the front-locking lugs of the Mauser system. In theory this meant that the Lee system was less safe than that of the Mauser, but in service it caused no problems at all, and the smooth action of the Lee-Enfield mechanism made the British rifle easy and extremely fast to use.

The detachable box magazine held ten rounds, which was twice the capacity of many contemporary rifles. There was also a cut-out device that held all the rounds in the magazine while

single rounds were fed into the chamber by hand; this meant the user had a reserve of 10 rounds for rapid fire when needed.

The main sights were of the ramp type and calibrated to well over 1,000 yards (915m), and on the left-hand side of the rifle stock was a long-range sight that was used in the generation of really long-range fire; it was used only under careful volley-fire control.

Although the No. 1 Mk. III was an excellent service rifle, it was expensive and ill-suited to mass production. In 1916, in order to meet the ever-increasing wartime demand for rifles, a new, simplified, design was introduced to speed manufacture. Several production shortcuts were made including the removal of the magazine cut out and long-range sights, and the new model was known as the No. 1 Mk. III*.

Effectively the standard British rifle of World War I, the Mk. III* was produced in substantial numbers not only in the UK (over three million) but also in Australia and India. Production was not halted in the UK until 1943, two years after the introduction of the No. 4 Mk. I in 1941, which was itself derived from the SMLE.

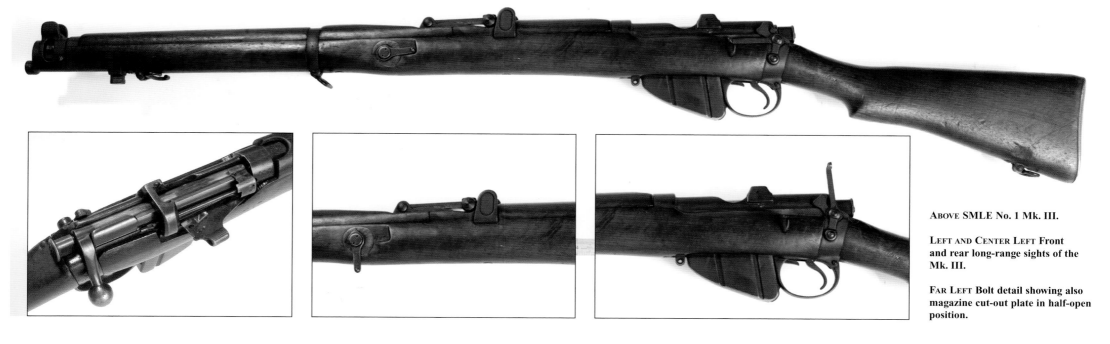

ABOVE SMLE No. 1 Mk. III.

LEFT AND CENTER LEFT Front and rear long-range sights of the Mk. III.

FAR LEFT Bolt detail showing also magazine cut-out plate in half-open position.

ABOVE SMLE No. 1 Mk. III*. Note the absence of long-range sights.

LEFT AND FAR LEFT On the left is a close up of the action and magazine of the Mk. III showing magazine cut-off. Compare this with the close up of the Mk. III* at far left.

Lee-Enfield No. 2 Mk. IV rifle

ABOVE AND BELOW SMLE No. 2 Mk. IV—a .22 caliber training rifle. The No. 2 and No. 8 rifles were both reduced caliber training rifles.

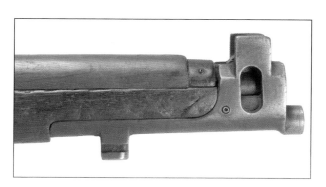

LEFT Front sight detail of a No. 1 Mk. III SMLE made in India at Ishapore in 1930.

CENTER LEFT Manufacturing marks from the Indian No. 1 Mk. III.

FAR LEFT Manufacturing marks from a 1910 No. 1 Mk. III made in Enfield for New Zealand forces.

De Lisle Silent Carbine

Caliber: .45
Length: 37.8in (960mm)
Weight: 8lb 2oz (3.7kg)
Barrel: 8.27in (210mm), four grooves, left-hand twist
Feed system: Eight-round removable box magazine

System of operation: Turning bolt action
Manufacturer: Sterling Armament Co., Dagenham, Essex, England
Values: $5,000–$$6,000

This must rank as one of the most unusual modifications of any rifle and its origins date back to 1942 when William de Lisle and Sir Malcolm Campbell (of British Combined Operations HQ) began work on a totally silent rifle for use on covert operations. By 1943 three designs had been produced and these were submitted to the Ordnance Board in 1943 by de Lisle, two in .22 RF caliber and one in .45 ACP. The .22 rifles were an auto-loader and a machine carbine, which featured a waxed paper belt, but these were rejected. The De Lisle carbine that was accepted made use of the American .45 Automatic Colt Pistol (ACP) round. A subsonic round, it did not make a distinctive crack as it reached the speed of sound, and was already in British service for the Thompson submachine gun and the Colt Model 1911 pistol. It

was found that the magazine for the Colt could be modified and used in the De Lisle rifle. Despite the fact that the .45 ACP round was only a pistol cartridge, the De Lisle had a barrel length of 8.27in (210mm), compared with the five inches of the Colt 1911, in order to increase range and accuracy.

Prototypes of the De Lisle were made at the Sterling factory in Dagenham, East London, for testing by the ordnance board in 1943–44. They were tested against the silenced Sten Mk. II and fared very well in the endurance and sound level tests. Production was begun at the Stirling factory as an order for 500 carbines was placed. There were two planned models, one with a folding metal stock and one using the standard SMLE stock (weighing 7lb 2.5oz (3.25kg) and 8lb 4oz (3.75kg) respectively). Of these, only 130 of the standard model were built.

Used or condemned SMLE rifles were employed as the basis for the De Lisle. The receiver had the charger guide removed and an ejector set into the left of the body. The magazine housing was modified to take Colt 1911 magazines and it was rechambered for .45 ACP ammunition. The bolt was shortened to 3.6 inches and the bolt head recessed and extractor modified. A Bakelite insert was fitted into the cocking handle using a dovetail joint to reduce the noise made when closing the bolt. Beyond the muzzle of the barrel was an expansion chamber and a series of thirteen baffles inside a two-inch diameter tube. The baffles were posi-

tioned on two locating rods to align the bullet passage holes. The baffles were cut and joined into a spiral to form an archemedes screw, the shape found to be most effective in reducing noise.

The De Lisle had a conventional leaf back sight graduated at 50, 100, 150 and 200 yards, the base of which was riveted to the silencer casing. The blade foresight had two protecting walls. The woodwork of the SMLE was cut off level with the receiver and an 8-inch long fore wood was attached beneath the silencer. The butt trap contained a cleaning rod. The De Lisle is still the world's only truly silent rifle and though it saw limited uses in Europe it was very effective in the jungles of the Far East.

BELOW The ancestry of the De Lisle silent carbine is apparent in this artwork by the Author. Everything from the barrel back, except the magazine, was from the SMLE. The magazine was from the Colt M1911 pistol.

Lee-Enfield No. 4 Mk. I rifle

Caliber: .303 British
Length: 44.43in (1.13m)
Weight: 9lb 1oz (4.10kg)
Barrel: 25.19in (522mm), five grooves, left-hand twist
System of operation: Lee turn-bolt
Feed system: 10-round, detachable box magazine
Manufacturers:
Royal Ordnance Factory, Fazakerley, England
Royal Ordnance Factory, Maltby, England
Birmingham Small Arms Co., England
Tyseley Savage Arms Corporation, Chicopee Falls, Mass., U.S.
Long Branch Arsenal, Ontario, Canada
Values: $100–$300

The No. 4 was developed from the Short Magazine Lee-Enfield in an order to produce a rifle that overcame the two main defects of the SMLE—namely its unsuitability to mass production and the excessive amount of training required to master the open 'U' rear sight. The resultant weapon was very similar in appearance but with an aperture fore sight, hinged at the rear of the body; the deletion of the nose cap; and the muzzle exposed for about three inches and fitted with lugs for a simple spike bayonet. All screw threads were to national standards instead of being to the Enfield standard, and the action was redesigned to facilitate mass production with unskilled labor. The No. 4 Mk. I was also fitted with a heavier barrel for improved accuracy.

VARIANTS

No. 4 Mk. I(T)
This 1942 variant saw the No. 4, Mk. I fitted with a tangent rear sight and prepared for a telescopic sight; the butt was fitted with a check rest.

No. 4 Mk. I*
Similar to the Mk. I pattern, this 1941 variant saw a simplified method of removing the bolt. Most of these rifles were made in the United States or Canada and were marked U.S. Property or Long Branch.

No. 5 Mk. I
A shortened version of the No. 4, designed for use in the jungle. The weapon was five inches shorter and had a prominent flash hider on the muzzle. The woodwork was shortened, leaving a more exposed barrel, and a rubber shoulder pad was fitted to the butt. Although light to carry it was violent to shoot and was never notable for its accuracy—neither was it very popular.

There were numerous postwar variants of the No. 4, the final ones being those rifles reworked to take the 7.62mm round used by the FN FAL of the 1950s.

BELOW No. 4 Mk. I(T) in transit case.

CENTER No. 4 Mk. I(T) with Mk. III sniper scope fitted.

BELOW RIGHT (INSET): Close up of action and magazine. Stamp reads No. 4 Mk. I* Long Branch, indicating that it is one of the rifles made in Canada at Canadian Arsenals Ltd., Long Branch, Ontario.

BOTTOM No. 4 Mk. I with grenade discharger fitted and a No. 94 anti-tank training grenade.

LEFT No. 4 Mk. I(T) with No. 32 sight fitted. Note cheek rest on butt.

BELOW LEFT No. 4 Mk. I(T) with Mk. III sniper scope in case.

BELOW AND BOTTOM Spotting telescope typical of those issued to snipers. The textured brown coating was to prevent any reflections that may give away the sniper's position.

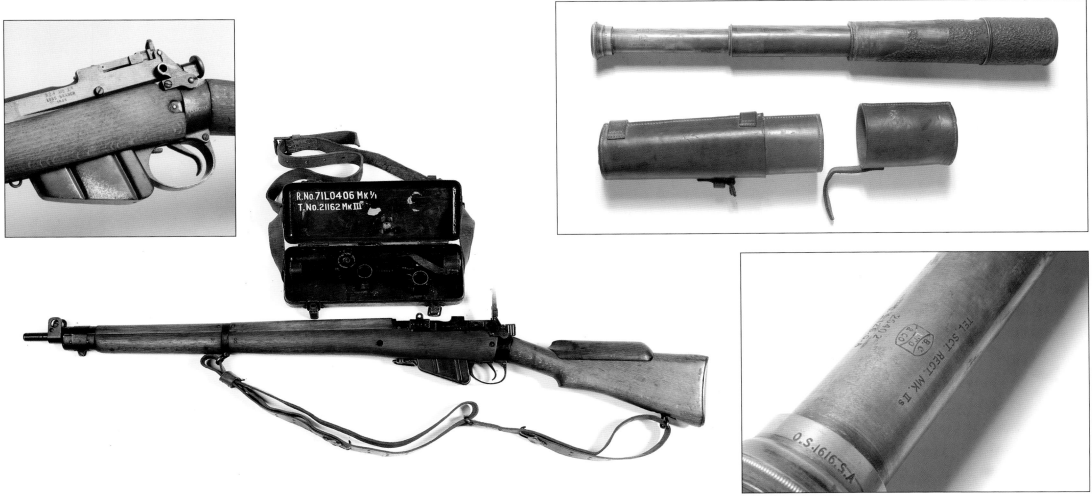

Lee-Enfield No. 5 Mk. I carbine

Caliber: .303 (7.7mm)

Length: 39.5 in (1m)

Weight: 7lb 2.4oz (31.5kg)

Barrel: 18.75in (476mm), five grooves, left-hand twist

Feed system: 10-round, detachable box magazine

System of operation: Lee turn-bolt

Manufacturers:
Birmingham Small Arms, England
Royal Ordnance Factory, Fazakerley, Liverpool, England

Values: $300-$500

The Rifle No. 5 Mk. I was designed in response to the need for a weapon more suited to the jungle fighting in which British troops were involved in Burma and the Far East. The No. 1 and No. 4 Lee-Enfield rifles were too long and awkward for use in heavily overgrown terrain and it was decided to produce a shortened version of the No. 4. The new design included a shorter barrel and fore stock (altogether some five inches shorter than the No. 4), and sights modified to suit the changed ballistics of the weapon. The Jungle Carbine—as it was designated—was also provided with a flash hider and a rubber pad on the butt, both intended to offset the effects of firing a normal rifle bullet from a short barrel—particularly the large muzzle flash and ferocious recoil. The new weapon was never very popular in service, but it was much handier in a jungle environment, and more than 100,000 were produced.

At one point it looked as if the No. 5 carbine, with some development, was to be the standard British Army rifle after the war. In the end, this did not happen, largely because the weapon gradually lost accuracy after being zeroed. This problem was never satisfactorily cured and the No. 4 remained in service until replaced by the FN self-loader in the 1950s.

ABOVE AND OPPOSITE PAGE Two examples of the Lee-Enfield No. 5 Mk. I. Note the rubber shoulder pad to offset the effects of the vicious recoil, shortened stock, and the flash hider. For comparison, the lower photograph at left is of a No. 4 Mk. I(T).

M1 Garand rifle

Caliber: .30	**Manufacturers:**
Length: 43.5in (1.1m)	Springfield Arsenal, Mass., U.S.
Weight: 9lb 8oz (4.37kg)	Winchester Repeating Arms Co.,
Barrel: 24in long, four grooves, right–hand twist	New Haven, Conn., U.S. Harrington & Richardson Arms Co., Worcester, Mass., U.S.
Feed system: Eight–round integral magazine, clip-loaded	**Values: $600–$1,500** (Many variations)
System of operation: Gas piston, turning bolt	

John C. Garand first produced a repeating rifle for trial in 1920, but it used an unusual system of operation, relying on the expansion and set-back of the primer cap in the cartridge to unlock the bolt action. While the system worked, it was not practical. Garand later joined the design staff of Springfield Arsenal and went on to develop the rifle which will always be associated with his name. In 1929 a series of tests of competing designs of rifle were held at Aberdeen Proving Ground, as a result of which a Garand design of gas-operated rifle was selected as the most promising. Further development took place, and in 1936 it was standardized as the U.S. Rifle M1: over five million had been built when production stopped in the 1950s.

Operation is by gas tapped very close to the muzzle end of the barrel, driving a long-stroke piston backward. This, by means of a cam, rotates and opens the bolt and cocks the firing hammer. The return spring is carried in the gas piston, an arrangement that keeps the action body short and compact. Feed is from a magazine loaded by an eight-round clip, and upon the last round being fired the clip is ejected and the action held open for reloading. This is probably the least desirable feature of the Garand, because single rounds cannot be loaded to "top up" the magazine; it has to be a full clip or nothing. It also led to a tactical disadvantage in that the ejected clip made a distinctive noise if it fell on hard ground, alerting the enemy to the fact that the rifleman was holding an empty rifle. In spite of this defect, the Garand proved reliable and accurate in service all over the world. Indeed the postwar rifle, the M14, is largely based on Garand's design.

VARIANTS

M1E1
An experimental model with slight changes in the cam angle of the bolt-opening section of the operating rod.

M1E2
An M1 fitted with an International Industries' telescope sight for trials as a sniping rifle.

M1E3
The bolt was fitted with a roller cam and the operating rod altered accordingly. Experimental only.

M1E4
Altered to cut off supply of gas and allow expansion in the gas cylinder to operate the action. Experimental only.

M1E5
Shortened, with a folding stock and 18in barrel. Intended for airborne use, it gave excessive muzzle blast and was not adopted.

M1E6
M1 fitted with an offset sighting telescope to allow use of either the standard sights or the telescope without adjustment. Not accepted.

M1E7
M1 fitted with a Griffin & Howe telescope mount, a Lyman, Alaskan, or Weaver 330 telescope, and a leather cheek pad on the butt. This was standardized in June 1944 as Rifle M1C (Sniper's) and some models were fitted with a flash-hider in January 1945.

M1E8
As for the M1E7 but using a telescope mount evolved by Springfield Arsenal and a Lyman telescope. Standardized as Rifle M1D (Sniper's) Substitute standard in September 1944.

M1E9
Similar to the M1E4 but had the piston head separate from the rest of the piston so as to act as a tappet. Experimental only.

T26
Action and barrel of M1E5 in a conventional wooden stock. In July 1945 HQ Pacific Theater ordered 15,000, but canceled in August 1945. A small number were made and these appeared on the surplus market described as the "Tanker's Model."

BELOW From top to bottom: M1 associated equipment—grenade discharger; M9A1 hollow charge anti-tank grenade; practice round.

M1, M1A1, M2, and M3 carbines

Data: M1	**Winchester Repeating Arms Co., New Haven, Conn., U.S.**
Caliber: .30	**Underwood-Elliot-Fisher, Hartford, Conn., U.S.**
Length: 36in (905mm)	
Weight: 5lb 7oz (2.48kg)	**Rochester Defense Corp., Rochester, N.Y., U.S.**
Barrel: 18in (457mm) long, four grooves, right-hand twist	**Quality Hardware Corp., Chicago, Ill., U.S.**
Feed system: 15 or 30-round, detachable box magazine	**National Postal Meter Corp., Rochester, N.Y., U.S.**
System of operation: gas, rotating bolt	**International Business Machines Corp., Poughkeepsie, N.Y., U.S.**
Manufacturers:	**Standard Products Co., Port Clinton, Ohio**
General Motors Corp., Dayton, Ohio, and Grand Rapids and Saginaw, Mich., U.S.	
Rock-Ola Corp., Chicago, Ill., U.S.	**Values:** $500–$1,200 (Many variations)

The U.S. Carbine M1 originated in 1938 with a request from the Army for a light rifle, which could replace the standard rifle and the pistol in arming drivers, machine gunners, mortar squads, cooks, clerks, and others whose primary function was not rifle shooting but who, in an emergency, might need a weapon with a better reach than the pistol. The request was initially turned down, but was revived in 1940 and this time met with a more favorable reception, because the U.S. Army was now expanding and the production of standard rifles was stretched to its utmost. In October 1940 a draft specification was issued for the new weapon, and the Winchester company was contracted to develop a special round of ammunition, using a 110-grain bullet and giving a velocity of 1,860ft/sec. This was officially called the .30 Short Rifle Cartridge and was based on a commercial round, the Winchester .32 automatic sporting rifle cartridge.

Eleven companies submitted weapons for test; of these seven models were subjected to trial. The Winchester design, using a modification of the Garand bolt with a short-stroke gas piston originally developed for a potential military rifle, was selected for adoption and was standardized as the Carbine M1 late in 1941.

The gas action uses a captive piston. This strikes an operating slide, delivering sufficient energy to drive the slide back to cam the bolt open against the power of the return spring. The rearward movement of the bolt also cocks a hammer before the spring returns it, loading a fresh round and locking the bolt.

It has been estimated that more than six million carbines were made during the war, and they were widely distributed throughout the army. Opinions as to their utility differ; they were without doubt very handy weapons, light and easy to use, but the bullet was a pistol bullet rather than a rifle bullet and consequently their accuracy at anything other than short range was far from satisfactory; it was also somewhat deficient in stopping power.

VARIANTS

M1A1
Same as the M1, but with a pistol grip and folding skeleton stock; this pattern was intended primarily for airborne troops.

M2
Full automatic fire version. It resembles the M1 except for having a fire selector lever on the left of the receiver. Standardized in September 1944, a special 30-round magazine was developed for it. The cyclic rate of fire was approximately 750 rounds per minute.

M3
An M2 with the open sights removed and fitted with an infra-red Sniperscope sight. Standardized August 1945.

T3
The development model number of the design standardized as M3.

T4
The development model number of the design standardized as M2.

Right and Opposite Page
The M1 carbine—more than six million were produced as personal weapons for troops not primarily intended as riflemen such as drivers and artillery crew.

M1A1 Airborne carbine

Caliber: .30

Length: 35.63in (905mm) butt extended

Weight: 5lb 9oz (2.35kg)

Barrel: 18in (457mm) long, four grooves, right-hand twist

Feed system: 15 or 30-round, detachable box magazine

System of operation: Gas, rotating bolt

Manufacturer:
Inland Mfg. Division of General Motors, Dayton, Ohio, U.S.

Values: $1,200-$2,000

This is the airborne model of the M1 carbine and was one of the US airborne troops' favorite weapons. It is identical to the M1 except for the pistol grip and folding stock. Its compact size when folded meant the M1 carbine could actually be tucked inside the paratrooper's harness during the descent, greatly reducing the chance of a landing injury.

RIGHT AND BELOW The M1A1 carbine, standard weapon of U.S. Airborne forces.

M1903 Springfield rifle

BELOW AND BELOW LEFT details of the M1903A4 fitted with Weaver 330C scope.

Caliber:.30
Length: 43.25in (1.09m)
Weight: 8lb 11oz (3.94kg)
Barrel: 24in (610mm) long, four grooves, left–hand twist
Feed system: Five-round integral box magazine
System of operation: Mauser turn-bolt

Manufacturers:
Springfield Arsenal, Springfield, Mass., U.S.
Rock Island Arsenal, Rock Island, Ill., U.S.
Remington Arms Co., U.S.
L. C. Smith Corona Typewriter Corp., U.S.
Values: $300–$400 (Many variations)

Although the M1 Garand was the standard rifle of the U.S. Army during World War II, many thousands of the older bolt-action M1903 remained in use. In the earlier part of the war they were still carried by first-line troops before production of the M1 reached sufficient quantities, and later the M1903 was relegated to reserve and guard use, as well as for initial training of recruits.

The M1903 is commonly known as the "Springfield" since it was designed and developed, and largely manufactured, at Springfield Arsenal. The first magazine rifle of the U.S. Army was the Krag-Jorgensen, but after a few years of using this weapon, work began on developing a replacement. After considering all the designs then available, it was decided to adopt the Mauser system of bolt-action and magazine, and for $200,000 the U.S. government purchased a license from the Mauser company. The original design was a long rifle with a 30in (762mm) barrel, but while work was in progress, the British Army introduced its "Short" Lee-Enfield and the U.S. Army decided that it would adopt this idea of one rifle for all troops. The design was modified to use a 24in (610mm) barrel and the first models were issued in 1905.

The original bullet for which the rifle was designed was a 220-grain round-nosed pattern, but in 1905 the German Army introduced its "Spitzer" or pointed bullet, which promised improved performance, and the rest of the world hurried to follow suit. The U.S. Army adopted a 150-grain pointed bullet, and the rifle sights were modified to match its ballistics. Although basically of Mauser pattern, there are one or two features that made the Springfield unique. The firing pin is in two pieces; the ejector is not spring-loaded; and an ingenious bolt stop allows bolt removal and acts as a cut-off, so that the rounds in the magazine can be held there while the rifle is used as a single-loader.

VARIANTS

M1903A1
Same as M1903 but with a new stock of pistol-grip pattern, the forward finger grooves omitted, and the surface of the trigger milled to give surer grip.

M1903A2
A proposed barrel and action fitted into a special mounting for use as a sub-caliber training weapon for tank guns. The requirement was subsequently canceled.

M1903A3
The rear sight was moved back to the rear of the receiver. Various small changes were made in construction to simplify and speed up manufacture. This model may have a straight or pistol-grip stock, and may have a barrel with only two rifling grooves. The design was standardized on May 21, 1942.

M1903A4
Same as A3 but with a Weaver 330C sighting telescope and the iron sights removed. The bolt handle was also modified by cutting and bending so that it did not foul the telescope when operated. Like many bolt-action rifles with telescopes mounted centrally, this could only be used as a single-loader, because the location of the telescope prevented the magazine from being charged by the usual charger system.

ABOVE, BELOW, AND ABOVE RIGHT
The M1903A4 fitted with Weaver
330C scope.

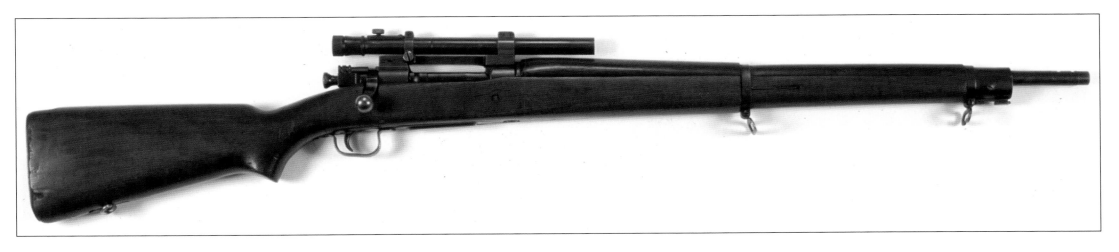

ABOVE AND BELOW Left and right-hand views of the standard M1903.

Mannlicher-Parravicino-Carcano M91 rifle and carbine

Caliber: 6.5mm

Length: 50.79in (1.29m)

Weight: 8lb 6oz (3.8kg)

Barrel: 30.71in long (780mm), four grooves, right-hand twist

Feed system: Six-round integral box magazine, clip-loaded

System of operation: Turnbolt

Manufacturer: Italian State Arsenals

Values: $125-$225

This basic Italian Army rifle was developed at the Turin Army Arsenal in 1890 and is essentially a form of modified Mauser—the names referring to: Austro-Hungarian designer Ferdinand von Mannlicher; General Parravicino, who oversaw the procurement of the weapon; and Salvatore Carcano at the Turin arsenal. On the whole the M91 was a serviceable enough weapon and on a par with its contemporaries, and it served as a basis for a host of variations over the years. Its principal drawback was its somewhat weak 6.5mm cartridge, and in 1938 a 7.35mm cartridge was introduced. Unfortunately, the planned change of caliber did not take place to the extent that had hoped for, and while a small number of rifles and carbines in 7.35mm were eventually issued, the 6.5mm weapons were by far the most common throughout World War II, leaving Italian troops undergunned.

VARIANTS

Carbine M1891/24

After World War I the Italians decided to fall in line with the major powers and do away with the separate long rifle and carbine models; the 1891 rifles were cut down to a barrel length of 17.7in (450mm), the bolt handle bent down, and the sights improved. This then became the standard army rifle.

Moschetto modello 91 per cavalleria

This was a cavalry model of the standard carbine and differed only in that it was fitted with a folding bayonet in place of the

THIS PAGE Left and right-hand side views of the M91 rifle.

usual knife type. It was used by many special troops such as gunners and signalers.

M1938

The introduction of the 7.35mm cartridge demanded a slight re-design since it was too powerful to be fired comfortably through a barrel as short as that of the 1891/24. A new rifle with a 21in (534mm) barrel but otherwise much the same as the 1891/24 was developed. With the failure of the 7.35mm changeover, numbers of this pattern were made in 6.5mm caliber.

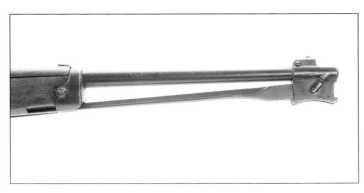

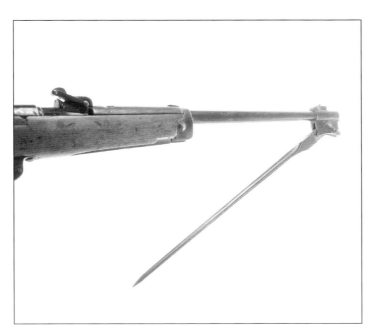

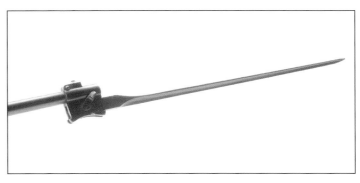

THIS PAGE *Moschetto M91 per Cavalleria* with details of the folding bayonet and (above and below left) rear sight and maker's mark.

MAS Mle 1936 rifle

Caliber: 7.5mm

Length: 40.25in (1.02m)

Weight: 8lb 4.3oz (3.75kg)

Barrel: 22.6in (575mm), four grooves, left-hand twist

Feed system: Five-round internal charger-loaded box magazine

System of operation: Turning bolt

Manufacturer:

Manufacture d'Armes de St. Étienne (MAS), France

Values: $150–$250

The origins of the Modèle 36 date to 1924 when the introduction of a rimless 7.5mm cartridge, ballistically bettter than the existing 8mm rimmed pattern, forced the French to reexamine their infantry weapons. Their service rifles, originally developed in the 1880s, needed replacement; a development program was started.

In 1929 prototype rifles were produced by MAT (Manufacture d'Armes de Tulle, France) and MAS. From these the MAT 1932 was developed and the design was further modified to produce the MAS 34, the B1 version being accepted for service in 1935. The production model was to be known as the MAS 36, and by now the shape of the MAS 36 was already apparent. The pistol-grip butt was separated from the forend and hand guard by a massive slab-sided receiver containing the one-piece bolt. No safety catch was provided, and the bolt was bent forward so that it came easily into the firer's hand. The back sight lay on the rear of the receiver, immediately ahead of the firer's eye. There was a single-barrel band, which carried a swivel ring and a machined nose cap, that mounted the front sight. The butt was fitted with a recessed strap clip. The spike bayonet lay in a channel in the forend and a stack-

ing spike protruded from the right side of the nose cap. Though the first deliveries had been made in 1937, and these rifles were used by the French Army and the forces of former French colonies in Africa and the Far East, comparatively few MAS 36 rifles had reached French infantrymen when the Germans invaded. The MAS 36 and its derivatives were sturdy and durable, and though the bolt was harder to operate than some of its rivals and safety features were poor, they remained service for many years.

VARIANTS

MAS 36 CR 39

Adopted for airborne and ski troops, the CR 39 was a shorter-barreled version with a two-piece aluminum butt, foldable forward on either side. It was 34.8in (885mm) long had a 17.7 (450mm) barrel.

ABOVE AND BELOW Left and right-hand side views of the MAS Mle 1936, which was just entering service with the French army at the time of the German invasion.

LEFT AND FAR LEFT Details showing bayonet stowage and bayonet fixed.

Mauser rifles

Data: Swedish m/1896

Caliber: 6.5mm

Length: 49.5in (1.26m)

Weight: 8lb 12oz (3.98kg)

Barrel: 29in (740mm) later
   shortened to 24in (610mm),
   four grooves, right-hand twist

Feed system: Five-round internal
   charger-loaded box magazine

System of operation: Bolt action

Manufacturers:
   Husqvarna Vapenfabrik AB,
      Sweden
   Carl Gustavs Stads Gevärfactori,
      Eskilstuna, Sweden

Values: $75–$400
   (Many variations)

RIGHT This Mauser is marked "Danzig 1899."

FAR RIGHT The markings on this Turkish Mauser of 1935 identifies it as having been built at ASFA (*Askari Fabrika*) Ankara—Ankara Military Factory.

The entries on the Gewehr 98 and Kar 98k (pages 76–77) identified the Mauser bolt-action weapon designed by the brothers Mauser as being one of the most important twentieth century weapons. The Mauser designs were used by German forces for over 50 years, and many other countries produced versions; hugely collectible, Mauser rifles are are still in use today as sporting weapons.

The main producers of Mauser rifles include Argentina, Belgium (see illustrations on page 99), Brazil, Chile, China, Czechoslovakia, Mexico, Poland, Serbia, Spain, Sweden (see illustrations overleaf), Turkey and Uruguay. Many of these weapons were in use in various armies around the time of World War II, although the biggest user by far was Germany.

The illustrations on this and pages 98–99 cover just a few of the Mauser types to provide merely a flavor of what is available today.

RIGHT Mauser carbines.

ABOVE AND BELOW Left and right-hand side views of the Swedish Mauser carbine, manufactured by Husqvarna Vapenfabrik.

ABOVE AND BELOW Left and right-hand side views of the Swedish Mauser rifle, manufactured by Husqvarna Vapenfabrik.

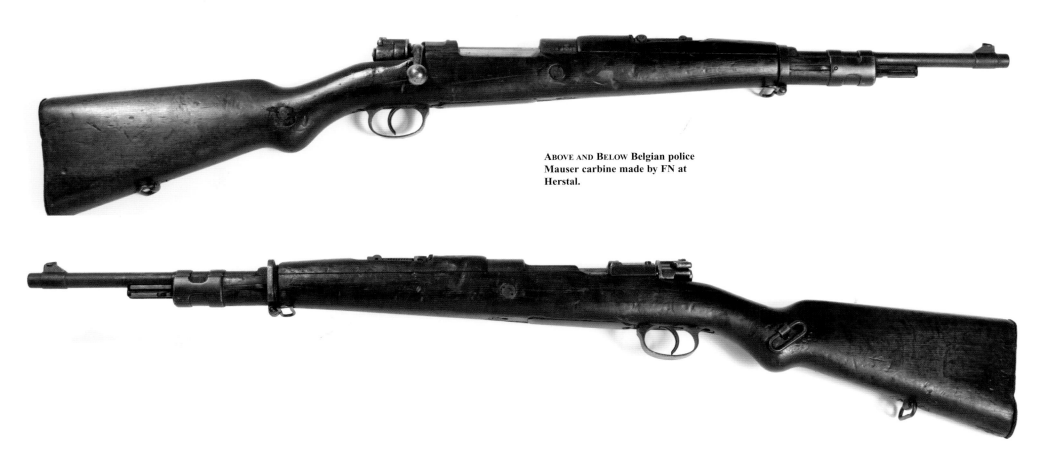

ABOVE AND BELOW Belgian police Mauser carbine made by FN at Herstal.

RIGHT Maker's mark detail of a Swedish Model 1896—"KARL GUSTAFS STADS GEVÄRS FACTORI 1908."

CENTER AND FAR RIGHT Details of the Belgian police carbine. The maker's mark identifies the manufacturer "FAB NAT D'ARMES de GUERRE HERSTAL-BELGIQUE"—better known as FN.

Meiji 38 (Arisaka) rifle

Caliber: 6.5mm
Length: 50.25in (1.27m)
Weight: 9lb 8oz (4.31kg)
Barrel: 31.45in (800mm) long, six grooves, right-hand twist
Feed system: Internal, charger loaded, five-round, box magazine

System of operation: Turnbolt action
Manufacturer: Imperial artillery arsenal, Koishikawa, Tokyo
Values: $125–$175 (Many variations)

The Rifle Type 38 entered Imperial Japanese service in 1905, (the 35th year of the Meiji reign) and was a development of two earlier rifles selected by a commission headed by Colonel Arisaka, who gave his name to all subsequent Japanese service rifles. The Type 38 employed features taken from both Mauser and Mannlicher designs, combined with some Japanese innovations. The result was a successful weapon that was used by all the Japanese armed forces and also widely exported across the Far East. The Type 38 was a fairly conventional weapon of 6.5mm (0.256in) caliber. An unusual addition, though rarely found on specimens today, was a sheet-metal bolt cover which moved with the bolt but served to keep rain and dust out of the mechanism. While it did all that was claimed, it was flimsy and prone to rattle, giving away the owner's location, and most were removed at the earliest opportunity.

The relatively small caliber of the Type 38, coupled with a cartridge of modest power, produced a rifle with a small recoil that suited the smaller Japanese stature. The length of the Type 38 rifle compensated to some extent for the Japanese soldier's slight build when used with a bayonet, as it gave the Japanese soldier a considerable reach advantage for close-in warfare, but it also made the Type 38 a rather awkward rifle to handle.

From 1942, as the war turned against Japan, the production standards of Japanese arms, from rifles to aircraft, deteriorated rapidly; any pieces that could be removed were, and simplifications

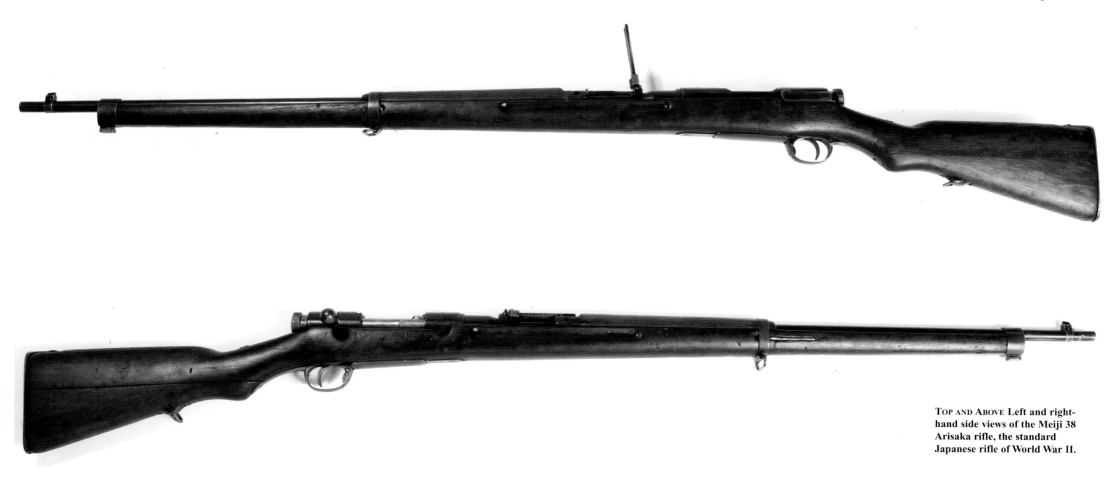

TOP AND ABOVE Left and right-hand side views of the Meiji 38 Arisaka rifle, the standard Japanese rifle of World War II.

were introduced onto the production lines. Overall standards went down to the point where some of the late-production rifles were unusable, many of them being constructed from such low-quality materials, they were dangerous to those who fired them.

VARIANTS

Carbine Type 38
This was a shortened version of the Type 38, that was otherwise identical; it saw widespread service. The Type 38 was also produced with a folding butt for use by airborne troops.

Sniper's Rifle Type 97
Another version of the Type 38 rifle that had provision for a telescopic sight and was fitted with a bipod. It also had a revised bolt handle to avoid the firer's hand fouling the bolt.

Rifle Type 99
During the 1930s the Japanese adopted a new cartridge of 7.7mm (0.303in) caliber, and the Type 38 was revised as the Rifle Type 99 with several new features, including an antiaircraft sight, and a folding monopod. Problems in the ammunition changeover meant that relatively few of the new-caliber rifles reached the front.

Paratroop Rifle Type 100
A special paratroop model that could be broken down into two , but the joining mechanism proved to be unreliable.

Paratroop Rifle Type 2
This was similar to the Type 100 but featured a revised joining mechanism.

Type 99 Arisaka carbine

Caliber: 7.7mm
Length: 45in (1.43m)
Weight: 9lb 2oz (4.14kg)
Barrel: 18.5in (469mm), four grooves, right-hand twist
Feed system: Internal, charger-loaded, five-round box magazine.
System of operation: Turning-bolt action

Manufacturers:
Toriimatsu factory of the Imperial army arsenal, Nagoya, Japan
Dai-Nippon Heiki Kogyo, Notobe, Japan
Kayaba Kogyo, Tokyo, Japan
The Imperial army arsenal, Kokura, Japan
Toyo Juki, Hiroshima, Japan
Tokyo Juki, Tokyo, Japan
Jinsen arsenal, Korea
Values: $100–$175

THIS PAGE Left and right-hand side views of the Type 99 Arisaka carbine. Note wire monopod and rear sight. Compare with anti-aircraft sight on page 102.

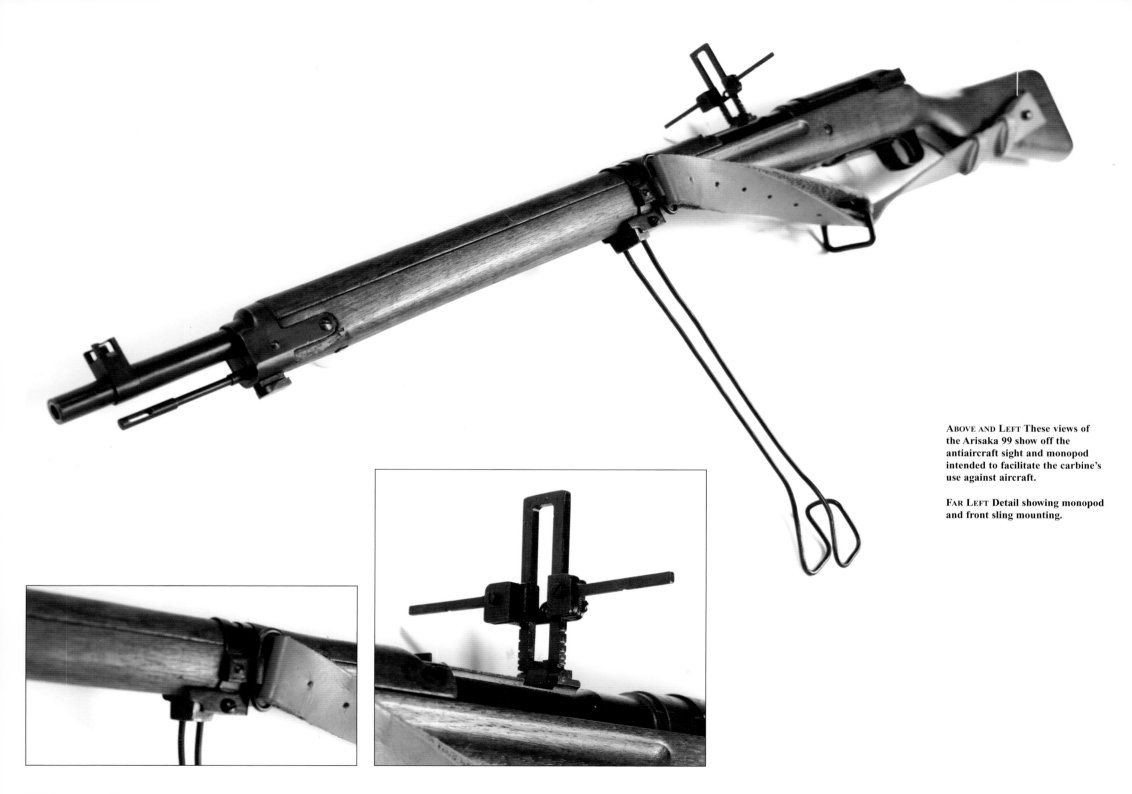

ABOVE AND LEFT These views of the Arisaka 99 show off the antiaircraft sight and monopod intended to facilitate the carbine's use against aircraft.

FAR LEFT Detail showing monopod and front sling mounting.

Mosin-Nagant rifles and carbines

Vintovka obrazets (obr) 1930g rifle

Caliber: 7.62mm

Length: 48.5in (1.23m)

Weight: 8lb 12.8oz (4kg)

Barrel: 28.7in (730mm), four grooves, right-hand twist

System of operation: Turning-bolt action

Feed system: Integral, five-round charger-loaded box magazine

Manufacturer: Russian state ordnance factories in Tula, Izhevsk, Sestroretsk and elsewhere

Values: $100-$150

The *Vintovka* (rifle) *Obrazets* (model) *1930g* (sometimes called the 1891/30g) is one of a series of rifles based on the Mosin-Nagant Model 1891 that were the standard rifles of the Russian Army until 1945. They were called Mosin-Nagants because they were designed by the Belgian Nagant brothers with modifications by Colonel S. I. Mosin of the Imperial Russian Army. The rifle won of a competition in Imperial Russia to replace the Berdan single-shot breech-loading rifles then in use. The resulting rifle had an action based on a French-style bolt inspired by the Lebel, with a detachable head and a cocking piece that could be retracted and turned to the left as a safety measure. An unusual feature of the design was the provision of an interrupter. One of the difficult problems of weapon design is the efficient feeding of rimmed cartridges from a magazine; the pressure of the magazine spring tends to jam the rims together and give rise to stoppages. The Mosin-Nagant used a spring-loaded latch, controlled by the operation of the bolt, to hold down the second round in the magazine and thus take pressure off the top round so that it could be easily loaded into the chamber by the closing bolt without the danger of the rim of the second round interfering because of the upward pressure of the spring.

The original 1891 model was a long rifle (51.25in), and was always used with its bayonet attached. It was partnered by two shorter weapons, the Dragoon and Cossack rifles, but at 48.75in neither was as short and handy as the contemporary carbines in use by other armies. In 1931 the Soviet Army introduced the 1930g which was more or less the Dragoon Rifle with improved sights and with the design somewhat simplified so as to make production easier. It became the standard infantry rifle and remained so throughout the war , although it was widely supplemented by the later model of carbine and, of course, by vast numbers of submachine guns which were a lot cheaper and quicker to make. Numbers of the Model 1891/30 were fitted with telescopic sights for use by snipers.

VARIANTS

Carbine 1938g/Carbine 1944g
See page 106.

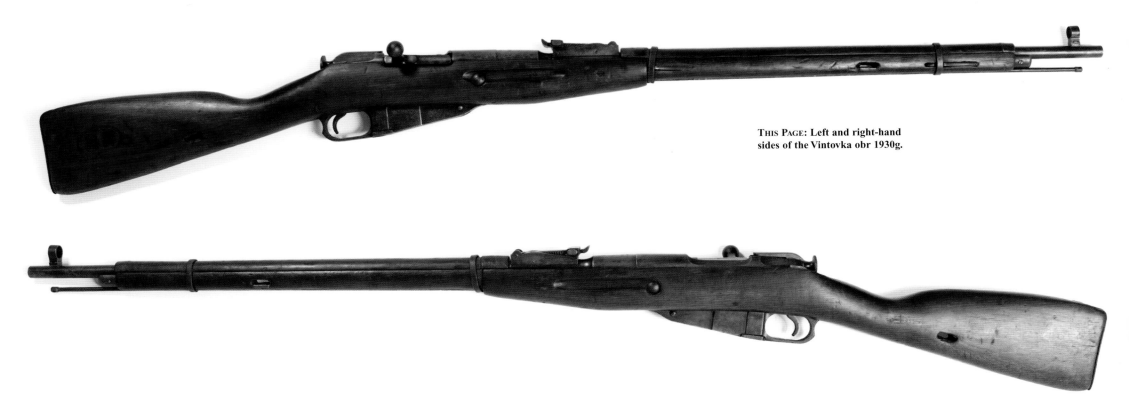

THIS PAGE: Left and right-hand sides of the Vintovka obr 1930g.

Dragunskaya vintovki obr 1891g rifle

Caliber: 7.62mm

Length: 48.75in (1.24m)

Weight: 8lb 12oz (3.98kg)

Barrel: 28.75in (730mm), four grooves, right-hand twist

System of operation: Turning-bolt action

Feed system: Integral, five-round charger-loaded box magazine

Manufacturer: Russian state ordnance factories in Tula, Izhevsk, and Sestroretsk

Values: $125–$200

The Mosin-Nagant 1891 Cossack Rifle was little more than a shortened infantry rifle with a handguard extending as far as the back sight base. The barrel bands were retained by springs, the majority of weapons had sling slots cut laterally through the butt and the forend (protected by oval blued steel washer) and a modified cleaning rod was provided. The serial numbers had a distinctive 'KA3' prefix. The Dragoon Rifle was almost identical to the Cossack Rifle but was fitted with a different cleaning rod. It was issued without a bayonet, although the standard pattern would fit. Serial numbers were given no particular distinction. In 1908 the introduction of the obr 1908g ball cartridge led to the 3,200-arshin (a Russian measurement equal to 28in/711mm) sights being fitted. The work continued until 1911 or later. By January 1, 1914, the inventory contained 204,390 cossack and 540,270 dragoon rifles, as production of cossack models was slowed in favor of the dragoon type. In 1915 production of cossack rifles ceased altogether, and in 1922 the Red Army standardized the dragoon rifle as a substitute for the full-length infantry pattern. Production continued into the early 1930s, consequently, guns will be found with imperial or Red Army markings.

ABOVE AND BELOW Left and right-hand sides of the Dragoon Rifle

RIGHT Curved rear sight in arshins.

CENTER RIGHT Hex receiver and the Sestroretsk factory marking.

FAR RIGHT Rounded receiver and the Izhevsk factory marking.

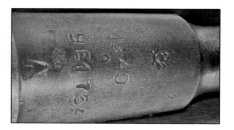

Vintovka obr 1930g rifle with telescopic sights

Caliber: 7.62mm

Length: 48.58in (1.23mm)

Weight: 8lb 1.14oz (3.8kg)

Barrel: 28.74in (730mm), four grooves, right-hand twist

System of operation: Turning-bolt action

Feed system: Integral, five-round charger-loaded box magazine

Manufacturer;
Russian state ordnance factories in Tula, Izhevsk, Sestroretsk, and elsewhere

Values: $700-$1,200
(50% premium for PE scope)

On April 28, 1930, the Red Army adopted the perfected Soviet version of the Tsarist Dragoon Rifle as its standard service rifle. In 1932 it was also chosen to form the basis of a new sniper rifle (*Snayperskaya Vintovka*) being produced as part of a determined effort to develop marksmanship as part of the first Five-Year Plan. Guns selected for accuracy had their bolt handles turned downward to clear the telescope sights, the side of the stock being cut away to accept the handle.

Russian sights were made in a factory equipped by Carl Zeiss of Jena. The 4 x PE type had a 30mm objective lens, a field of view of 8° 30'; azimuth and elevation adjustments were internal. It gave good optical performance for its day, but was comparatively heavy. The earliest sights were mounted in a single-piece

twin split-ring mount held on the receiver ring above the chamber, but this was replaced by a twin split-ring mount fitted to a dovetailed base plate on the left of the receiver. In 1940 use of the PU telescope, introduced for the Tokarev sniper rifle, was extended to the obr 1891/30g. Shorter and lighter than the PE pattern, the 35 x PU was carried in a twin-ring slab side mount locking onto the left side of the Mosin-Nagant receiver.

A few rifles were used with 26mm (1.02in) diameter rubber baffle silencers weighing about 480gm (1lb 1oz). Silenced weapons could only fire subsonic "partisan" ammunition, with green marks on the bullet, case or primer; otherwise, baffles were wrecked after a few rounds. In all some 185,000 sniper rifles were produced during the war.

RIGHT Left and right-hand sides of the Model 1891/30g sniper rifle fitted with 1940 PU telescope sight. Sniper rifles were selected from production examples for accuracy and fitted with a down-turned bolt handle to clear the sight.

Karabina obr1938g carbine

Caliber: 7.62mm
Length: 40.16in (1.02m)
Weight: 7lb 9.8oz (3.45kg)
Barrel: 20.01in (510mm), four grooves, right-hand twist
System of operation: Turning-bolt action

Feed system: Integral, five-round charger-loaded box magazine
Manufacturer: Russian state ordnance factories
Values: $150–$375

Karabina obr1944g carbine

Caliber: 7.62mm
Length: 40.16in (1.02m)
Weight: 8lb 9.6oz (3.9 kg)
Barrel: 20.01in (510mm), four grooves, right-hand twist
System of operation: Turning-bolt action

Feed system: Integral, five-round charger-loaded box magazine
Manufacturer: Russian state ordnance factories
Values: $125–$200

In 1939 the Karabina obr 1938g was introduced to replace any obr 1891/30g rifles and surviving ex-Tsarist carbines in the hands of the cavalry, artillery, signals, and motor transport units. Unlike the 1910 pattern, the 1938 type carbine was basically a shortened infantry rifle, and would accept the standard socket bayonet Production exceeded two million, and 687,430 were made in 1942 alone. In May 1943 a range of eight different bayonets were tested on obr 1938g carbines. The Semin system, a special cruciform blade bayonet pivoting on a block attached to the right side of the muzzle, was selected in November of that year. On January 17, 1944, the obr 1944g was standardized as the new service carbine. It was identical with the 1938 model except for the bayonet.

ABOVE AND BELOW The Karabiner obr 1944g. Note markings on barrel (above) and bayonet folded back on right side of barrel. The three details show the bayonet being deployed.

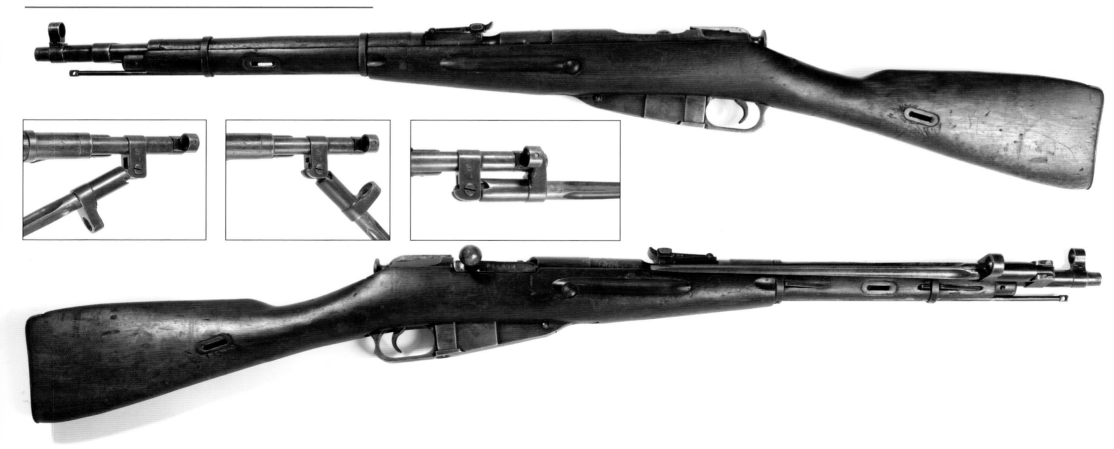

MP43/Sturmgewehr StG44 assault rifles

Caliber: 7.92mm (short)
Length: 37in (940mm)
Weight: 11lb 5oz (5.13kg)
Barrel: 16.5in (418mm) long, four grooves, right-hand twist
Feed system: 30-round detachable box magazine
System of operation: Gas, tipping bolt

Manufacturers:
C. G. Haenel Waffen und Fahrradfabrik, Suhl, Germany
B. Geipel GmbH, Waffenfabrik 'Erma', Erfurt, Germany
Mauserwerke AG, Oberndorf, Germany

Values: $7,000–$8,500 (Class III)

During the 1930s the German Army spent some time assessing the basic requirements for an infantry rifle, and came to the conclusion that the traditional rifle cartridge was unnecessarily powerful. Analysis revealed that the vast majority of infantry rifle fire was over short ranges. As a result work began by the Deutsche Waffen & Munitionsfabrik to develop a short 7mm caliber round; while this promised well, it was eventually stopped in favor of a 7.92mm design by Polte of Magdeburg, since this was of standard caliber and utilized a shortened version of the normal cartridge case, features which simplified production since much of the work could be done on existing machinery.

With the design of cartridge finalized, contracts were placed with Haenel and Carl Walther for the production of suitable rifles. The resulting weapons were known respectively as the Maschinenkarabiner 42, or Mkb42(H) and Mkb42(W). The Walther design used an annular gas piston surrounding the barrel to operate a tipping bolt, while the Haenel pattern used a more conventional gas cylinder and piston mounted below the barrel, also operating a tipping bolt. About 4,000 of the Walther and 8,000 of the Haenel model were produced in 1942–43 and issued to selected units on the Eastern Front for evaluation. As a result of their reports the Haenel pattern would eventually be selected for further development, particularly as far as simplification for mass production was concerned, and the finalized design was issued as the *Maschinenpistole MP43*.

However, this took time. In spite of favorable reports from the trials, Hitler rejected them because he demanded longer ranges for infantry weapons. He based this decision on his experiences in World War I and because he wanted, particularly for the battles in North Africa, a rifle capable of long-range fire. Moreover, according to a statement by Hauptdienstleiter Saur, then chief of the Technical Office of the German Ministry of Munitions, it was also rejected on the grounds that there were, at the time, eight billion rounds of standard 7.92mm ammunition in stock.

The Army Weapons Office continued the development and eventually experience with the first models of the MP43 on the Russian Front led to demands for this improvement to existing close-range weaponry. After initial service trials fittings for a grenade launcher cup were added to the muzzle and the designation became MP43/1. In 1944 the designation was changed to

ABOVE AND OVERLEAF, TOP StG44 left and right-hand sides. The StG44 was also used with an infra-red night sight and, in its strangest form, as the *Krummlauf*—with a curved barrel. Although often said to have been developed to fire around corners, its main use was by tank crews to ensure that blind spots around their vehicle could be kept clear of tank-killers. There were two experimental versions of the *Krummlauf*—the StG44(P) and StG44(V) with curved barrels of 90° and 45° respectively.

MP44 and later, after Hitler had dropped his opposition to the weapon, it was again renamed becoming the *Sturmgewehr*, or assault rifle, StG44. The assault rifle nomenclature has ever since been associated with this type of weapon.

The MP43/StG44 was one of the first German weapons in which production was put before finish, no importance being attached to fine appearance or close tolerances except where they were vital. Indeed the original design had to be considerably modified by the Merz Company of Frankfurt, who were specialists in metal pressing and stamping, to enable production to be done on simple presses. Nevertheless the design was exceptionally robust and reliable; one German report stated, "Of all infantry weapons, the *Sturmgewehr* was the only one which always worked in Russia's dirt, cold, and snow, had no misfires, and was resistant to stoppages."

In spite of this, a contract was issued in 1944 to develop an even better weapon, tentatively known as the *Sturmgewehr* 45. Numerous designs were put forward, the most successful being that by Mauser. The war ended before development was very far advanced and the design was later taken to Spain where it was developed into the CETME rifle. It then returned to Germany where, considerably improved, it is now produced as the Heckler & Koch Gewehr 3; as well as being the standard rifle of the Bundeswehr, it is widely used throughout the world.

BELOW Detail of StG 44 trigger, triggerguard, and magazine. The receiver, trigger housing, and pistol grip are made from steel stampings. The trigger housing and grip is hinged to the receiver and folds down for stripping.

BELOW Detail of the front sight. By modern standards the StG44 was heavy, uncomfortable to fire when lying down, and the butt was too easily damaged in close combat, but it was the first assault rifle and the Russians would use its novel approach in the development of the postwar AK-47.

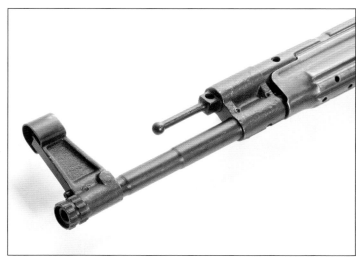

ABOVE LEFT Right-side view of another StG44. Note slightly modified front sight.

BELOW Details showing magazine housing and (below) MP44 barrel stamp.

P14 and P17 "Enfield" rifles

Rifle, Magazine, 1914 Mk. I

Caliber: .30

Length: 46.25in (1.17m)

Weight: 9lb 10oz (4.37kg)

Barrel: 26in (660mm) long, two, four, or five grooves, left-hand twist

Feed system: Five-round integral magazine

System of operation: Enfield (modified Mauser) bolt action

Manufacturers:
Remington Arms Co., U.S. (Mk1e and Mk1r)
Winchester Repeating Arms Co., New Haven, Conn., U.S. (Mk 1w)

Values: $100–$250

The Rifle No. 3 Mk. 1 evolved from a weapon that was produced as a back up, in case the innovative new SMLE did not live up to expectations. There was some concern that the SMLE would lack accuracy and would not be a match for the rifles of other nation's armed forces. In the event the SMLE more than justified its supporters' confidence but, in the mean time, work had begun on a fresh design, using a longer barrel and a bolt action with frontal locking lugs based more or less on the Mauser system. The new rifle was in .276 caliber, and small numbers were issued for trial in 1913 as the Pattern 1913. They were not particularly successful, most of the troubles stemming from the exceptionally powerful cartridge, and when war broke out the development was shelved, never to be revived.

However, because of the shortage of rifles, and since the "P13" had been designed with an eye to rapid production in wartime, the design was changed to accept the standard .303 cartridge and several thousand were made on contract in the United States as the "Pattern 14." When the U.S. entered the war it, too, had a rifle problem, and solved it by redesigning the Pattern 14 to take the standard U.S. .30 cartridge. The same manufacturers

RIGHT Detail of P14 sight and bolt.

ABOVE AND TOP Left and right-hand side views of the P14.

were asked to continue with production, this version being called the "Pattern 17" by the British and the "M1917" or "Enfield" by the Americans. In all, 2,193,429 Pattern 17 rifles were produced before the contracts were terminated in 1918.

After the war they were placed in storage and were brought out once more in 1940 when more than one million were sent to Britain to arm the Home Guard (who also were given large numbers of Pattern 14s that had been stored in Britain). The remaining M1917s were issued to the U.S. Army to fill its needs until sufficient Garand rifles were produced. It is, in fact, doubtful if any Pattern 17 (or Pattern 14) rifles were ever used in combat, but they were certainly widely used for training.

As military rifles the Pattern 14 and 17 were not among the world's best, which is probably why it was never revived after World War I; it was, certainly in comparison to the Lee-Enfield,

a cumbersome and badly balanced weapon. But as a target rifle it is worthy of respect, which rather reflects the target-shooting bias of the people who originally clamored for the design to replace the Lee-Enfield. It was used as a sniping rifle during World War I, but when it came to fighting the British troops were in no doubt about which rifle they preferred.

BELOW AND BOTTOM Left and right-hand sides of the P17. The red stripe was applied when the weapons were issued to the British Home Guard in to show it fired American .30 ammunition rather than the standard UK .303 fired by the P14.

U.S. Rifle Cal .30, M1917

Caliber: .30-06

Length: 46.3in (1.17m)

Weight: 9lb (4.08kg)

Barrel: 24.48in (622mm) long, five grooves, right-hand twist

Feed system: Five-round integral magazine

System of operation: Enfield (modified Mauser) bolt action

Manufacturers:
Remington Arms Co., Eddystone, Pa., and Ilion, N.Y., U.S.
Winchester Repeating Arms Co., New Haven, Conn., U.S.

Values: $150-$500

RIGHT Detail of P17 marking— "U.S. Model of 1917 Remington."

Ross Mk. III rifle

Caliber: .303
Length: 50.36in (1.28m)
Weight: 9.85lb (4.47kg)
Barrel: 33.25in (845mm) long, four grooves, right-hand twist
Feed system: Five-round, integral box magazine

System of operation: Bolt operation
Manufacturers: Ross Rifle Co., Quebec, Canada
Values: $275–$500

Designed by Sir Charles Ross in 1896, the weapon was supplied to the Royal Canadian Mounted Police from 1905. The Ross M1910 was adopted to replace the 1905 pattern in 1911. It bore little resemblance to the earlier weapon either in appearance or mechanically, and was destined to have a very short career as a standard service rifle. This was in spite of the fact that the British Army acquired large numbers of the Mk. IIIB version, with a magazine cut-off. In use it proved unwieldy to handle and the Ross action, although extremely strong, was far too easily jammed by the mud and dirt encountered in battle. In addition there was a serious design flaw that meant that it was possible to reassemble the bolt with the head incorrectly positioned. When the rifle was fired this could cause the bolt to be ejected backwards into the firer's face. The fault was quite easily remedied by armorers in the field, but by then the Ross was already being replaced as the standard service rifle by the SMLE. Many guns were scrapped, some were passed on to the Russians and some to the Royal Navy. A few were retained by the army for use as sniping rifles, a role for which their long barrel, such a hinderance in the trenches, made them ideally suited.

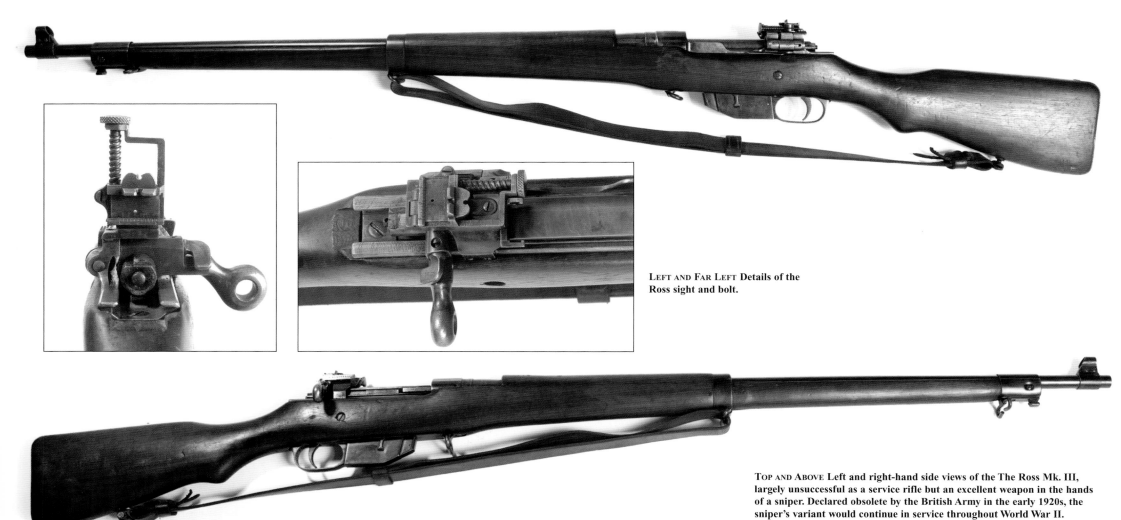

LEFT AND FAR LEFT **Details of the Ross sight and bolt.**

TOP AND ABOVE **Left and right-hand side views of the The Ross Mk. III, largely unsuccessful as a service rifle but an excellent weapon in the hands of a sniper. Declared obsolete by the British Army in the early 1920s, the sniper's variant would continue in service throughout World War II.**

Shotguns in World War II

United States forces have a long history of using shotguns in warfare, dating back to the 1850. The U.S. military turned again to shotguns when the nation became embroiled in World War I. The tried and proven Model 1897 was slightly modified by the

ABOVE AND BELOW Marlin 94 pump-action shotgun—this one was used in by a member of the British Home Guard.

addition of a ventilated metal hand guard and bayonet adaptor and was referred to as the "trench gun." The Winchester Model 1897 12-gauge trench guns, along with a smaller number of Remington Model 10 trench guns, saw action in the trenches of France during the closing months of the war. The trench gun soon acquired a reputation as a fearsome close-range arm.

Following the Armistice in 1918, the trench guns remained in the inventories of the U.S. Army and Marine Corps where they saw use in limited actions in the Caribbean and China between the wars. The supply of shotguns left over from World War I was sufficient to meet the demand until the eve of World War II.

The attack on Pearl Harbor found the United States military woefully short of all manner of arms—not helped by the quantities that had been shipped to Britain after Dunkirk. In 1940 the British Army had abandoned most of its firearms in northern France and the British

longer barreled guns for training aerial gunners. Winchester Repeating Arms Co. supplied Model 97 and Model 12 shotguns of all three types. Ithaca Gun Co. produced a small number of Model 37 trench guns and a larger number of Model 37 riot guns and training guns. The Stevens Arms Co. delivered trench guns, riot guns and training versions of its Model 520-30 and 620A shotguns. Remington Arms Co. turned out riot and training gun variants of its Model 11 auto-loading shotgun, and Savage Arms Co. produced a number of the almost-identical Model 720 riot guns and training guns. Shotguns saw combat use in most theaters of the war and, as was the case in World War I, they proved to be highly effective for close-range combat applications.

Records show a total of 39,176 Winchester M97s of all types were purchased between 1941 and 1944 when the contracts ended. 80,574 Winchester M12s were also supplied. Thousands of other "militarized" shotguns were also purchased from Steven, Savage, and Ithaca for a total of 150,000 supplied by the end of

Marlin 94 shotgun

Caliber: 12 gauge	System of operation: Pump action
Length: 49in (1.24m)	
Weight: 7lb 6oz (4.08kg)	Manufacturers: Marlin Firearms Co., New Haven, Conn., U.S.
Barrel: 30in (762mm) long	
Feed system: Tube magazine under barrel	Values: n/a

types of ammunition: .45 ACP, .30, .30-06, .50 as well as 12 gauge to infantry units.

Shotguns are effective in close areas and trenches but not effective when the range exceeds 30m. Most armed forces have a shotgun on their inventory today; whether they are used depends on the expected action. For the most part, they remain second-line weapons for use by second-grade troops.

Government was forced to purchase every and any type of firearm including shotguns. The World War I vintage shotguns were about a quarter century old by that time, and the supply was insufficient to meet the burgeoning demand.

The Ordnance Department gave contracts to several commercial firms for shotguns. There were three basic types procured during World War II: trench guns with bayonet adaptors and hand guards—riot guns—plain, short barreled guns, and

the war. About 130,000 were used within the United States by the National Guard. The remainder were used mostly in the Pacific by the Marines, but also in Europe after the Normandy landings—many by U.S. Military Police behind the lines. The burden placed on the U.S. supply system sped the demise of the shotgun as a front-line weapon because of the need to provide four different

Remington Model 10 shotgun

Caliber: 12 gauge
Length: 39.25in (997mm)
Weight: 7lb 13oz (3.5kg)
Barrel: 19.75in (502mm)
Feed system: Tube magazine under barrel

System of operation: Pump action
Manufacturer: Remington Arms, Co., Ilion, N.Y., U.S.
Values: n/a

BELOW AND BOTTOM Left and right-hand sides of the 12 Gauge Remington Model 1910. Introduced in 1908 and discontinued in 1929, more than 275,500 were manufactured—including numbers of the Model 10 Trench Shotgun.

RIGHT AND FAR RIGHT Remington Model 1910 and Model 1911 maker's marks.

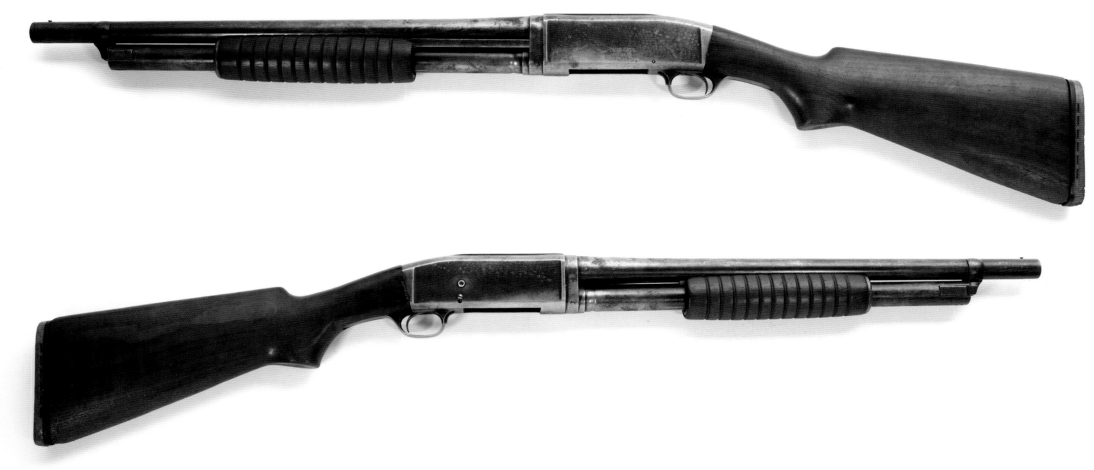

Remington Model 11 shotgun

Caliber: 12, 16, and 20 gauges
Length: 45in (1.14m)
Weight: 7lb 12oz (3.52kg)
Barrel: 26in (660mm)
Feed system: Five-round tube magazine under barrel

System of operation: Autoloading shotgun
Manufacturer: Remington Arms Co., Ilion, N.Y., U.S.
Values: n/a

RIGHT, BELOW, AND BOTTOM Left and right-hand sides of the Remington Model 1911. Introduced in 1905 and discontinued in 1947, over 850,000 were manufactured including some 65,000 by Browning for use in World War II.

Winchester Model 97 shotgun

Caliber: 12 gauge
Length: 39.5in (1m)
Weight: 7lb 10oz (3.46kg)
Barrel: 24.5in (622mm)
Feed system: Six-round tube magazine under barrel

System of operation: Pump action
Manufacturer: Winchester Repeating Arms Co., New Haven, Conn., U.S.
Values: n/a

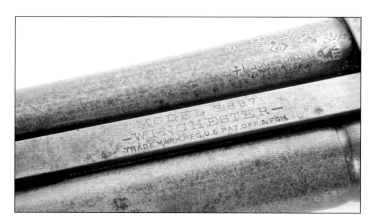

LEFT Maker's mark detail.

BELOW AND BOTTOM Left and right-hand side views of the 12 Gauge Winchester Model 1897 pump-action shotgun.

BELOW AND BOTTOM Left and right-hand sides of a Winchester Model 97 pump action shotgun that has had a barrel extension of four inches in an attempt to improve accuracy. The weight addition (some 2oz/57gm) was minimal.

Stevens Model .22/.410 combination rifle–shotgun

Caliber: .22 rifle; .410–gauge shotgun

Length: 40in (1.02m)

Weight: 6lb 5oz (2.86kg)

Barrel: 24in (610mm)

Feed system: Manual

Manufacturer: J. Stevens Arms & Tool Company of Chicopee Falls, Mass., U.S. (later Savage Arms Co.)

Values: n/a

The weapon shown here is typical of the many unnofficial arms carried by aircrew in World War II for use as a survival weapon in the event of a forced landing or bail out.

It is a .410/.22 combination rifle-shotgun made by J. Stevens Arms & Tool Co. of Chicopee Falls, Massachusetts. Produced as a sporting gun, this type of weapon was particularly popular with aircrews, to the extent that in 1949 the Savage Model 24 .22/.410 Rifle-Shotgun Survival Gun (Stevens had been absorbed by Savage in 1939) was procured on a limited basis by the U.S. Air Force for use as survival weapons by aircrew operating in remote areas. These were marked USAF on the bottom of the frame.

Later, specially designed survival guns were adopted (the M4 bolt action rifle in .22 Hornet caliber, and the M6 over-under .22 Hornet rifle/.410 gauge shotgun).

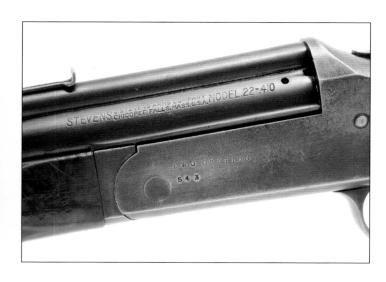

LEFT, RIGHT, AND BELOW LEFT The Stevens .22/.410 combination rifle-shotgun. Popular as a survival gun with aircrew, this particular weapon is said to have been carried on missions by a crewman of a B-17 Flying Fortess.

Training equipment

A number of rifles and handguns were used as training equipment (for example, see page 80): the equipment identified here and on page 120 shows a different slant. The Swift Training Rifle and the equipment overleaf were used for the initial training of new recruits in a time when there was a desperate shortage of weapons and ammunition in Britain.

Swift Training Rifle

This complicated apparatus was designed to develop shooting skills without a rifle. The user had to pull the stock tight against their shoulder to release the lock in the butt and then sighted on a small paper target mounted at the muzzle of the "gun." Pulling the trigger caused the spring loaded prongs in the muzzle (see detail at right) to prick holes in the target. There was a prism on the sight to enable the instructor to see where the student was aiming.

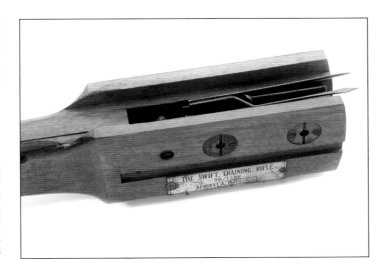

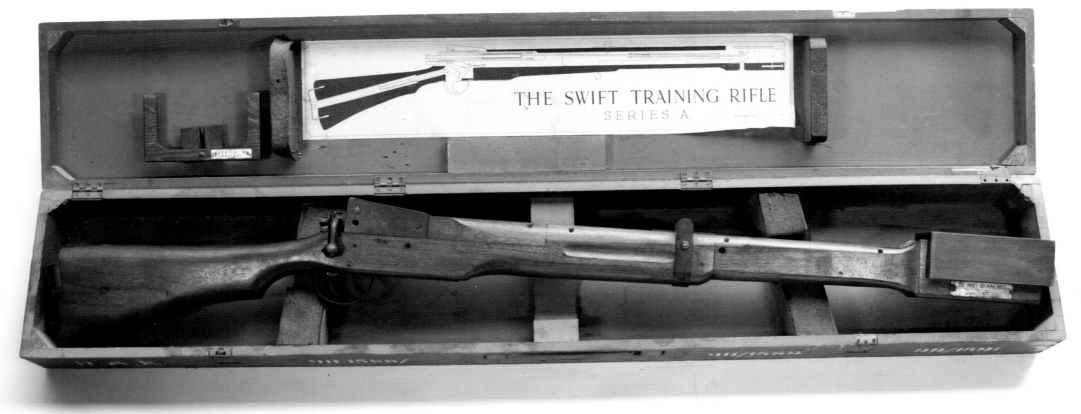

British Army Bayonet Practice Weapon and Mask

Shown here is a dummy weapon and mask typical of those used in bayonet practice during the war, particularly in Home Guard units deprived of weapons in 1940.

Tokarev SVT40 rifle

Caliber: 7.62mm

Length: 48.1 in (1.22m)

Weight: 8lb 8oz (3.86kg)

Barrel: 24.60in (625mm) long, four grooves, right-hand twist

Feed system: 10-round detachable box magazine

System of operation: Gas; tipping bolt

Manufacturers: Russian state arsenals

Values: $300–$400

The SVT40 was the third self-loading rifle to see service in the USSR. The first was the AVS36, or *Automaticheskaya Vintovka Simonova 36*, designed by S G. Simonov for introduction in 1936. This was not a great success as it produced excessive muzzle blast and recoil, and it was all too easy for dust and dirt to get into the complex mechanism. 1938 saw the introduction of the *Samozariadnyia Vintovka Tokareva 38*, or SVT38, designed by F V Tokarev. This had its own share of problems, for although the basic design was sound, the components had been made too light for the stresses imposed on them in an effort to reduce weight. This inevitably led to breakages and poor reliability and

in 1940 it was replaced by the improved SVT40 in which the basic mechanism was retained but everything was made more robust. The Model 40 was issued in relatively small numbers during the war and can be distinguished from the Model 38 thus: first, it has more of the barrel exposed; second, it has a two or three-baffle muzzle brake instead of the six-baffle pattern of the earlier one; third, it used a shorter bayonet. The action was by gas, this being tapped off close to the muzzle to drive a gas piston operating in a cylinder above the barrel. This, in turn, drove an operating rod to the rear, and this protruded above the breech to strike the face of a bolt carrier and drive it to the rear against a return spring. Bolt movement was imparted by the bolt carrier by means of cam tracks which lifted and unlocked the bolt and then held it firmly to be withdrawn by the remaining rearward movement of the carrier. The return spring was in the bolt carrier and receiver body, which accounted for the length of the action, and this returned carrier and bolt, loading a fresh round as it did so. A separate spring returned the operating rod and gas piston. Mechanically speaking, this is a sound and commonplace design, but there seem to have been numerous teething troubles.

In service the SVT40 proved not to be the most rugged of weapons. Generally the rifles were issued to NCOs of infantry regiments, but they were later withdrawn and the majority were converted to sniping rifles, an application where the self-loading action was advantageous and where the sniper could devote some time to careful maintenance of the weapon.

Although the SVT40 was not produced in sufficient numbers to meet demand, it had a considerable influence on future Soviet small arms development, leading ultimately to the AK-47.

VARIANTS

SKT40 Carbine

This was a shortened version of the rifle. It was not produced in great numbers.

BELOW Right-hand side view of the SVT40.

Winchester Rifles

M69 rifle

Caliber: .22

Length: 42.5in (1.08m)

Weight: 6lb 13oz (3.09kg) inc scope

Barrel: 24in (610mm) long, six grooves, right-hand twist

Feed system: Magazine

System of operation: Bolt-action

Manufacturers: Winchester Repeating Arms Co., New Haven, Conn., U.S.

Values: n/a

In 1940s' Britain, faced the threat of imminent invasion, there was a desperate shortage of weapons after the evacuation at Dunkirk. Many men had been recovered from France but most of their weapons had been left behind. The Home Guard was equipped with all sorts of improvised weapons and any and all types of guns. Many of these dated from World War I and many were never intended for military use but for sports shooting. Winchester .22 rifles, in particular, were extremely popular between the wars and a good many were impressed into military service. Illustrated here are two examples of sporting .22s adapted for military use. Both are fitted with telescope sights and the M94 is also fitted with a silencer and a ready ammunition pouch on the butt. It is doubtful if weapons such as these would have been much use in the face of the full onslaught of the German Army, but they were useful in training Home Guard troops until more suitable weapons were available and, if nothing else, served to boost morale when it mattered most.

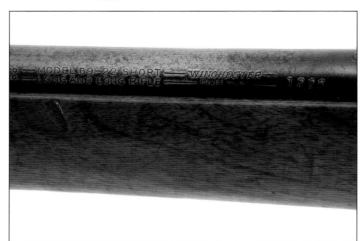

LEFT Winchester trademark on Model 69 barrel.

ABOVE AND BELOW Typical of the type of weapons pressed into service with the Home Guard in the desperate months following Dunkirk, this Winchester M69 sports rifle is fitted with a silencer and scope, and has a ready ammunition pouch on the butt. The silencer was seven inches long and weighed seven ounces.

M94 rifle

Caliber: .22
Length: 43.75in (1.11m)
Weight: 8lb 4oz (3.74kg) including scope
Barrel: 24in (610mm) long, six grooves, right-hand twist

Feed system: Magazine
System of operation: Bolt-action
Manufacturers: Winchester Repeating Arms Co., New Haven, Conn., U.S.
Values: n/a

TOP RIGHT Detail of the scope on the Winchester Model 94.

ABOVE AND BELOW Another Winchester .22 sports rifle, a Model 94, impressed into military service.

SUBMACHINE GUNS

The submachine gun was first developed at the end of World War I. But it was not until the Spanish Civil War that the capabilities of the weapon in the hands of poorly trained troops became apparent.

Soviet Russia and Germany were the first to take heed—not unnaturally because both nations had effectively used Spain as a testing ground for new weapons. Both countries produced enormous numbers of these weapons, the most prolific being the PPSh (see page 139) in the USSR and the MP40 (see page 129) in Germany. The United States and Britain came to appreciate the benefits of the submachine gun a little later. The Thompson was produced in the United States as a private venture in the 1920s, but was not taken up by the military until some time later. There was some resistance in the military, both in the U.S. and Britain, as the submachine gun was seen as a gangster's weapon. With the outbreak of war these objections were soon forgotten, and cheap, easily produced designs appeared in both countries: the M3 "Grease Gun" in the States, and the Sten in the UK, and these were produced in ever-increasing numbers.

The submachine gun made levels of firepower possible that were undreamed of in World War I and transformed infantry tactics, particularly in urban fighting.

ABOVE Sten Mk. II—see page 142.

RIGHT Sten seven-magazine bandolier.

BELOW M3 Grease Gun—see page 136.

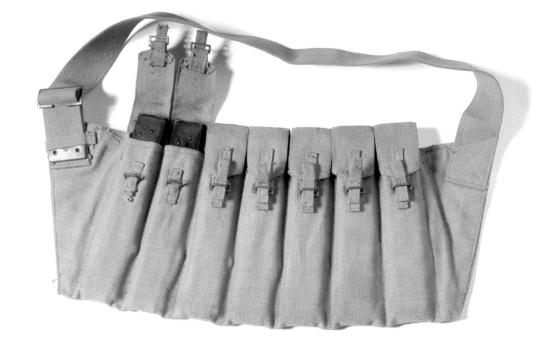

Right MP40 Schmeisser—see page 126.

Far Right Thompson submachine gun detail—see page 146.

Below Right Lanchester submachine guns—see page 134.

Australian submachine guns

Austen

Caliber: 9mm
Length: 33.25in (845mm) stock extended
Weight: 8lb 12oz (3.98kg)
Barrel: 7.75in (196mm) long, six grooves, right-hand twist
Feed system: 28-round detachable box magazine
System of operation: Blowback, selective fire
Rate of fire: Cyclic, 500rpm
Manufacturers: Diecasters Ltd., Melbourne, Australia
W. J. Carmichael & Co., Melbourne, Australia
Values: $4,500–$5,500 (Class III)

In 1941 the Australian armed forces decided to produce a new submachine gun that was suitable for mass production. The design was based on that of the Sten gun, the first examples of which had just arrived in Australia. Indeed, the name is a contraction of Australian Sten. The barrel, body, and trigger mechanism came straight from the Mk. II Sten, but the bolt mechanism was copied from the German MP38, using a telescopic cover over the return spring and a separate firing pin. The butt stock was also copied from the MP38 but with a slight improvement to the locking system. The magazine was a smaller capacity version of the Sten's, and a front pistol grip was added.

Although specifically intended for mass production, no more than about 20,000 were manufactured between mid-1942 and early 1945, for although it was a sound and reliable weapon it was never as popular as the Owen gun.

VARIANTS
Mk. II
Although called the Mk. II this was effectively a new weapon. It was put into production in late 1944 but very few were made before the contract was cancelled at the end of the war.

Owen

Caliber: 9mm
Length: 32in (813mm)
Weight: 9lb 5oz (4.21kg)
Barrel: 9.75in (247mm) long, seven grooves, right-hand twist
Feed system: 33-round detachable box magazine
System of operation: Blowback
Rate of fire: Cyclic, 700rpm
Manufacturer: Lysaght's Pty, Port Kemble, NSW, Australia
Values: $6,500–$7,500 (Class III)

The decision to design an indigenous submachine gun for the Australian Army came about as a response to the lack of alternative sources. Britain had none in 1940 and America only a few Thompsons. The task fell to Lt Evelyn Owen, who produced the prototype of the Owen gun in 1940. Pre-production models in a variety of calibers were made for troop trials, and on November 20, 1941, the 9mm version was authorized for production and issue. Over 45,000 of the Mk. I model were made before production ceased in September 1944.

The most prominent feature of the Owen was the top-mounted magazine. This arrangement was less awkward than it looked, and meant the feed was working with gravity rather than against it. The magazine was a two-column type, easy to fill, and had the ejector machined as an integral part of the magazine mouth. The mechanism was of blowback type, but the bolt travel was remarkably short, and this made the action rather more violent than most. The bolt was carefully sealed in to prevent dirt entering the action, and the cocking handle was isolated from the bolt for the same purpose. An odd form of construction was used in which an inserted ring in the rear of the gun body acted as a stop to the breech block's travel. To dismantle the weapon it was necessary to remove the barrel in order to take the bolt out through the front of the body; to make this easier a quick release plunger on top of the body held the barrel in place.

Manufacture was by traditional methods of machining, which made production slower than it might have been, and also meant that the gun was unnecessarily heavy. An interesting report, in view of the weapon's eventual success and popularity, was made in February 1942 after a specimen had been sent to Britain for assessment. After discussing the various features of the gun, the report stated, "the tests carried out on the Owen are the standard tests . . . and we consider it passed them satisfactorily. The accuracy is well within acceptance limits but the rate of fire is unfavorably high." The conclusion was that, "The Owen gun has very few genuine new features to recommend it. Most of the parts which are novel are poor in design and have not been studied from the production angle. We anticipate, before this gun comes from the factory in larger quantities, much development work will be required and many teething troubles will be experienced which will involve radical re-design."

The Owen gun became the principal submachine gun of the Australian Army, it was highly effective and popular with everyone who ever used it. The Owen remained in service, substantially unchanged, until 1962.

VARIANTS

Mk. I/42
The basic model, described above. Had cooling fins on the barrel and a frame-type buttstock. Later models had holes cut in the frame behind the pistol grip to lighten the weapon.

Mk. I/43
The first of these were identical with the later Mk. I/42s, but then the barrel cooling fins were omitted in favor of a plain barrel. This version had a wooden buttstock.

Mk. II/43
A rare model. The frame behind the triggerguard was removed and a new design of wooden buttstock secured beneath the body by a knurled screw fitted with a bayonet that slid over the muzzle compensator. Some 200 were made early in 1943.

Mk. I/44
Generally the same as the I/43 but later models had a bayonet lug on the barrel.

German MP (*Maschinenpistole*) submachine guns

MP18 and MP28 submachine guns

Data: MP28
Caliber: 9mm
Length: 32in (812mm)
Weight: 8lb 12oz (3.97kg)
Barrel: 7.75in (196mm) long, six grooves, right-hand twist
Feed system: 32-round detachable box

System of operation: Blowback, selective fire
Rate of fire: Cyclic, 500rpm
Manufacturer: C. G. Haenel Waffenfabrik, Suhl, Germany
Values: $5,500–$6,500 (Class III)

The MP28 was a development of the earlier MP18, a few of which had been retained for use by the police after World War I. It was redesigned in the 1920s by Hugo Schmeisser to provide selective fire. At the same it was fitted with improved sights and the magazine feed was altered so that the magazine entered at 90 degrees instead of 45, making the gun easier to handle. In spite of the limitations placed on the German arms industry at the time, the MP28 was successfully developed as a commercial venture by Theodor Bergmann Waffenfabrik AG of Suhl. As a result, it was produced in various calibers and was made under license in Belgium and Spain. It saw widespread use in the Spanish Civil War where the Germans and Russians both gained a good deal of battlefield experience with the submachine gun as, indeed, they did with many other weapons. Its use in the German Army was restricted to the early part of the war, since its manufacture demanded a lot of milling and machining, and was not suited to mass production. It was soon replaced by weapons of more modern construction, produced in in larger quantities. It was copied to make the Lanchester, used by the Royal Navy. It had also very nearly been selected to be the standard British Army submachine gun but lost out to the Sten.

MP34 and 35 submachine guns

Data: MP35
Caliber: 9mm
Length: 33in (840mm)
Weight: 8lb 15oz (4.05kg)
Barrel: 7.75in (196mm) long, six grooves, right-hand twist
Feed system: 32-round detachable box
System of operation: Blowback, selective fire

Rate of fire: Cyclic, 650rpm
Manufacturer:
Carl Walther Waffenfabrik, Zella-Mehlis, Germany
Junker & Ruh AG, Karlsruhe, Germany
Values: $5,500–$6,500 (Class III)

In 1934 T.E. Bergmann formed Theodor Bergmann GmbH in Berlin, with the intention of exploiting the patents of Theodor Bergmann, Senior. This enabled them to develop the existing prototype MP34 submachine gun, but because of the new company's lack of facilities, manufacture was contracted out to Carl Walther of Zella-Mehlis. The production MP34 was first adopted by the German police. It was wooden stocked and had a barrel jacket perforated with long slots and with a built-in compensator at the muzzle. The cocking handle resembled a rifle bolt and protruded from the rear of the receiver end cap. An unusual feature was that the magazine fed from the right, ejection being to the left, and instead of the magazine protruding at 90 degrees to the axis of the weapon, it was slightly angled forward. A double trigger for selective fire was fitted; pulling the front trigger gave single shots, but further pressure also pulled the second trigger to give automatic fire.

The MP34 was in production for about year (arround 2,000 were made) and in mid-1935 a small number of changes were made to simplify production. The revised model, the MP35, was available with long or short barrels, the long-barreled models often being fitted for a bayonet. In subsequent years these guns were sold to Spain, Sweden, and Poland as well as Ethiopia.

In 1940 the Waffen-SS adopted the weapon as its standard submachine gun, from then on the entire production, this time contracted out to Junkers & Ruh, went to the Waffen-SS units. It appears to have been mostly used on the Eastern Front, and the few MP35 specimens found in the west generally have SS runes engraved on them.

RIGHT **The MP40 Schmeisser, a classic Wehrmacht weapon. Note the stock folded under the body of the gun.**

MP38, 38/40, 40, and 41

Data: MP38

Caliber: 9mm

Length: 32.75in (832mm) stock extended

Weight: 9lb (4.14kg)

Barrel: 9.75in (247mm) long, six grooves, right-hand twist

Feed system: 32-round box magazine

System of operation: Blowback, automatic only

Rate of fire: Cyclic, 500rpm

Manufacturers: Erfurter Maschinenfabrik B. Geipel GmbH, Erfurt, Germany

Values:
MP38: $17,000–$20,000
MP40: $7,000–$8,000
MP41: $10,000–$13,000
(Class III)

LEFT AND BELOW The MP41.

The MP34 was designed by a team from the Erfurter Maschinenfabrik—the Ermawerke—factory using various patents of Heinrich Vollmer, under the direction of owner Berthold Geipel. In 1938 the German Army issued a specification for a new submachine gun that drew on the battlefield experience gained in the Spanish Civil War. The new specification tallied closely with the project that was already in hand at Ermawerke and, with a few slight changes, this was accepted as the MP38.

The MP38 broke new ground in weapon design by having no wood anywhere in its construction and by having a folding stock. The bolt was driven by a return spring contained in Vollmer's telescoping tube and it carried a spring-retracted firing pin. The muzzle was threaded to take a blank-firing attachment or a combined muzzle cover and cleaning-rod guide. Beneath the barrel was a hook-like steel bar that prevented damage to the barrel when firing through the gun-port of an armored vehicle and also prevented the gun being pulled inadvertently inboard during firing should the gunner lose his footing.

Although it was a great success, the MP38 was still largely made by conventional methods. The army was pleased with it, but demanded a weapon more easily mass-produced. As a result the MP38 was redesigned to make the maximum use of stampings and welded assemblies. The principal changes were that the body was made of stamped sheet steel, formed and welded; the magazine housing was ribbed instead of plain; and the body top was plain instead of ribbed. The cocking handle was redesigned so that it could be pressed inward when the bolt was forward to engage an enlarged portion of the handle in a slot milled in the receiver, thus locking the bolt forward as a type of safety.

The new model was known as the MP40 and replaced the MP38 as the standard submachine gun. The MP40—or Schmeisser as it was popularly, though erroneously, known—became synonymous with the German Army.

VARIANTS

MP38/40

A modification of the MP38 to bring it up to the safety standard of the MP40 by fitting it with the MP40's cocking handle and cutting a suitable slot in the receiver.

MP40/1

The first model of the MP40 had a smooth-surfaced magazine housing and the cocking handle of the MP38. When these were changed by a retrospective modification to use the cocking handle of the MP40 and the ribbed magazine housing, the official designation became the MP40/1.

MP40/2

During the Russian campaign the German troops complained that the Russian soldier with a 71-round drum on his submachine gun had a considerable edge over the German with a 32-round box magazine. As a result, a special magazine housing was produced that allowed two magazines to be inserted side by side; one was aligned with the barrel and fired, after which the second could be slid across into alignment and fired. It was cumbersome and only produced in limited numbers. The main drawback was that the weapon with two loaded magazines weighed over 12lb (5.44kg), while the Russian weapon weighed less and still had a seven-shot advantage.

MP41

This was basically the body and barrel of the MP40 fitted to the wooden butt of the MP28 and provided with a Bergmann-type fire selector.

EMP submachine gun

Caliber: 9mm
Length: 35.5in (902mm)
Weight: 9lb 2oz (4.14kg)
Barrel: 10in (254mm) long, six grooves, right-hand twist
Feed system: 25 or 32-round detachable box magazine
System of operation: Blowback, selective fire

Rate of fire: Cyclic, 500rpm
Manufacturer:
Erfurt Maschinenfabrik B Geipel GmbH, Erfurt, Germany
Values: $5,000–$6,500 (Class III)

ABOVE The MP40 was constructed from steel pressings to ease mass production.

BELOW Detail showing this MP40 maker's mark (bnz—Steyr-Daimler-Puch AG, Werk Steyr, Steyr, Austria) and date of manufacture—1943.

BELOW RIGHT Detail of the cocking handle, variant (MP41) and manufacturer (C.G. Haenel GmbH). Note the PATENT SCHMEISSER. Hugo Schmeisser's name has become popularly used as a shorthand for various German submachine guns.

The Erfurt Maschinenfabrik company entered the submachine gun field about 1930, making a gun designed by Heinrich Vollmer and Berthold Geipel and known as the Vollmer submachine gun. After some commercial success with this weapon it was slightly redesigned and marketed as the "*Erma*" *Maschinenpistole Modell 35*. This had a long barrel and was fitted to take a bayonet. Then came a shorter model without bayonet fittings, and another with a rifle-type fore end replacing the front pistol grip of the two earlier designs.

The second model, with short barrel and forward pistol grip, was produced in the greatest numbers and was adopted by the German Army in small numbers from about 1936. It has a barrel jacket with long slots, a magazine entering from the left, and—its most easily recognized feature—a wooden buttstock, the front end of which is formed into a pistol grip. The mechanism uses a simple bolt but has the return spring carried in a telescoping tube, the unique Vollmer design which reappeared on the MP38 and MP40.

The EMP remained in production from about 1932 to mid-1938 when the Ermawerke factory was turned over entirely to the production of the MP38. Quite a large number of these weapons were used during the Spanish Civil War. In German service they were largely replaced in the army by the MP38 and MP40.

Italian submachine guns

Beretta Model 1918

Caliber: 9 mm	System of operation: Retarded blowback, automatic only
Length: 43in (1.1m)	
Weight: 7lb 3oz (3.26kg)	Rate of fire: Cyclic, 900rpm
Barrel: 12in (305mm) long, six grooves, right–hand twist	Manufacturer: P. Beretta, Brescia, Italy
Feed system: 25–round box magazine	Values: $8,000–$9,500 (Class III)

The Beretta 1918, like the OVP (see page 133), was essentially a reworked Villar Perosa (VP). Beretta and OVP were both requested to redesign the cumbersome VP into a more practical weapon. The result of Beretta designer Tullio Marengoni's efforts was the Model 1918—his first submachine gun. His modifications included fitting a new trigger mechanism based on that of the standard Italian service rifle of the day; a long wooden stock, with an ejection port underneath; and a folding bayonet similar to that used on Italian service carbines. The result was a practical and handy weapon. The mechanism remained unchanged, still using the rotating-bolt system, and the slotted, curved magazine fitted into the top of the action.

The Model 1918 was preferred to the OVP but there were manufacturing problems. The weapon couldn't be output in quantity, immediately. The solution was to hand over to Beretta the existing Villar Perosa machine guns and their spare parts. From these Beretta built Model 1918 submachine guns.

The Model 1918 was issued to the elite regiments of the Italian Army early in 1918. They became the first units to receive submachine guns as a standard issue, because they predate the German issue of the Bergmann by a few weeks. They remained in service until World War II—although their carbine-like appearance means that their opponents often did not recognize them for what they were. Numbers were used in the Spanish Civil War and the Italo–Abyssinia War and were frequently encountered in the early phases of the Libyan campaign in 1941.

VARIANTS

Model 18/30
Rarely used as a military weapon, this was derived from the 1918. A fifteen-round magazine was mounted below the gun, ejecting at the top; cocking was by a ring-shaped handle at the rear end and the mechanism was altered to allow single-shot firing only. Intended as a police weapon it was not produced in very large numbers.

Beretta Model 1938A

Caliber: 9mm	System of operation: Blowback, selective fire
Length: 37.5in (953mm)	
Weight: 9lb 4oz (4.26kg)	Rite of fire: Cyclic, 600rpm
Barrel: 12.5in (318mm) long, six grooves, right–hand twist	Manufacturer: P. Beretta, Brescia, Italy
Feed system: 10, 20, 30, or 40-round detachable box magazines	Values: $6,000–$7,000 (Class III)

Developed from the Model 1935 semiautomatic carbine, the Model 1938A was redesigned as a selective-fire weapon and went into production in 1938. The first model was fully stocked, similar to the Model 1918, but had the magazine below the weapon, had a folding bayonet of special design, and had a cooling jacket with long slots surrounding the barrel. It also had an entirely new firing mechanism with two triggers; the front trigger for firing single shots and the rear trigger for firing automatic. The front end of the barrel jacket was formed into a rudimentary compensator with two large holes in its top.

Although quite a serviceable design, it was only produced in small numbers during 1938 and was soon replaced by the second version, which had no distinctive model number. This version added a fire-selector lever in the shape of a crossbolt locking bar behind the rear trigger which, when pushed in, prevented the rear trigger being depressed and so restricted fire to single shots. The barrel jacket had smaller, circular holes, but the compensator and bayonet of the first model were retained.

A third version was designed at the end of 1938 and went into mass production in 1939 concurrently with the second version; the main difference was the deletion of the bayonet and a change in the design of the compensator to give four upward-facing slots.

BELOW The Beretta Model 1938/42, the major production version of the Italian submachine gun.

The two mass-production versions were turned out in large numbers for the Italian, German, and Romanian armies until 1944, after which production lapsed for some time until taken up again when the war was over. In 1940 the Model 1938 was redesigned to ease production. Several previously machined components were replaced with stamped alternatives and the two-part bolt was replaced with a simpler, one-piece design. While this weapon was originally intended for 9mm Glisenti ammunition, it could fire the German 9mm Parabellum round equally well. To extract the utmost performance from the Model 1938, a special cartridge known as the 9mm M38 was

ABOVE The Beretta Model 1938/42. Note the twin triggers for single shot and automatic fire.

issued; identified by a green surround to the cap, it was issued in ten-round chargers that could be loaded into the magazine using a special loading tool. The 1938A was widely used throughout the war; it saw service in North Africa and Russia with the Italian Army, and was adopted by the German Army as the *Maschinenpistole (Beretta) 38(i)*.

The model 1938 underwent various minor modifications during its life but remained in production until 1950 before being superseded by more modern designs.

VARIANTS
Model 38/42
The move to simplify manufacture of the 1938A was taken further by the development of the Model 38/42. While it was basically the same weapon as the 1938A, the body and magazine housing were of metal stampings, the barrel jacket was discarded, and the compensator reverted to a two-slot model. The first version had the barrel milled with longitudinal grooves for cooling, but this was found to be unnecessary and was soon abandoned in favor of a smooth barrel. The stock was also shortened.

Model 38/43
Sometimes used to distinguish later, smooth-barrelled, 38/42s.

Model 38/44
Much the same as the 38/43 but with a slight change in the design of bolt and return spring, as a result of which the receiver end cap is plain, whereas the 38/42 and 38/43 models had a raised center on the cap to act as an anchor for the return spring.

Model 39A
Made in very small numbers, it resembles the 39M but has the buttstock hinged behind the trigger guard so as to fold sideways and lie alongside the receiver.

Model 43M
Mechanically much the same as the 39M but has a skeleton folding stock similar to that of the MP38—folding beneath the gun. The magazine is slightly altered, having a distinctive forward rake, and a pistol grip is fitted. Numbers of these weapons were used by German troops on the Eastern front under the nomenclature MP43(u).

FNAB-43

Caliber: 9 mm	**System of operation:** Delayed blowback, selective fire
Length: 31.15in (790mm)	
Weight: 8lb 12oz (3.25kg)	**Rate of fire:** Cyclic, 400rpm
Barrel: 7.8in (198mm) long, six grooves, right–hand twist	**Manufacturer:** Fabrica Nazionale d'armes, Brescia, Italy
Feed system: 20 or 40-round detachable box magazine	**Values:** n/a

Designed and developed in Italy during the war, about 7,000 FNAB-43s were made during 1943 and 1944. All were issued to Italian and German units fighting in Northern Italy. Unusually for a weapon produced at this stage of the war, its design called for expensive and time-consuming methods of precision engineering at a time when the general tendency was to make weapons as cheap and easy to produce as possible. Although this undoubtedly limited the number that were produced, it was a well-made and efficient weapon.

The action is a delayed blowback of unique design, firing from the closed-bolt position. The bolt is a two-piece unit with a pivoted lever interposed between bolt head and body. On firing, the bolt head moves back and begins to rotate the lever, the toe of which abuts against a lug in the body; this lever is pivoted in order to delay the opening movement by operating at a mechanical disadvantage, allowing the bullet to leave the barrel and breech pressure to drop before the lever has completed its rotation. The movement of the lever then presses the free end against the bolt body and accelerates the bolt to the rear; the toe of the lever pulls clear of the lug and the whole bolt unit can recoil as one component in the usual way. On returning, the lever engages once more with the body lug and pivots forward, and in doing so removes an interlock which allows movement of the firing pin only when the bolt is fully forward. This unusual and complicated system allows the rate of fire to be kept down to very practical limits without using a heavy bolt or strong spring.

Other features of this weapon include a muzzle brake and compensator built into the barrel casing in the manner of some Russian weapons, and a magazine housing that is hinged so that the magazine can lie beneath the barrel. The stock, a single metal bar, also folds, so that the weapon can be carried as a very compact unit.

Villar Perosa OVP

Caliber: 9 mm

Length: 35.5in (901mm)

Weight: 8lb 1oz (3.67kg)

Barrel: 11in (279mm) long, six grooves, right-hand twist

Feed system: 25-round detachable box magazine

System of operation: Delayed blowback, selective fire

Rate of fire: Cyclic, 900rpm

Manufacturer: Officina di Villar Perosa, Villar Perosa, Italy

Values: $8,000–$9,000 (Class III)

The Italians were the first army ever to adopt a submachine gun, the Villar Perosa, and although it ceased to be a service weapon in 1918 the mechanism of the VP was a sound design. Shortly after the end of the war the manufacturers of the VP were asked to produce a more practical weapon that became known as the OVP . Basically it is little more than the barrel and action of the VP attached to a wooden buttstock and provided with a trigger and some small refinements. Although formally classed as a delayed blowback, the delay is minimal and certainly has little practical effect, as might be deduced from the high rate of fire. The mechanism consists of a bolt and return spring, but the bolt is controlled by a track in the receiver body that causes the bolt to rotate 45 degrees as it closes. The striker carries a lug bearing on the receiver track that also bears on a cam face on the bolt, so that the firing pin, driven by the return spring, cannot go forward to fire the cartridge until the bolt has rotated. When the gun is fired, recoil of the cartridge case moves the bolt back, causing it to rotate to the unlocked position, during which movement the pin is withdrawn by the action of the bolt's cam surface. Once unlocked, the bolt is free to recoil and complete the firing cycle.

An unusual feature of the OVP that was not on the original VP gun was the use of a cylindrical sleeve surrounding the receiver for cocking the weapon. This was pulled to the rear to retract the bolt and then pushed forward again to remain in the forward position during firing. One design feature that was carried over from the VP, was the provision of a slot in the rear edge of the top-mounted magazine which allowed the firer to see how many rounds remained inside it, unfortunately this also allowed dust and dirt to enter the magazine..

The OVP was issued in the early 1921 and by the time of World War II had been largely replaced by the various Beretta models. However, it saw use in the Italo-Abyssinian War and was used in small numbers by some Italian units in the Western Desert in 1941, but after this it was withdrawn from service.

TZ-45

Caliber: 9 mm

Length: 33.5in (901mm)

Weight: 7lb 3oz (3.26kg)

Barrel: 9in (229mm) long, six grooves, right-hand twist

Feed system: 40-round detachable box magazine

System of operation: Blowback, selective fire

Rate of fire: Cyclic, 550rpm

Manufacturer: Tonone et Zorzola, Gardoneval-Trompe, Italy

Values: n/a

This is another Italian wartime design produced in small numbers by a small company. No more than 6,000 were made during 1944–45. In comparison with the FNAB-43, the TZ-45 is much more in keeping with other weapons of the time. It was cheaply made from metal stampings, welded together in parts, and crudely finished. In spite of this, it worked, and was reasonably successful in action, although not as reliable as it could have been.

The action is simple blowback, but the return spring is assembled around a guide rod which is in two pieces and telescopes as the bolt returns. A muzzle compensator is fitted, and the shoulder stock is formed of steel rods which slide alongside the receiver when retracted. Two separate safety systems are fitted: the fire-selector lever has a safe position that locks the bolt in either the forward or rearward positions; and there is a grip safety fitted behind the magazine housing.

The entire issue of the TZ-45 appears to have gone to various units of the Italian Army operating against guerrilla forces in the mountains. It was offered to the British and U.S. armies but neither took up the weapon.

BELOW Beretta Model 1938/3 muzzle compensator.

BOTTOM Beretta Model 1938/3 maker's marks.

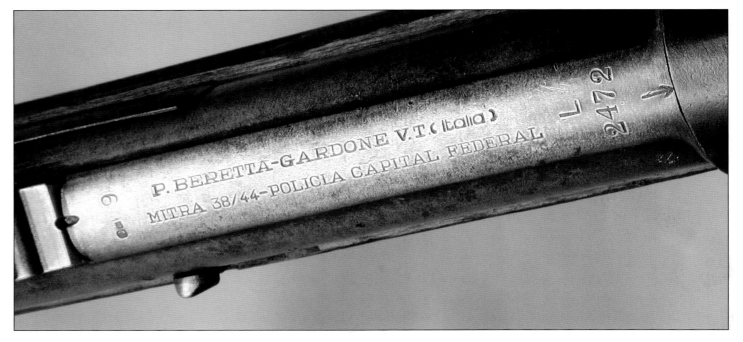

Lanchester submachine gun

Caliber: 9mm	**System of operation:** Blowback
Length: 33.5in (851mm)	**Rate of fire:** 625rpm
Weight: 8lb 8oz (4.37kg)	**Manufacturer:**
Barrel: 7.9in (200mm), six grooves right–hand twist	Sterling Armament Co., Dagenham, Essex, England
Feed system: 50–round, detachable, box magazine	**Values:** $4,000–$5,000 (Class III)

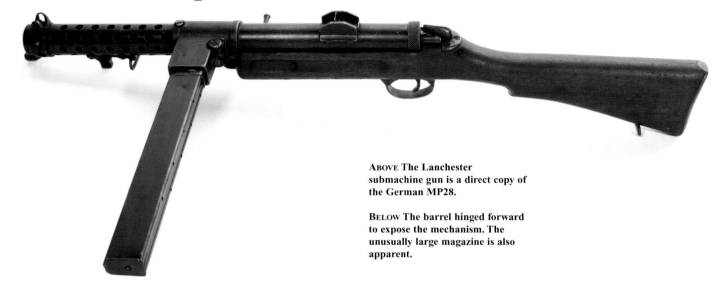

In 1940, in the face of imminent invasion, the Royal Air Force decided to adopt a submachine gun for airfield defense. With no time to spare for the development of a new weapon, it decided to produce a direct copy of the German MP28. The Admiralty decided to join the RAF in adopting the new weapon, and ultimately were the only service that did.

The British copy of the German MP28 was called the Lanchester after George H. Lanchester, who was charged with producing the weapon at the Sterling Armament Company at Dagenham. The Lanchester emerged from its British development as a sound, sturdy weapon, well suited to use by boarding and raiding parties It was a very solid, soundly engineered weapon: the blowback mechanism was well made of the finest materials, the breechblock well machined, and the magazine housing was fabricated from solid brass. A mounting on the muzzle for a long-blade British bayonet was added, and the rifling differed from that of the German original to accommodate the different type of ammunition fired by the Lanchester. The magazine for the Lanchester was straight and carried a useful load of 50 rounds. Stripping was aided by a catch on top of the receiver.

The first model was the Machine Carbine, 9mm Lanchester, Mk. I capable of single-shot or automatic fire. On the Lanchester Mk. 1* this was changed to automatic fire only, and many Mk. 1s were converted to Mk. 1* standard at Royal Navy workshops. The Lanchester was an unashamed copy of a German design, but gave good service to the Royal Navy throughout and after World War II. Its one serious fault was that if the butt was given a hard knock when the gun was cocked and loaded it would fire. The Lanchester remained in service until the 1960s.

ABOVE The Lanchester submachine gun is a direct copy of the German MP28.

BELOW The barrel hinged forward to expose the mechanism. The unusually large magazine is also apparent.

Top The Lanchester with bayonet fitted.

Below The Lanchester could also accept the smaller Sten magazine.

Bottom, Left and Right Maker's marks.

Bottom, Center Muzzle with flash suppressor, fore sight, and bayonet socket.

M3 and M3A1 submachine guns

Caliber: .45 (or 9mm Parabellum)

Length: 30in (762mm) stock extended; 22.75in (577mm) stock stowed

Weight: 8lb 15oz (4.05kg)

Barrel: 8in (203mm) long, four grooves, right-hand twist

Feed system: 30-round detach-able box magazine

System of operation: Blowback

Rate of fire: Cyclic, 450rpm

Manufacturer Guide Lamp Division of General Motors, Anderson, Indiana, U.S.

Values: $9,000–$12,500 (Class III)

The United States entered the war with only one submachine gun in its arsenal—the Thompson—and because this weapon had not been designed for mass production, it would not be available in sufficient quantity. In October 1942 work on the design of a replacement was started by the Small Arms Development Branch of the U.S. Ordnance Corps Technical Division, with the emphasis on simplicity of production. The first prototype, the Machine Pistol TI5, was capable of single-shot or automatic fire, but the single-shot facility was dropped to turn it into the T20. This was tested in late November 1942 and on Christmas Eve 1942 it was formally approved as the Submachine gun M3.

The design was relatively simple; the barrel projects from the front cap of a cylindrical body, the ejection port is covered by a hinged flap, the pistol grip is, as the rest of the weapon, steel, and a simple collapsible wire stock is fitted. Cocking was performed by a crank on the right side and was one of the less successful features; another was the design of a single-column magazine that inevitably gave stoppages and misfeeds throughout the gun's life. One very ingenious feature was the provision of a conversion kit of barrel, bolt, and magazine adapter whereby the normal .45 gun could be rapidly converted to fire 9mm Parabellum ammunition, feeding from a standard Sten magazine.

The M3 did what it set out to do: provide a cheap and efficient weapon which could be stamped out by the thousands in a short time. Over 606,000 of them were made at an average cost of about $25 each.

VARIANTS

M3A1

In January 1944 there were complaints from various users that the cocking crank mechanism was beginning to exhibit defects caused by wear. The solution was simple: the entire cranking mechanism was removed and a large hole was drilled in the bolt into which the firer inserted his finger and pulled the bolt back. To permit this, the ejection port and its cover were extended rearward. Other small refinements to aid production were incorporated and the resulting weapon entered service in December 1944 as the M3A1. Over 15,000 were produced before the war ended, at a cost of $22 each.

ABOVE LEFT AND RIGHT M3—note bolt-retracting handle on right-side view. Retraction of the stock reduces the 30in length of this compact weapon by 7.25in. The M3/M3A1 "Grease Gun" was the forerunner of the smaller modern submachine guns such as the Ingrams or Uzi.

Reising Model 50 submachine gun

Caliber: .45

Length: 35.75in (907mm)

Weight: 6lb 12oz (13.1kg)

Barrel: 11in (279mm) long, six grooves, right-hand twist

Feed system: 12 or 20-round detachable box magazine

System of operation: Retarded blowback

Rate of fire: Cyclic, 550rpm

Manufacturer: Harrington & Richardson Arms Co., Worcester, Mass. U.S.

Values: $2,500-$3,500 (Class III)

This weapon was designed by Eugene Reising and patented in June 1940. After testing by various authorities it was put into production, and a quantity estimated to be in the region of 100,000 of this and the similar Model 55 were produced before manufacture ceased in 1945.

The Reising was a rather unusual weapon in that it fired from a closed bolt at all times and the bolt was locked to the receiver before the round was fired. Upon firing the recoil of the cartridge case forced the bolt back, but opening was delayed while the bolt was unlocked and lowered by cams working in paths in the gun body. The bolt then recoiled in the usual way, returning under spring pressure to chamber a fresh round and then being cammed back into the locked position. A hammer was then released to strike the firing pin and fire the next round.

There were many complaints of unreliability in service particularly the weapon's vulnerability to dirt; nevertheless, the greater part of the production of the Reising submachine gun was taken by the U.S. Marine Corps and it was extensively used by them in the campaigns in the South Pacific. A small number of weapons was also purchased by the British government for issue to the Canadian Army and for supply to the Soviet government.

VARIANTS

Model 55

This is mechanically the same as the Model 50 but dispensed with the muzzle compensator and had a wooden pistol grip and a folding wire stock. It was primarily intended for airborne use.

Russian submachine guns

PPD-1940

Caliber: 7.62mm

Length: 31in (787mm)

Weight: 8lb 2oz (3.69kg)

Barrel: 10.5in (267mm) long, four grooves, right-hand twist

Feed system: 71-round detachable drum magazine

System of operation: Blowback, selective fire

Rate of fire: Cyclic, 800rpm

Manufacturers: USSR state arsenals at Tula and Sestroretsk

Values: $7,500-$8,500 (Class III)

PPD, *Pistolet-Pulyemet Degtyarev* (machine pistol designed by Degtyarev), was one of a series of weapons designed by a team led by Vasily Degtyarev from 1934 onward. Not many were made before 1937, but after that a small number appeared in Spain, where they proved their worth, and quantity production began. The original model was very similar to the German Bergmann design of 1928 but used a drum magazine. This magazine had a box-like extension which slipped into a housing on the underside of the foreend. There were a number of small variations of this model, known as the 1934/38, but in 1940 it was decided to simplify the design to speed production. The peculiar drum was changed for the Finnish Suomi pattern of drum and the weapon altered to allow the drum to be pushed into place from the side, rather like the Thompson drum. The earlier intricate cooling slots in the barrel jacket were simplified into a few long cuts, and one or two other small changes were made for ease of manufacture.

Like all Soviet submachine guns the barrel was internally chromium-plated, a practice rarely followed in weapons of any other country, but one which makes the barrel more resistant to wear and more tolerant of poor maintenance. The caliber is 7.62mm Soviet Pistol, a cartridge derived from the German 7.63mm Mauser round, and is one of the few bottle-necked cartridges used with submachine guns. Of smaller caliber than the average submachine gun round, it compensates to some degree by having a rather higher velocity than average.

The number of PPD submachine guns produced is not known, but it was probably small by Russian standards. Production only lasted from the autumn of 1940 to late 1941, at which point the arsenals producing the PPD were overrun by German ground forces.

PPS-42 and PPS-43

Caliber: 7.62mm

Length: 32.25in (819mm) stock extended; 25in (635mm) stock stowed

Weight: 7lb 6oz (3.39kg)

Barrel: 10in (254mm) long, four grooves, right-hand twist

Feed system: 35-round detachable box magazine

System of operation: Blowback, automatic only

Rate of fire: Cyclic, 700rpm

Manufacturers: USSR state arsenals

Values: $6,500-$7,500 (Class III)

This was the third standard submachine gun adopted by the Red Army during the war (following the PPD and the PPSh), and was designed by A. I. Sudayev (PPS means *Pistolet-Pulyemet Sudayeva*). In view of the Soviet system of selecting one design and mass-producing it to the exclusion of every other, it is unusual that this weapon was produced at the same time as the PPSh, but this was because of the exigencies of war. When Leningrad was besieged by the German Army in 1941–42, weapons were in short supply. The PPS was designed and put into production inside the besieged city, being sent straight from the factory to the nearby front line. It was a remarkable design, entirely stamped from steel except for the barrel and bolt, and spot-welded together. The only non-metal parts were the wooden grips and a small piece of leather acting as a buffer for the bolt. The perforated barrel jacket extended beyond the muzzle to act as a muzzle brake and compensator. It shared the curved box magazine of the PPSh, and the skeleton steel butt was hinged to fold across the top of the gun. A simple safety catch was fitted in the front edge of the triggerguard, and there was no provision for firing single shots. There was no cosmetic finishing; welds were left rough or crudely ground off where necessary. Most importantly it worked well and reliably, and many thousands were turned out during the siege.

The PPS-42, tried and tested in the heat of battle, proved to be an exceptional weapon. It was effective, cheap, and easy to produce. Not long after the lifting of the siege it was adopted as a standard weapon of the Red Army—with a few minor alterations, mostly concerning the degree of finishing, it entered service as the PPS-43. In 1944 it also became the standard service submachine gun of the Finnish Army. The PPS-43 continued in service after the war and was used in action in the Korean War.

THIS PAGE The PPS-43. Its extremely functional design and simple construction are readily apparent. This is a postwar (the markings inset right show 1948) production example. Wartime models exhibited a far rougher finish. Note the stock folds onto the top of the weapon.

PPSh 1941G submachine gun

Caliber: 7.62mm

Length: 33.1in (841mm)

Weight: 8lb (3.63kg)

Barrel: 10.5in (267mm) long, four grooves, right-hand twist

Feed system: 71-round detachable drum, or 35-round detachable box, magazine

System of operation: Blowback, selective fire

Rate of fire: Cyclic, 900rpm

Manufacturers: USSR state arsenals

Values: $7,500–$8,500 (Class III)

THIS PAGE Left and right-hand sides of the PPSh-41. Note the 71-round drum magazine and solid construction.

The *Pistolet Pulyemet Shpagina* (machine pistol designed by Shpagin—Georgi Shpagin) was developed in 1940–41 in an effort to design a weapon more suited to mass production than the PPD-40 model it replaced. Although the PPD was good, it was not entirely suited to fast production in huge quantities, which was the Soviet's primary concern in 1941. The PPSh used stamped steel for the body and jacket, although the barrel was still chromium-lined and the weapon still used a wooden stock. At one point in a desperate bid to speed up production old Mosin-Nagant rifle barrels were used to provide barrels for the submachine gun, as one rifle barrel could be cut up to make two submachine gun barrels with a considerable saving in time and machinery. The entire assembly was by pinning and welding, and the barrel jacket extended beyond the muzzle to act as a muzzle brake and deflector. The first models had a tangent sight, but this was soon discarded for a simple open sight.

The 71-round drum magazine of the PPD was retained, since it was already in production. It also gave the firer a good reserve of ammunition, always useful in house-to-house combat. The mechanism was simple blowback—a bolt with fixed ring pin and a return spring being almost the only components apart from a basic firing mechanism. In addition to the 71-round drum a 35-round box magazine was later made for this weapon, but it was much less common than than the drum pattern. Large numbers of the weapon were captured by the German Army on the Eastern Front; so large, in fact, that the Germans found it worth their while to convert the captured PPShs to fire 9mm ammunition, replacing the barrel and altering the magazine housing to take the standard MP38 magazine.

The PPSh submachine gun came to be identified with the Russian soldier, as much as the MP38 was with the German. Whole divisions were armed with nothing else, since it was a weapon which well suited aggressive Soviet tactics. The PPSh was rugged, simple, cheap and effective and more than five million were made.

Solothurn S1-100 submachine gun

Caliber: 9mm

Length: 33.5in (851mm)

Weight: 8lb 8oz (3.87kg)

Barrel: 7.75in (196mm) long, six grooves, right-hand twist

Feed system: 32-round detachable box magazine

System of operation: Blowback, selective fire

Rate of fire: Cyclic, 500rpm

Manufacturers:
  Waffenfabrik Solothurn AG, Switzerland
  Waffenfabrik Steyr, Steyr, Austria

Values: $7,500–$8,500 (Class III)

This weapon, used by the German Army among many others, was originally designed in 1924 by Herr Louis Stange of the Rheinmetall Company of Dusseldorf. Since, by the terms of the Versailles Treaty, Rheinmetall was forbidden to develop or manufacture such a weapon, it acquired a Swiss company—Solothurn AG—in 1929 to produce the prototypes and carry out developmental engineering. But Solothurn was not equipped for mass production, so Rheinmetall now took a controlling interest

in Waffenfabrik Steyr, a well-established Austrian company, and arranged for the weapon to be put into production as the Steyr-Solothurn submachine gun. It went on to be sold throughout the world in a variety of calibers, and was a commercial success.

The SL-100 was made of the finest available materials and finished to the highest possible standard. Its mechanism was quite simple, the bolt having its return

spring housed in the wooden butt stock, and the firing pin being separate. It fired from an open bolt in blowback mode. One of the most unusual features is the incorporation of a magazine loading device in the magazine housing.

The first specimens of this weapon were generally made in 7.63mm Mauser caliber or 9mm Steyr, and ammunition of these types was always supplied in pre-packed ten-round chargers for use in pistols. So that these chargers could be used for loading the submachine gun magazine, the magazine housing has a slot in top and bottom; the empty magazine could be withdrawn from its housing and slipped into the bottom slot. Chargers of cartridges were then inserted into guides in the top slot and the rounds stripped down into the magazine, one of the easiest and quickest systems of magazine loading ever devised.

The SL-100 was first adopted by the Austrian police in 9mm Steyr chambering, and then by the Austrian Army as the MP34, chambered for the powerful 9mm Mauser Export cartridge. When Austria was incorporated into the Third Reich, the weapon was taken into German Army service as the MP34(o) (o for Österreich). After a relatively short front-line service it was relegated to use by German MPs. However, it did see front-line use in China in the hands of troops from both the Chinese and Japanese armies.

RIGHT The Solothurn featured a unique integral magazine charger.

BELOW AND OPPOSITE PAGE Left, right and top views of the Steyr-Solothurn.

Sten submachine guns

Data: Mk. II

Caliber: 9mm

Length: 30in (762mm)

Weight: 6lb 8oz (2.95kg)

Barrel: 7. 75in (196mm) long, two or six grooves, right-hand twist

Feed system: 32-round detachable box magazine

System of operation: Blowback, selective fire

Rate of fire: Cyclic, 550rpm

Manufacturers: Royal Ordnance Factory, Fazakerley, England Birmingham Small Arms Co., Tyseley, England Long Branch Arsenal, Ontario, Canada

Values: $4,000-$5,000 (Class III)

In the summer of 1940, after the evacuation of Dunkirk and with the British Army short of weapons, the British Government began to look seriously at acquiring a submachine gun for the armed forces. Such was the desperation of the time that in August the decision was made to put into production a copy of the German MP28 (see page 127). An acceptance trial of the new weapon, known as the Lanchester (see page 134), was carried out on November 28, 1940, and arrangements for production were put in hand.

In the meantime a simplified weapon had been designed by Major R. V. Shepherd and Mr. H. J. Turpin of the Royal Small Arms Factory at Enfield Lock. The new weapon, loosely based on the German MP38, was much better suited to mass production. It was constructed mainly of steel pressings, spot-welded together, and machining was kept to a minimum. Although crude, it was effective. The prototype was demonstrated during January 1941, and instructions were given for an immediate trial and a rapid decision as to whether the manufacture of the Lanchester should proceed as planned or whether its production should be curtailed in favor of the new design.

The new weapon was tested and passed satisfactorily. Arrangements were made immediately to organize production and the first weapons came off the production lines in June 1941. The Lanchester was produced solely for the Royal Navy.

The new weapon was known as the Sten Mk. I, ST from the names of the two designers (Shepherd and Turpin) plus EN from Enfield. While the Mk. I was a crudely functional weapon, it still made some concessions to tradition: there was a wooden fore-end and a folding grip for the forward hand, a barrel jacket and protectors for the foresight, and a combined flash hider and muzzle compensator. A safety slot at the rear of the cocking

handle slot allowed the lever to be turned down and locked as a rudimentary safety measure. The Mk. I was soon replaced by the Mk. I* that dispensed with the flash hider, the fore-grip, and the wooden forend, and a simple metal cover was provided for the trigger mechanism both speeding production and lightening the gun. But further simplification was possible, and the Mk. II, probably the most common of all the marks, soon entered

service. This dispensed with the barrel jacket, instead retaining the barrel in a large perforated sleeve that doubled as a forward hand grip; the magazine housing was modified so that it could be swung down through 90 degrees to close the feed and ejection openings against dirt; and the safety slot was repositioned at the

Continued on page 145

LEFT Sten Mk. II showing stock and magazine removed. Note rotated magazine housing.

BOTTOM The Mk. II showing bayonet and scabbard.

LEFT AND BELOW LEFT Sten Mk. II. Note skeleton stock, lack of pistol grip, and cleaning rod kept in lower strut of stock. It is said that the name Sten was a combination of the first letters of the names of its designers—Sheffield and Turpin—and the first two letters of Enfield.

BELOW Canvas seven-magazine bandolier as issued to Airborne troops.

RIGHT AND BELOW Sten Mk. III—the two main distinguishing features of this mark are the length of the welded-steel tube that covers almost all of the barrel and the stiffening rib at the top of the tube. Note sling attachment (on the versions with a perforated barrel the clip was attached through a perforation) and rod stock that was introduced as an alternative on the Mk. II.

BOTTOM RIGHT A montage of Sten manuals, magazines with loaders attached, and 9mm Parabellum rounds.

top rear of the cocking handle slot. Over two million of this pattern were made, and at one stage they were being turned out at a rate of more than 20,000 per week from one factory alone, and the price of manufacture went down to £2.50 (then $4.30) per gun. The Mk. II was first used in action during the Dieppe raid of August 1942, and though the operation was not a success, the Sten gun proved its worth.

The Mk III was further simplified. It dispensed with the removable barrel and movable magazine housing, containing everything within a welded steel tube with a stiffening rib along the top, which also aided quick sighting.

A Mk. IV, intended for Airborne troops, was designed next but never put into production. In 1944 the Mk. V was issued. This was rather more carefully made than the previous marks and had a wooden butt and pistol grip. The muzzle and front sight were of the same pattern as those of the No. 4 rifle, allowing a bayonet to be fitted. This model was first issued to Airborne troops and had its baptism of fire at Arnhem, after which it became the standard-issue model and gradually replaced the earlier versions. A silenced version of the Mk. II, known as the Mk. IIS, was developed for Commando use, and there was also a silenced version of the Mk. V, the Mk. VI.

The Sten was a highly successful weapon; its introduction was greeted with some reserve by soldiers who were accustomed to a higher degree of finish, but it proved itself in battle. It did have faults—probably the worst was the design of the magazine, which was never entirely satisfactory and was prone to damage resulting in misfeeds—but in spite of this it was one of the most effective submachine guns of the war.

ABOVE RIGHT AND RIGHT Mk. V Sten gun—this example lacks its front pistol grip.

Thompson submachine guns

Data: Model 1928

Caliber: .45

Length: 31.8in (807mm)

Weight: 10lb (4.28kg) without magazine; 12lb 8oz (5.42kg) with 50-round drum mag

Barrel: 10.5in (263mm) long, six grooves, right-hand twist

Feed system: 20 or 30-round detachable box magazine, or 50 or 100-round detachable drum magazine

System of operation: Delayed blowback, selective fire

Rate of fire: Cyclic, 800rpm

Manufacturers:
Colt's Patent Firearms Co., Hartford, Conn., U.S.
Savage Arms Co., Utica, N.Y., U.S.

Values: $8,000–$15,000 (Class III)

The Auto-Ordnance Corporation was founded in America in 1916 with the intention of developing a variety of weapons, the most well known of which is, surely, the Thompson submachine gun. Named for General John T. Thompson, the company's design director, the first models were built in prototype form in 1919. The first production models appeared in 1921 and from then on manufacture was small but continuous throughout the 1920s and 1930s. The first official military recognition came when the U.S. Marine Corps was issued with a number of the 1927 model, which were officially named the M1928.

In 1939 the Thompson was the only submachine gun in production outside Europe, and as a result the governments of Britain, France, and Sweden hurriedly placed orders. Shortly afterwards the U.S. Army also ordered a large quantity. But the Thompson was a difficult gun to manufacture; the engineering processes were numerous and complicated, and the materials used were of the best quality, a fact which was reflected in the price of almost £50/$86, as compared to the later Sten's £2.50/$4.30. By the end of 1940 orders for more than 318,000 guns had been placed; previous production had been by the Colt Co. under license from the Auto-Ordnance Corp., but now Auto-Ordnance built its own factory and by late summer of 1941 was producing guns. The Savage Arms Co. was also given a license to manufacture, and between these two plants over 1.25 million Thompson guns were produced during the war.

In order to make production easier the gun was redesigned in 1941 as a simple blowback gun. The facility of using a drum magazine was also discarded and a 30-round box became the standard. Various other simplifications were made, notably the abandonment of the carefully made front grip and its replacement

by a simple wooden fore-end. The resulting weapon was standardized by the U.S. Army as the M1 submachine gun in April 1, 1942. This was later modified into the M1A1 by making the firing pin integral with the bolt, and dispensing with the hammer .

The Thompson had a lot of drawbacks; it was difficult to make, it was expensive, and—even in its simplified form—it was heavy. But for all that, it had one great virtue in the eyes of soldiers: it was reliable. Trouble with a Thompson was a rare event, provided it was properly cared for. It was a favorite weapon with British Commandos and U.S. Rangers throughout the war and for many years afterward.

BELOW AND BOTTOM M1928A1 late-production model with a simple wooden foregrip instead of the original front pistol grip. Note finned barrel, Cutts compensator on muzzle brake, wooden butt, and large rear sight. This example is fitted with the 20-round box magazine. Compare this weapon with that on page 147.

RIGHT AND BELOW RIGHT Another M1928A1: note front wooden pistol grip; smaller, late-production rear sight; and 20-round box magazine.

BELOW M1928A1 maker's mark: Auto-Ordnance Corporation of Bridgeport, Connecticut, U.S.

BELOW CENTER M1928A1 patents detail.

BOTTOM Detail of the Cutts compensator.

ABOVE AND BELOW M1928A1 early model with front pistol grip and 50-round drum magazine.

RIGHT AND **CENTER RIGHT** Rear (right) and front of the 50-round drum magazine. Note winding handle on front.

FAR RIGHT Top view showing ejector port.

BELOW RIGHT Drum magazine detail on an M1928A1.

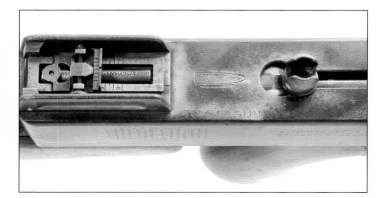

TOP LEFT Magazine receiver of the M1928A1.

CENTER LEFT M1928A1 removable butt detail.

LEFT M1928A1 rear sight and cocking lever details.

TOP AND ABOVE Left and right-hand side details of the M1A1. Note position of cocking lever.

TOP AND CENTER RIGHT M1A1 maker's mark details.

RIGHT Muzzle and fore sight detail of the M1A1.

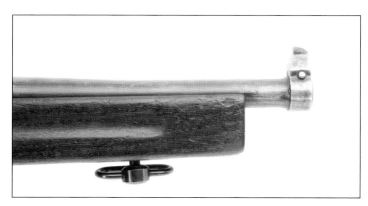

LEFT AND BELOW M1A1
—a simplified M1928A1 with a plain barrel, fixed butt, no muzzle compensator, and smaller rear sight. This example carries a 30-round box magazine.

MACHINE GUNS

The majority of heavy machine guns used at the beginning of World War II were either models that had seen action in World War I or were based on designs from that period. In Britain the Vickers was still in service and the American M1917 Browning and Russian Maxim were both of World War I vintage. The notable exceptions to this were Germany and Japan. After the Treaty of Versailles, which had tried to stop German developing armaments, the emerging, clandestine, German Army of the 1930s in many ways had to start from a clean slate. It did so brilliantly and entered World War II with the classic MG34 (see page 203)—not a heavy machine gun, but not a light one either: rather an all-purpose weapon that could be mounted for the heavy role, but was portable. On the other hand, Japan's armed forces did not possess any machine guns until the 1920s, and when Japan did start producing them, they were largely based on existing Hotchkiss designs: they would develop heavy, medium, and light weapons along the lines of the western allies. It is interesting to note that the postwar world would see the German tactical thinking become the order of the day with the U.S. Army's M60 and NATO's General Purpose Machine Gun.

Light, portable machine guns represented the area of greatest change between the mainly rifle-equipped soldier of World War I and his World War II counterpart. This class of weapon had not existed at the start of World War I, and had been developed to increase mobility. The U.S. Army's Browning Automatic Rifle (see page 69) dates from that period. It was originally intended as a sort of assault rifle and came to be fitted with a bipod and fired from the ground since it was really too heavy to be used any other way. By the time the U.S. Army entered World War II, the BAR was the standard light machine gun and squad support weapon. Other, similar weapons were used by the British (the Bren, see page 156), the Czechs (see page 170), the French (the Châtellerault, see page 168), the Italians (see

page 188), the Japanese (see page 192), and the Russians (see page 174).

The concept of mobile firepower had led at the end of World War I to the first submachine guns—the Italian Beretta Model 1918 (see page 131) and the German Bergmann (see page 127). During World War II the submachine gun would be mass-produced and used in great numbers. By the end of the war the precursors of the assault rifles of postwar armies—the PPS (see page 137) and StG44 (see page 107)—had also entered the fray.

The massive reliance on armored vehicles during World War II meant that many of the infantrymen's weapons were adapted for use on AFVs. This section also includes one or two photographs of weapons taken from the infantryman's arsenal to be used in armored vehicles—such as the Browning M2 (see page 165) or the Besa 15mm (see page 156)—to show how the trend toward these weapons took place.

Top Besa 15mm used in British armored cars.

Left, Above, and Right Three answers to MG ammunition storage. From left to right: Lewis gun 47-round circular magazine (see page 156); Bren 20-round curved box magazine (see page 194); MG34 75-round saddle drum magazine (see page 205).

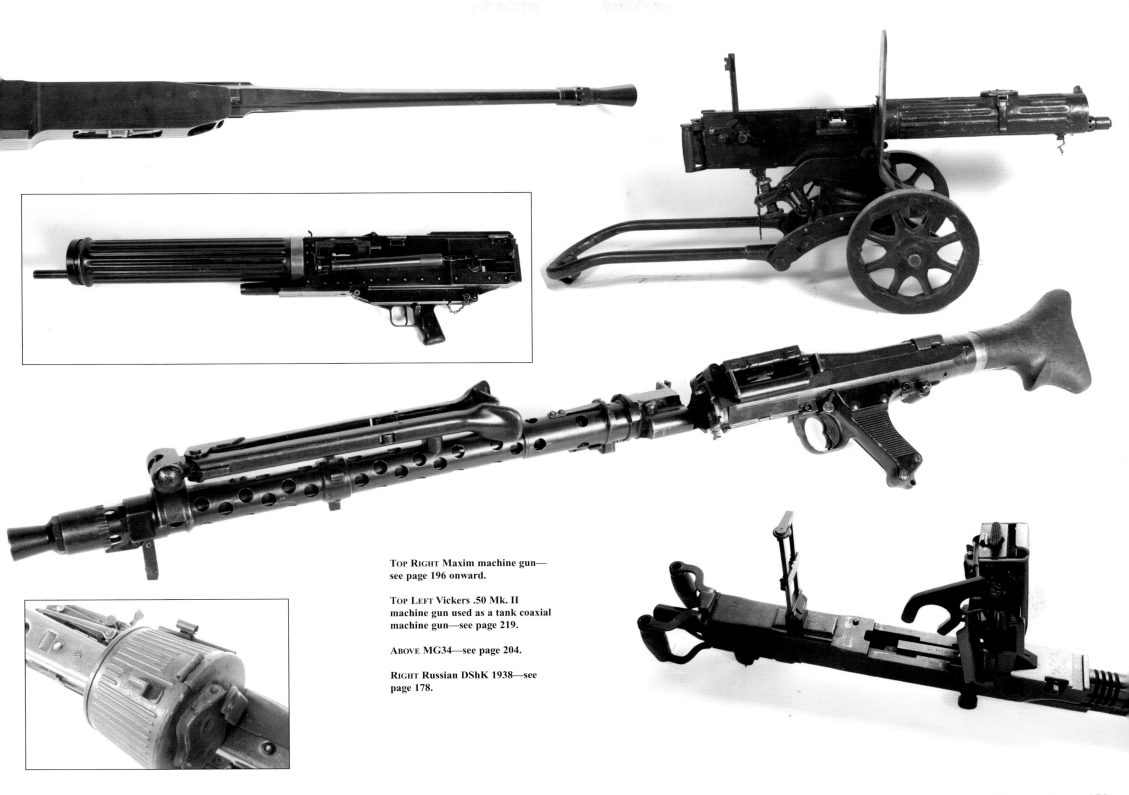

Top Right Maxim machine gun—see page 196 onward.

Top Left Vickers .50 Mk. II machine gun used as a tank coaxial machine gun—see page 219.

Above MG34—see page 204.

Right Russian DShK 1938—see page 178.

Besa machine guns

Besa 7.92mm medium machine gun

Caliber: 7.92mm

Length: 43.5in (1.1m)

Weight: 41lb (18.6kg)

Barrel: 26.7in (67.8in) long, four grooves, right-hand twist

Feed system: Belt

System of operation: Recoil and gas; tipping bolt

Rate of fire: 500 or 700rpm

Manufacturer:
British Small Arms Ltd, Birmingham, England

Values: $7,500–$8,500 (Class III)

This weapon is an adaptation of the Kulomet vz37, developed by Ceskoslovenska Zbrojovka of Brno in the early 1930s, and became the standard British tank machine gun of World War II. The main alterations were the provision of a solid machined front barrel support in place of the perforated one of the original and the replacement of the spade grips with a pistol grip and trigger. Mechanically the gun was unchanged and it was renowned for its accuracy, continuing in service for many years after the war.

RIGHT Although based on the design of the vz37, the 7.92mm Besa was of much sturdier construction, the majority of the components being machined from solid steel. Weight was not an important consideration in a vehicle-mounted weapon and the gun had to withstand the rigors of use as an AFV weapon.

BELOW Besa 7.92mm mounted coaxially on a British Daimler Mk. II armored car. The main armament is a two-pounder.

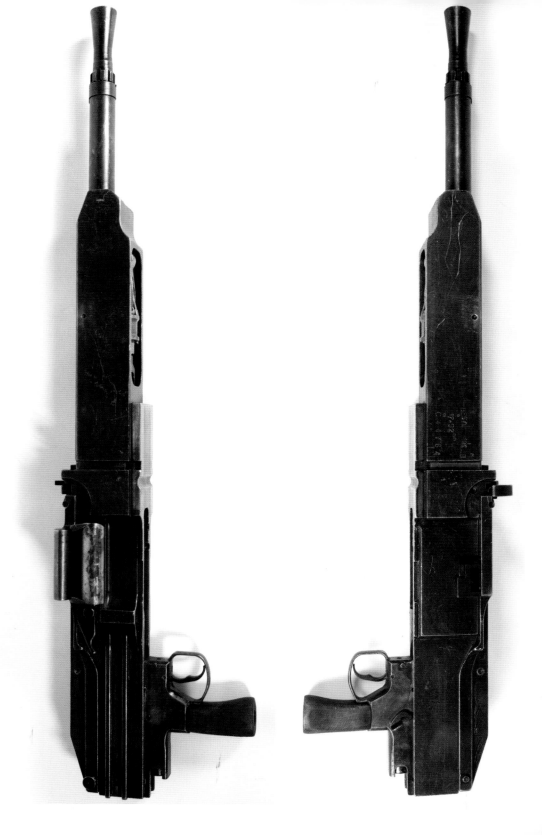

BELOW These close-up shots show the maker's marks and details of the action. In all of these the massive construction of the weapon is evident.

Besa 15mm heavy machine gun

Caliber: 15mm

Length: 80.7in (2.050m)

Weight: 125lb 8oz (56.9kg)

Barrel: 57.5in (1.46m) long, eight grooves, right-hand twist

Feed system: 25-round belt

System of operation: Recoil and gas tilting breechblock

Rate of fire: 450rpm

Manufacturer: British Small Arms Ltd, Birmingham, England

Values: n/a

This is the Czech ZB vz60 produced under license by BSA Ltd. as the main gun for armored cars such as the Humber armored car. A scaled-up 7.92mm Besa, it is mechanically much the same as the smaller weapon.

TOP AND ABOVE The similarities between the 15mm Besa and the 7.92mm Besa opposite are apparent although the 15mm version was of even heavier construction.

Bren light machine gun

Data: Mk. I

Caliber: .303

Length: 45.25in (1.15m)

Weight: 22lb 5oz (10.12kg)

Barrel: 25in (635mm) long, six grooves, right–hand twist

Feed system: 30–round, curved, detachable box magazine

System of operation: Gas; tipping bolt

Rate of fire: Cyclic, 500rpm

Manufacturer: Royal Small Arms Factory, Enfield Lock, Middlesex, England

Values: $20,000–$30,000 (Class III)

The Bren Gun evolved from the Czechoslovak ZB vz26 (see page 170) light machine gun, but the development path was one that involved as much British as Czechoslovak expertise. During the 1920s the British Army looked far and wide for a new light machine gun to replace the generally unsatisfactory Lewis Gun (see page 194). In 1930 there began a series of trials involving several designs, among them a slightly revised version of the vz26, the vz27. This emerged as a clear winner from these trials. However, it was made only in 7.92mm (.312in) caliber, and the British Army wanted to retain the .303 (7.7mm) cartridge with its outdated cordite propellant and its awkward rimmed case. Thus started a series of development models that involved the vz27, the later vz30 (see page 171) and eventually an interim model, the vz32.

Then came the vz33, and it was from this that the Royal Small Arms Factory at Enfield Lock evolved the prototype of what became the Bren Gun (Bren from the 'Br' of Brno, the place of origin, and the 'en' of Enfield Lock). Tooling up at Enfield Lock resulted in the completion in 1937 of the first production Bren Gun Mk. I, and thereafter the type remained in production at Enfield and elsewhere until well after 1945. By 1940 well over 30,000 Bren guns had been produced and the type was firmly established in service. The weapons left at Dunkirk by the British Expeditionary Force even gave the Germans a useful stock of Bren Guns, and these were designated *leichte MG 138(e)*.

The disastrous equipment losses of Dunkirk led to an urgent demand for new weapons of all types to reequip the British Army. As part of this process the design of the Bren was modified to speed production, and new lines were established The original gas-operated mechanism of the ZB design was retained, as were the breech-locking system and general appearance, but out went the rather complicated drum sights and extras such as the under-butt handle in the Bren Gun Mk. II. The bipod became much

simpler but the curved box magazine of the .303 Bren was retained. In time more simplifications were made (the Bren Gun Mk. III had a shorter barrel and the Bren Gun Mk. IV had a modified butt assembly), and there was even a reversion to the 7.92mm caliber when Bren guns were manufactured in Canada for China.

The Bren Gun was a superb light machine gun. It was robust, reliable, easy to handle and to maintain, and it was not too heavy for its role. It was also very accurate. In time a whole range of mountings and accessories was introduced, including some rather complex antiaircraft mountings that included the Motley and the Gallows mountings. A 200-round drum was developed but little used, and various vehicle mountings were designed and introduced. The Bren Gun outlived all these accessories, for after 1945 the type remained in service and the wartime "extras" were phased out as being irrelevant to the increasingly hi-tech modern battlefield, and also costly to maintain. The Bren Gun on its basic bipod did linger on, however, in limited service with some armies as the Bren Gun L4 series. It was modified to fire the NATO standard 7.62mm (0.3in) cartridge through a barrel chrome-plated to reduce wear.

VARIANTS

Bren Gun Mk. II
In 1940 various design modifications were made in order to simplify manufacture. The butt fittings were discarded, the drum sight replaced by a simpler tangent sight, the telescopic bipod replaced by a simpler fixed-length pattern, the cocking handle no longer folded, and certain lightening grooves on the body were omitted, resulting in the weight going up to 23.25lb (10.6kg). This mark was introduced on June 6, 1941.

Bren Gun Mk. III
Introduced on July 18, 1944, the Mk. III was identical to the Mks. I and II, except that the barrel was 22.25in (656mm) long.

Bren Gun Mk. IV
The Mk. IV was identical to the Mk. III except for a modified butt assembly.

ABOVE A British-made Bren Mk. I mounted on a tripod and fitted with a long-range sight for use in the medium machine gun role (see also next page).

RIGHT The tripod folded down to quite compact proportions and was often to be seen stowed on vehicles such as the Universal Carrier— more popularly called the Bren Carrier.

Above Detail of long-range sights.

Left The left-hand side of a British-made Bren Mk. I.

Far Left Maker's mark.

Left The gun could be locked on target to enable fire patterns to be set up on presighted targets.

LITHGOW
N.A.
1943

BREN Mk I 3/1

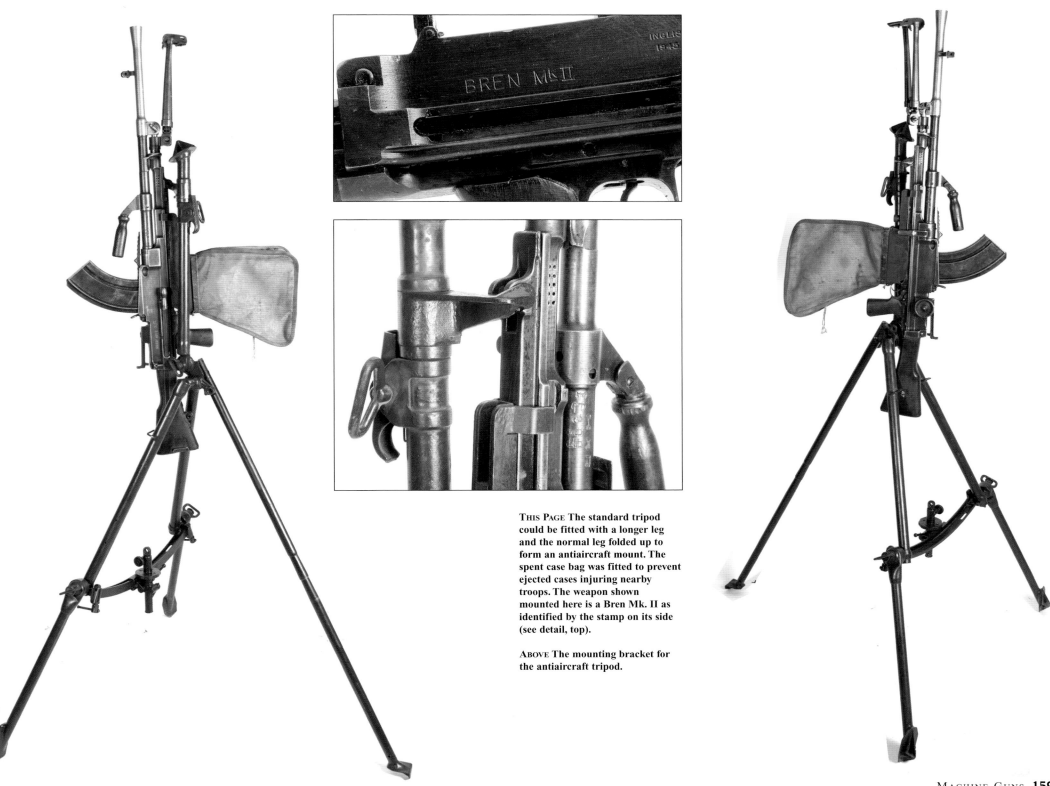

BREN Mk II

INGLIS
1945

THIS PAGE The standard tripod could be fitted with a longer leg and the normal leg folded up to form an antiaircraft mount. The spent case bag was fitted to prevent ejected cases injuring nearby troops. The weapon shown mounted here is a Bren Mk. II as identified by the stamp on its side (see detail, top).

ABOVE The mounting bracket for the antiaircraft tripod.

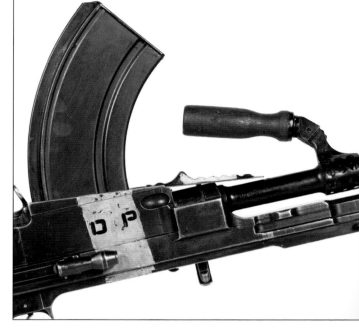

THIS PAGE Bren Mk. III. Worn out weapons were deactivated and retained for drill purposes. To prevent them being mistaken for active weapons they were painted with white bands and marked DP.

RIGHT Magazine, muzzle flash reducer, and trigger details.

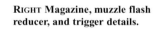

ABOVE AND BELOW Maker's marks—note fire selector: A for automatic; S for safe; R for single shot.

THIS PAGE The weapon shown here is a Bren Mk. IV. This differed from the Mk. III in the construction of the butt; the prominent mounting bolt can be seen projecting from the top rear face.

Browning .30-cal machine guns

M1917A1, M1919A4, M1919A6

	Caliber	Length	Weight	Barrel
M1917A1	.30	38.64in (982mm)	32.6lb (14.8kg)	23.9in (607mm)
M1919A4	.30	37.94in (964mm)	30.75lb (14kg)	24in (610mm)
M1919A6	.30	53in (1.35m)	32.5Lb (14.7kg)	24in (610mm)

Barrel: Four grooves, right-hand twist

Feed system: 250-round fabric belt

System of operation: Recoil, vertical sliding breech lock

Rate of fire:
M1917A1—400-550rpm;
M1919A4—400-450rpm;
M1919A6—450-600rpm;

Manufacturers:
Remington Arms, UMC, Bridgeport, Conn., U.S.
Winchester Repeating Arms Co., New Haven, Conn., U.S.
New England Westinghouse Co., Springfield Mass., U.S.
Colt's Patent Firearms Co., Hartford, Conn., U.S.

Values::
M1917A1: $16,000-$20,000
M1919A4: $9,000-$10,000
M1919A6: $9,000-$10,000
(Class III)

ABOVE AND BELOW The Browning M1917A1, the first service version of the ubiquitous Browning .30-cal., easily recognizable by its distinctive water-cooling jacket.

LEFT Detail of the sight.

The Browning .30 cal has its origins in a John Moses Browning design that was first patented in 1890. This early gas-operated gun was built by the Colt Company and became known as the Colt M1895. In 1900 Browning decided that recoil operation offered more possibilities than gas, and he began work on a completely new design. He took out his first patent the following year, but did not produce a prototype until 1910. The U.S. Army had no interest at that time, but in February 1917, with war looming closer and vitually no machine guns in the armories, the U.S. War Department finally allowed Browning to demonstrate his new weapon. Initially no decision was forthcoming, then in April the U.S. went to war. The following month saw Browning demonstrating his gun once more, giving spectacular proof of the gun's efficiency by firing 20,000 rounds non-stop. Contracts were placed for 45,000 guns and the Browning M1917 entered service. After the war changes were made—a new bottom plate, various steel components instead of bronze, and an improved water-cooling system; the weapon became the M1917A1.

The Browning mechanism relies on barrel recoil; this moves to the rear, carrying the bolt with it. After a short recoil a vertically sliding lock is withdrawn by cam surfaces in the gun body, unlocking the bolt. The final movement of the barrel's recoil causes an accelerator, a curved steel claw, to swing back and, because of leverage gain, flip the bolt backward very rapidly

ABOVE The right side of the Browning M1919A4. Note the locking mechanism on the tripod, enabling the gun to be trained on a presighted line of fire.

LEFT Detail of the maker's marks.

against a return spring. This movement of the bolt also drives the belt feed mechanism that moves the belt, strips rounds from it, and positions them in front of the bolt.

In addition to ground requirements the Browning was wanted as an aircraft gun, but water-cooling was neither necessary nor desirable in this role and an air-cooled model was developed, known as the M1918. From this stemmed the M1919, also air-cooled but with a heavier barrel and intended for use in tanks. During the 1920s it was found that this air-cooled weapon worked well as a ground gun, and eventually the M1914A4 was issued, tripod-mounted, to supplement and later largely replace the water-cooled M1917A1 model.

VARIANT

M1916A6

Little more than the 1919A4 gun with a shoulder stock, carrying handle, pistol grip, and bipod, the A6 was intended to fulfill the role of a light machine gun. It was an unfortunate design, heavy and cumbersome. It was adopted in February 1943 but classified as Substitute Standard and relatively few were issued.

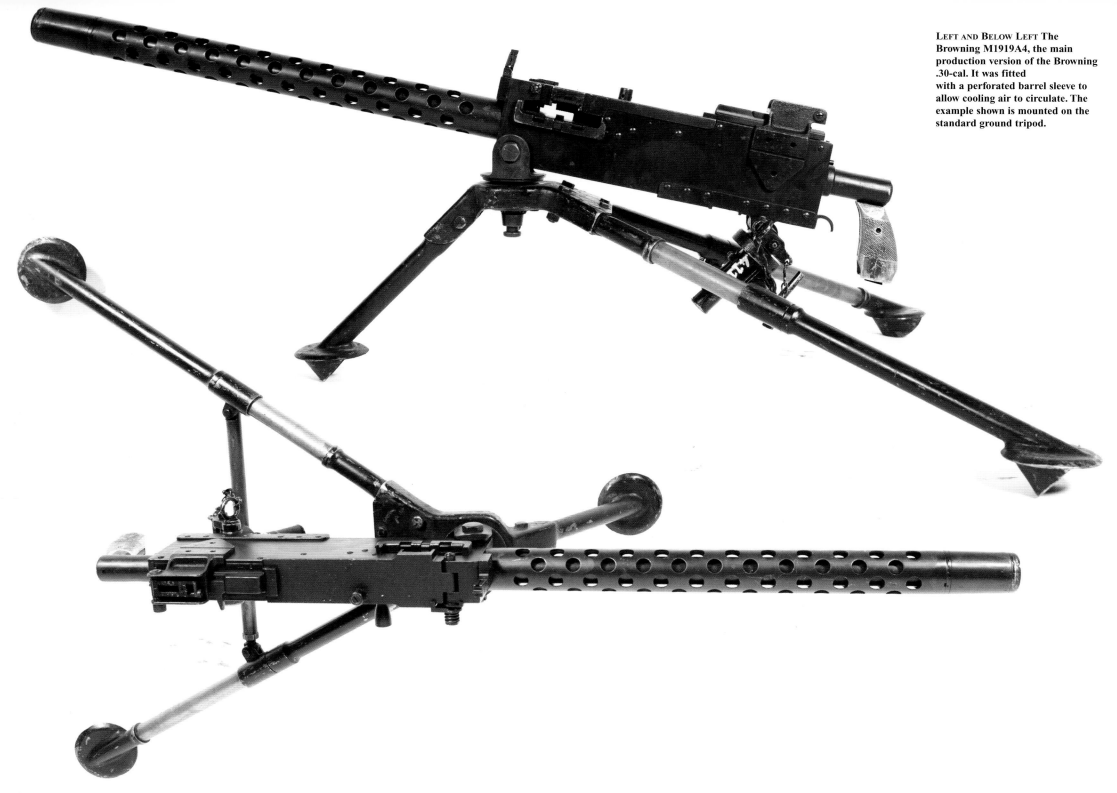

LEFT AND BELOW LEFT The Browning M1919A4, the main production version of the Browning .30-cal. It was fitted with a perforated barrel sleeve to allow cooling air to circulate. The example shown is mounted on the standard ground tripod.

Browning .50-cal heavy machine gun

Data: M2HB

Caliber: .50 (12.7mm)

Length: 65.1in (1.65mm)

Weights:
Gun 84lb (381kg)
M3 tripod 44lb (19.96kg)

Barrel: 45in (1.14mm) eight grooves, right-hand twist

Feed system: 110-round metal-link belt

System of operation: Recoil, vertical sliding breech lock

Rate of fire: Cyclic, 450-575 rpm

Manufacturer:
Colt's Patent Firearms Co., Hartford, Conn., U.S.

High Standard Mg. Co., Hamden, Conn., U.S.

Savage Arms Corp.,Utica, N.Y., U.S.

Frigidaire, U.S.

Buffalo Arms Corp., Akron N.Y., U.S.

AC Spark Plug, Div. of G.M., Mich., U.S.

Brown Lipe Chapin, Syracuse N.Y., U.S.

Saginaw Div. of G.M., Grand Rapids, Mich., U.S.

Kelsey-Hayes Wheel Co., Detroit, U.S.

Values: $13,000-$15,000 (Class III)

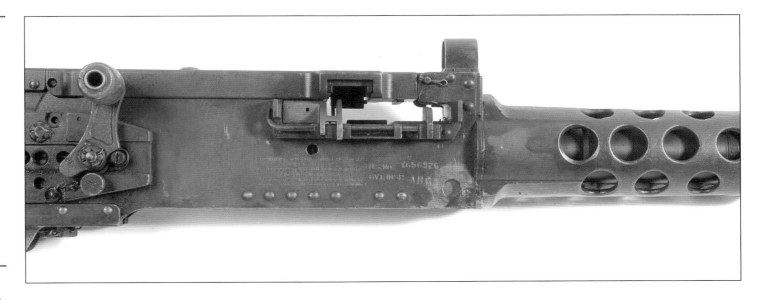

The first .50 caliber machine gun to enter service with the U.S. Army was the M1921 in 1925. This was essentially a scaled up M1917 .30 caliber and was designed around a new .50 caliber cartridge developed by the Winchester Arms Co. This was followed by two further water-cooled models, the M1921A1 and the M2. In 1928 the first air-cooled version, the M2 aircraft, was introduced for use—as its name suggests—as an aircraft weapon. This was followed by the M2HB (heavy barrel) which was fitted with a thick-walled barrel to absorb heat and dispense with the need for water-cooling. Early versions had 36in (914mm) barrels but from 1938 all M2HBs were produced with 45in (1.14m) barrels.

The M2HB became by far the most extensively produced version of the .50-cal and was found in a wide variety of roles. It has been employed as an infantry gun, as an antiaircraft gun, and also as a fixed and trainable aircraft gun. For infantry use the M2HB is usually mounted on a heavy tripod, but it can also be used mounted on vehicle pintles and ring mountings (see photos on page 167). The water-cooled models were mostly employed as antiaircraft weapons, especially on U.S. Navy vessels, and often in fixed multiple mountings for use against low-flying attack aircraft. These were crucial in fending off the massed Kamikaze attacks towards the end of the Pacific war. Single water-cooled mountings were often used to provide antiaircraft defence for shore installations. In addition to being lethal against personnel, the M2 Browning heavy machine gun is quite capable of bring-ing down aircraft and chewing through brick walls. The projectile fired by the type can also be used to defeat light armored vehicles, especially when firing armor-piercing rounds.

More 0.50-cal Browning machine guns have been produced in the United States than any other machine gun. The figure runs into millions, and the M2 has been put back into production on several occasions since the war, both in the U.S. and in Europe. By the end of August 1945 the M2 production total was 1,968,596. The cost per gun started at $750 although this figure had been reduced considerably by war's end. The M2 must surely rank as one of the most successful machine gun designs ever produced.

ABOVE Close-up of the receiver showing the ammunition feed, maker's marks and cocking handle. Note also the distinctive air-cooling sleeve.

BELOW The Browning M2HB—all five feet of it!—the main production version of the Browning .50-cal.

RIGHT The firer's view of the Browning. Note the sights, spade grips and unusual ambidextrous trigger

FAR RIGHT AND OPPOSITE PAGE As well as being used as a ground fired weapon, the M2HB was also mounted on a wide variety of vehicles—in this case on a skate rail pintle in a White Scout Car.

FAR RIGHT, ABOVE Detail showing ammunition box and metal-link belt ammunition.

FAR RIGHT, BELOW AND OPPOSITE PAGE INSET Details of the pintle mounting. The gun can elevate and pivot on the pintle and the pintle can slide along the skate rail. The rail ran around the entire top of the vehicle to permit the gun to be fired in any direction.

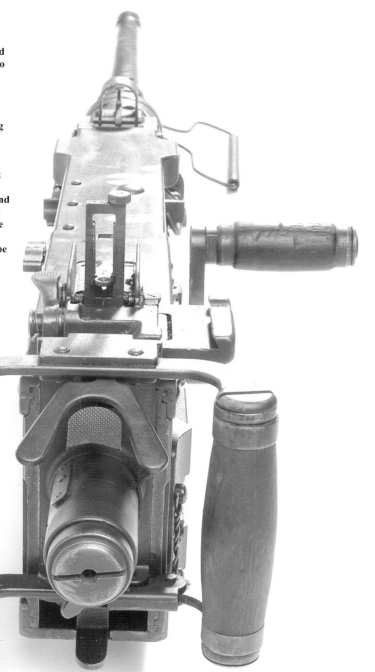

Châtellerault M1929 light machine gun

Caliber: 7.5mm
Length: 42.6in (1.08m)
Weight: 20lb 4oz (9.19kg)
Barrel: 19.7in (500mm) long, four grooves, right–hand twist
Feed system: 25–round detachable box magazine
System of operation: Gas

Rate of fire: Cyclic, 500rpm
Manufacturers:
Manufacture d'Armes de Châtellerault, France
Manufacture d'Armes de St. Etienne, France
Values: $7,500–$8,500 (Class III)

The French-designed machine guns that saw service during World War I were far from successful, and after the war the authorities were keen to find replacements. France had received a number of Browning Automatic Rifles from the U.S. Army and decided to develop a machine gun based on a similar action. At the same time a new cartridge, based on the Swiss Army 7.5mm round, was under development, and this was selected for the new weapon. The first model, the M1924, suffered from insufficient development, both of the new cartridge and the weapon itself,

before being issued, and had an unfortunate history of ruptured barrels and explosions. The solution to the problem was soon put in hand. The new model, firing a reduced power cartridge and with a strengthened barrel and action, was the Modèle 24/29 or M1929, and this remained France's standard light machine gun until the mid-1950s.

While using the basic Browning Automatic Rifle action, the bolt being locked by a bolt lock engaging in a shoulder in the roof of the receiver, the Châtellerault used a Bren-style top-mounted magazine rather than the bottom-mounted approach of the BAR. The gas was tapped close to the muzzle and a shock absorber fitted in the butt to produce a less violent action than that of the Browning. The M1929 had two triggers for selective fire control, the front one being for single shots and the rear for automatic fire. Supply of the M1929 was slow, but by about 1938 it had completely replaced all earlier machine guns. After the collapse of France in 1940 large numbers were captured by the German Army and put to use, mostly in arming the fortifications of the Atlantic Wall in France and the Channel Islands.

VARIANTS

Model 1931
This model used the same basic mechanism but was fitted with a side-mounted 150-round drum. It was intended for use in fortresses and other fixed defenses and was also used as a tank gun.

Model 34/39 aircraft
A belt-fed model intended for use as aircraft armament.

BELOW AND RIGHT The Châtellerault M1929, the standard light machine gun of the French army from its introduction in 1929 until the 1950s.

LEFT Top view showing magazine in place. Note also sights and magazine feed cover in open position.

FAR LEFT Close up of the M1929. Note closed magazine-feed cover, cocking handle and twin triggers for single shot and automatic fire.

CZ vz26 light machine gun

BELOW AND BOTTOM The CZ vz26, a great commercial success in the interwar period, and forerunner of the CZ vz30.

Caliber: 7.92mm

Length: 45.78in (1.16m)

Weight: 21lb 5oz (9.66kg)

Barrel: 23.7in (602mm) long, four grooves, right-hand twist

Feed system: 20-round, detachable box magazine

System of operation: Gas, tipping bolt

Rate of fire: Cyclic, 500rpm

Manufacturer: Ceskoslovenska Zbrojovka, Brno, Czechoslovakia

Values: $13,000–$15,000 (Class III)

Shortly after Czechoslovakia was established as a state, the Ceskoslovenska Zbrojovka company was set up in Brno to produce small arms. One of its first products was the Zbrojovka Brno vz26, a gas-operated light machine gun. This weapon was an immediate success, being adopted by the Czech Army and earning export sales all over the world, in particular China, Yugoslavia, and Spain. The weapon was based on a gas-operated, tipping bolt mechanism and the design placed great emphasis on ruggedness, ease of maintenance, and simplicity of use. With the annexation of Czechoslovakia by the Nazis in 1939 the ZB vz26 was adopted by the German forces as the MG 26(t).

CZ vz30 light machine gun

Caliber: 7.92mm

Length: 45.78in (1.16m)

Weight: 21lb 5oz (9.66kg)

Barrel: 26.5in (672mm) long, four grooves, right-hand twist

Feed system: 30-round, detachable box magazine

System of operation: Gas, tipping bolt

Rate of fire: Cyclic, 600rpm

Manufacturer: Ceskoslovenska Zbrojovka, Brno, Czechoslovakia

Values: $16,000-$18,000 (Class III)

ABOVE AND BOTTOM Left and right-hand side views of the CZ vz30, a great commercial success in the interwar period, and forerunner of the British Bren gun.

The ZB vz30 was a development of the vz26. It had new cam surfaces for the bolt and the design was modified to ease production. Like the vz26 it was a great export success and production facilities were set up in China and in Spain, where it was known as the FAO (*Fabrica de Armas de Oviedo*). The vz30 was also adopted by the German Army as the MG30(t) and was kept in production to meet German demand. A further development was the ZGB vz30 modified to fire British .303 ammunition and submitted for trials in the UK in 1931–32. As a result of these trials further changes were made to produce the ZGB33, the basis of the British Bren light machine gun (see page 156).

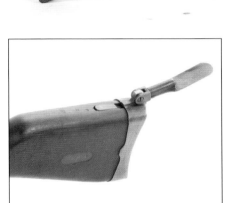

ABOVE AND ABOVE LEFT CZ vz30 maker's mark details.

FAR LEFT CZ vz30 butt detail.

CZ vz37 medium machine gun

Caliber: 7.92mm

Length: 43.5in (1.1m)

Weight: 41lb (18.6kg)

Barrel: 26.7in (678mm) long, four grooves, right-hand twist

Feed system: Belt

System of operation: Recoil and gas; tipping bolt

Rate of fire: 500 or 700rpm

Manufacturer: Ceskoslovenska Zbrojovka, Brno, Czechoslovakia

Values: $20,000–$30,000 (Class III)

This weapon is known under several designations: vz53—its factory nomenclature and that under which it was exported; in the Czechoslovak Army it was the *Kulomet vz37*; in the German Army it was the *Maschinengewehr 37(t)* and in the British Army it was the Besa machine gun. In all cases it was still the same gun, developed by Ceskoslovenska Zbrojovka of Brno in the early 1930s and put into production in 1937.

The mechanism was a peculiar mixture of recoil and gas operation, but it bore a distinct resemblance to the light machine gun designs that came from the same company. The barrel had an extension into which the bolt locked by having its rear end lifted to abut against shoulders. On recoil the whole unit moved rearward, and then the gas piston functioned in the usual way to unlock the bolt. The weapon was extremely reliable and, certainly in British service, was renowned for its accuracy.

In the British Army the gun was used only as a vehicle-mounted machine gun for tanks and armored cars but in the German Army, however, it was used in its original role as an air-cooled medium machine gun, in which its adjustable rate of fire was an unusual asset. In German Army use it was provided with a tripod of a rather complicated design. There is no record of how many VZ37s were manufactured, but large numbers of soldiered on for many years after the war, notably in a number of African countries.

ABOVE AND RIGHT The CZ tripod was an unusually complicated design as can be seen in these views of the traverse and elevation mechanisms.

RIGHT Looking down on the receiver.
FAR RIGHT The fire selector.

LEFT The CZ vz37 on its tripod. This was the standard medium machine gun of the Czech army and was also used by the German army under the designation *Maschinengewehr 37(t)*.

BELOW The zv37 was widely exported. This example saw service with the Venezuelan Army.

FAR LEFT AND CENTER LEFT With hand grips folded, the trigger is visible below the hand grip hinge. Note also the unusually small cocking handle.

BELOW In firing position with shoulder rest attached and hand grips extended.

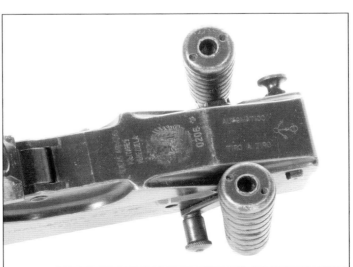

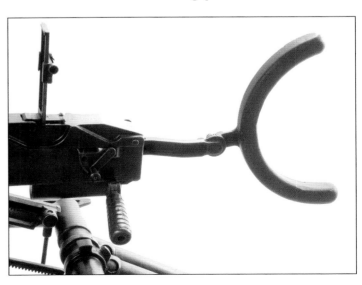

Degtyarev light machine guns

DP light machine gun

Caliber: 7.62mm

Length: 50.8in (1.29m)

Weight: 20lb 8oz (9.3kg)

Barrel: 23.8in (605mm) long, four grooves, right-hand twist

Feed system: 47-round detachable drum

System of operation: Gas; locking struts

Rate of fire: Cyclic, 550rpm

Manufacturer: Tula State Arsenal, USSR

Values: $9,000–$12,000 (Class III)

ABOVE AND TOP The Degtyarev DP. Note bipod attached to gas cylinder.

ABOVE AND BELOW RIGHT The DPM. Note bipod attached to barrel and return spring housing projecting from rear of receiver above stock.

In 1921 Vasily Alekseivitch Degtyarev began work on the first all-Russian machine gun. By 1926 it was perfected and it was trialed for an additional two years. In 1928, it was adopted by the Soviet Army as its standard light machine gun under the designation *Ruchnoi Pulyemet Degtyaryeva Pekhotnii* (automatic weapon, Degtyarev, infantry) better known by its abbreviation—DP. The gun was of simple, but reasonably robust, construction and contained only 65 parts, of which six were moving. The weapon had some deficiencies, particularly excessive friction in the action, susceptibility to the ingress of dirt, and overheating because barrel removal was slow and tedious (and useless as spare-barrel availability was rare). The first guns had finned barrels to help dissipate the heat, but the problem was never fully overcome. Rate of fire, therefore, had to be limited to the capacity of the barrel to disperse heat. Finally, the drum magazine was made of sheet steel and was liable to distort if dropped or roughly handled.

The gun was gas-operated, and its operation was rather unusual, though not original. The system was based on a patent taken out in 1872 and improved in 1907. Degtyarev was the first to put it to practical use. On each side of the bolt is a hinged lug lying in its own recess. When the bolt face is firm against the base of the round in the chamber, the bolt halts, but the piston continues briefly, taking with it a slider to which the firing pin is attached. During this final movement the firing pin cams the locking lugs into recesses in the receiver's side walls, thus locking the breech mechanism at the instant of firing.

The feed arrangement is reasonably good: rimmed cartridges usually cause problems in light automatic weapons, but are generally worse in those using box magazines. The large flat single-deck drum of the DP, driven by a clockwork mechanism rather than by the action of the gun, at least eliminates the problem of double feed. The magazine originally carried 49 rounds; in practice this was cut to 47 to reduce the chance of jams

The DP was a good design, particularly well-suited to the Soviet Army. It was uncomplicated, and did not demand highly skilled labor or complex machinery to produce. It was simple to operate and was, like most Russian equipment, extremely robust.

VARIANT

DPM (DP Modified)

The war in Russia revealed minor defects, as noted above. In 1944 the gun was modified to improve matters. The return spring was moved to a tube at the rear of the gun body, protruding over the butt. This made it difficult for the gunner to hold the gun in the usual way, so a pistol grip was fitted. The bipod was strengthened and attached to the barrel instead of the gas cylinder. The resulting DPM was an improvement: troops in the field found it better than the DP.

Far Left Detail of return spring housing.

Left The large, flat, 47-round drum magazine was common to both models and was driven by clockwork. This made misfeeds less likely and put less strain on the gun's mechanism.

DT light machine gun

Caliber: 7.62mm

Length: 47in (1.19m)

Weight: 28lb (12.7kg)

Barrel: 23.8in (605mm) long, four grooves, right-hand twist

Feed system: 60-round detachable drum

System of operation: Gas, locking struts

Rate of fire: Cyclic, 650rpm

Manufacturer: Tula State Arsenal, USSR

Values: $9,000–$12,000 (Class III)

RIGHT AND FAR RIGHT
The Degtyarev DT in tank-borne mode. The telescopic butt is retracted and the telescope sight is fitted. The padded headrest is to prevent injury in a violently moving vehicle.

BELOW A four-drum magazine bag.

The DT (*Degtyarev Tankovii*) was a modification of the DP for use in tanks. The magazine was deeper and carried 60 rounds; the barrel was heavier and not quickly changeable; a telescopic butt and pistol grip were fitted. A bipod was provided as an accessory so that the weapon could be used as a ground machine gun if the need arose. The DT saw service in virtually every Russian tank of the war including the famous T-34.

VARIANT

DTM (DT Modified)
This was the tank version of the DPM.

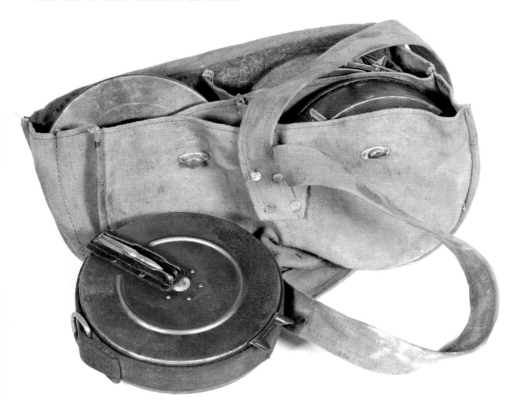

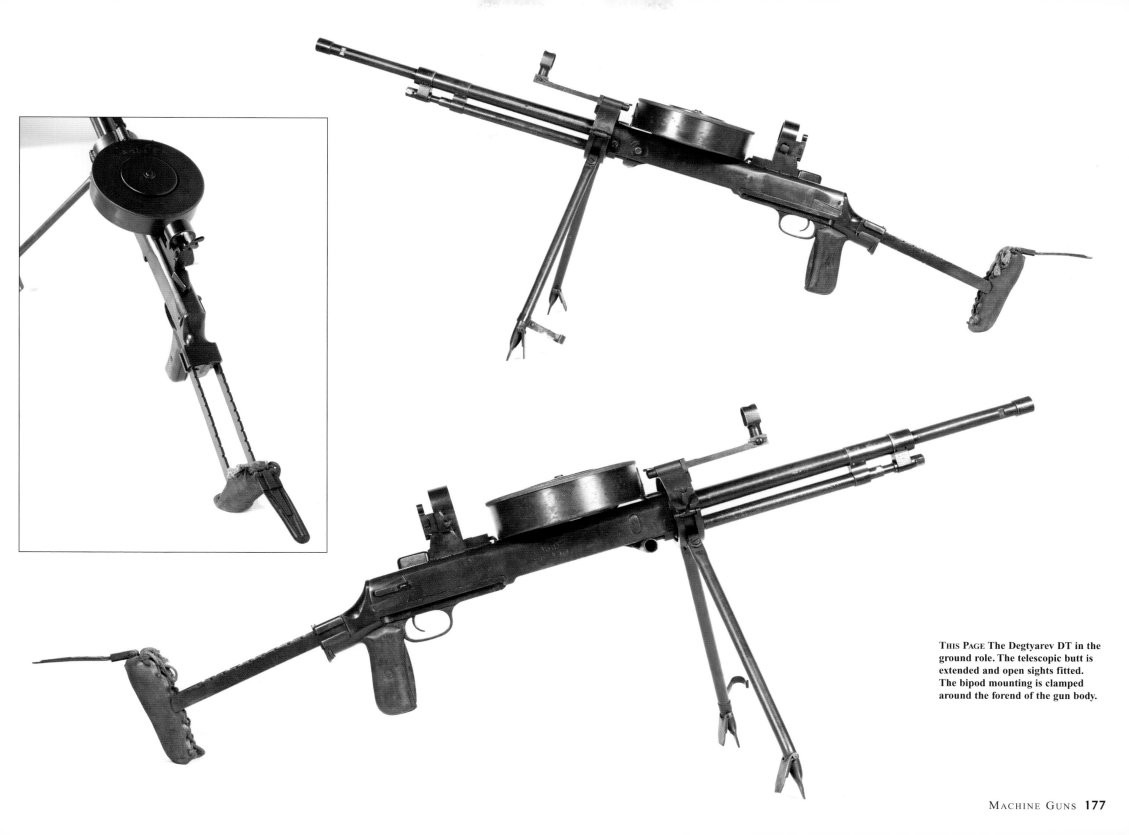

THIS PAGE The Degtyarev DT in the ground role. The telescopic butt is extended and open sights fitted. The bipod mounting is clamped around the forend of the gun body.

DShK 1938 heavy machine gun

Caliber: 12.7mm (0.50in)

Length: 62.5in (1.59m)

Weight: 78lb 8oz (35.6kg)

Barrel: 42in (1.08m) long, four grooves, right-hand twist

Feed system: 50-round belt

System of operation: Gas, hinged locking struts

Rate of fire: 550rpm

Manufacturer: USSR State Arsenals

Values: $30,000–$35,000 (Class III)

Degtyarev first developed a heavy machine gun, the DK, in 1934 but it was only made in prototype form and underwent further development before being adopted in 1938 as the DShK. During this period a second designer, Georg S. Shpagin, later a lieutenant general in the Red Army, was to play an integral role in the development of the weapon. Indeed the "D" and "Sh" of DShK are the initials of the two designers. Shpagin was later to go on to design the PPSh submachine gun. Degtyarev laid out the general design and basic mechanism, while Shpagin was responsible for the feed mechanism. Special attention to the feed was demanded by the fact that the weapon was designed to use the large 12.7mm (0.50in) cartridge, and the weight of a full belt of this placed a considerable strain on the feed system. Shpagin's solution was to mount a rotary "squirrel-cage" block above the bolt; the belt was fed into the gun, the cartridge withdrawn from the belt into a recess in the block, and the block indexed round. This process was repeated until the drum was almost filled and the first cartridge had moved around to the lowest position, from which it could be stripped by the forward movement of the bolt. Each subsequent stroke of the bolt loaded one cartridge from the drum, and at the same time took another from the belt and loaded it into the drum. The idea was not entirely original, having been used by Maxim in his first design of 1883, but Shpagin was the first to make it work successfully in or out of the Soviet Union.

The remainder of the mechanism was typical Degtyarev, using his well-tried system of hinged struts to lock the bolt by the movement of the striker, unlocking by movement of the gas piston. The long barrel was heavily finned to aid cooling and a single-baffle muzzle brake used to try to abate the recoil force. The mounting was a tripod which, for transport, folded and took on a pair of wheels so that it resembled the Maxim's "Sokolov" mounting. This tripod, when erected, was some five feet high so the weapon could be used as an antiaircraft machine gun, a role in which it was very prominent during World War II.

At the end of the war it was modified by removing the rotating drum feed and replacing it with a simple swinging-arm pattern which had been developed for a postwar gun, and as the DShKM it remained in service well into the postwae period. Numbers of DShKs were supplied to various satellite countries, and it was particularly prominent as an antiaircraft weapon during the Korean War.

BELOW LEFT AND RIGHT
The DShK38 used a rotary block mechanism that was housed under the distinctive cylindrical cover on the receiver. The DShKs were used extensively in the ground role as heavy machine guns and also as antiaircraft weapons on an upended tripod in a similar fashion to the Goryunov on page 182.

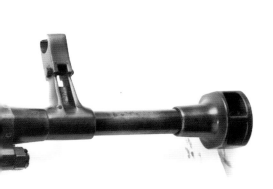

RIGHT AND ABOVE RIGHT The DShK
was aimed and fired using a two-
handed spade grip and
butterfly trigger. The example
shown is the latter version with the
rotary drum feed replaced with a
more conventional swinging arm
pattern.

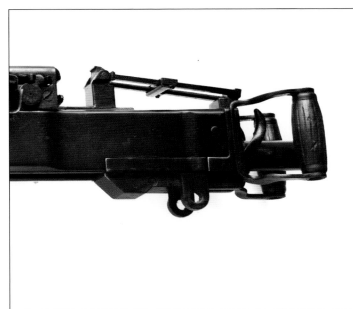

THIS PAGE AND OPPOSITE
The DShK38/46 was a postwar development of the DShK that dispensed with rotary block mechanism of the DShK38. The characteristic cylindrical receiver cover was replaced with a flat design shown here. Both models were also used as the main weapon of light tanks and armored cars and as the secondary armament of tanks such as the JSII "Joe Stalin" heavy tank.

Goryunov SG43 heavy machine gun

Caliber: 7.62mm

Length: 44.1in (1.12m)

Weight: 30lb 4oz (13.72kg)

Barrel: 28.3in (719mm) long, four grooves, right-hand twist

Feed system: Metallic link belt

System of operation: Gas, side-moving bolt

Rate of fire: 600rpm

Manufacturer: State Arsenals, USSR

Values: $12,000–$23,000 (Class III)

By the early 1940s it was obvious to the Red Army's general staff that a new heavy machine gun was required. The Maxim 1910, while still effective in some roles, was far too heavy and difficult to maneuver for modern mobile warfare and the Red Army demanded something to replace it. With the war in Finland just over, and a war with Germany not unlikely, this was a matter of some urgency. Design of the new weapon was entrusted to Peter Maximovitch Goryunov and the SG34 entered production in 1943. There is some evidence that Goryunov was working on a design for a tank machine gun at the time of the demand, and simply modified it to produce the ground gun. The barrel is much heavier than might be expected in this role, but it does lead to long life and is probably due to the tank influence. The mechanism was entirely new, representing the first Soviet departure from Degtyarev's designs. The bolt locks by moving sideways into a recess in the gun body, operated by a conventional gas piston. The feed system is unusually complicated because it has to withdraw the rimmed cartridge from the belt, move it forward in front of the bolt, and then move it sideways into line with the chamber. In spite of the complexity, the system is reliable and foolproof and will continue to work irrespective of the gun's attitude—upright, on its side, or even upside down, though this is more in the nature of a mechanical curiosity than a useful combat feature. Another feature of the SG is the extreme simplicity of its mechanism; there is, for example, only one large spring in the gun. It has been acclaimed by one authority as the most successful air-cooled machine gun ever made with the exception of the American Browning. Certainly the Soviets were satisfied with it, and although it never replaced the Maxim during the war because production could not keep up with the demand, in postwar years it became the standard medium gun and also went back to its origins to become the standard tank machine gun.

VARIANTS

SGM
This is a slightly improved SG43. Alterations include a fluted barrel, improved barrel lock and dust covers on feed and ejection ports. The cocking handle was moved to the right side of the receiver.

SGMT
Tank coaxial version of SGM.

SGMB
Alternative vehicle-mounted version.

RIGHT AND FAR RIGHT The Goryunov SG43 was one one of the most successful machine gun designs to come out of Soviet Russia and was widely used during World War II.

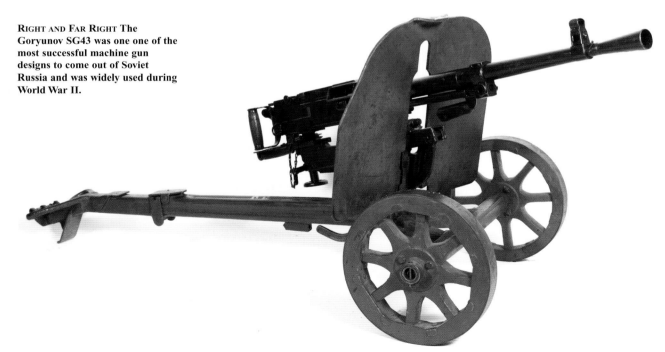

THIS PAGE The Goryunov SG43 was mounted on a wheeled carriage similar to that of the Maxim, although smaller. It was provided with elevation and traverse locks to permit sustained operation on a fixed line of fire.

TOP RIGHT The mount for the SG43 was similar in appearance to the Maxim's Solokov mount, but was smaller and lighter.

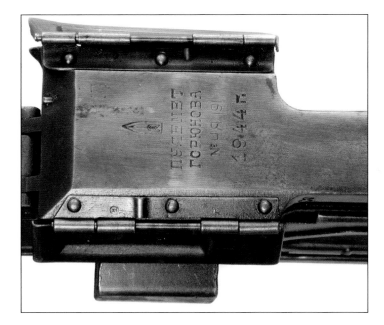

RIGHT AND LEFT The Goryunov SG43 was mounted on a wheeled carriage with a forward sloping shield that formed the third leg of a tripod when the carriage was tipped on end for use as an anti-aircraft mount.

ABOVE Maker's marks. Note also the dust covers for ammunition feed and ejection ports.

BELOW Close up of spade grips, trigger, and sight.

SGMT and SGMB Goryunov tank machine gun

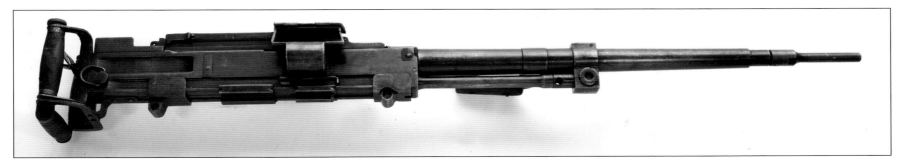

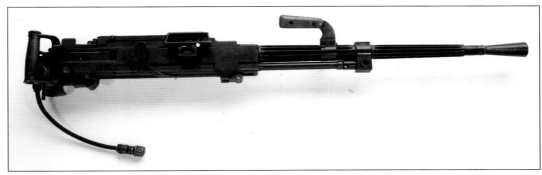

BELOW Three views of the SGM—a development of the SG43 that introduced a fluted barrel, and moved the cocking handle to the right side of the receiver. The example shown is an SGMT, a model intended for use as a coaxial tank machine gun and fitted with a solenoid trigger on the back plate.

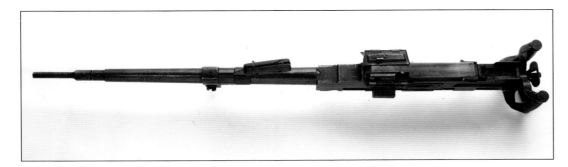

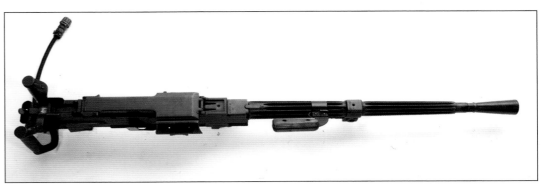

ABOVE Three photographs of the SGMB—an SG43 fitted with a modified muzzle for mounting in an armored vehicle.

Hotchkiss Mle 1909 machine gun

Caliber: .303
Length: 46.85in (1.19m)
Weight: 25.8lb (11.7kg)
Barrel: 23.6in (600mm), five grooves, right-hand twist
Feed system: 30-round metal strip

System of operation: Gas piston
Rate of fire: Cyclic, 500rpm
Manufacturer: Hotchkiss Enfield, England
Values: $7,500–$8,500 (Class III)

The Hotchkiss Mle 1909 was originally produced for use by the French cavalry and infantry units before World War I. It was not a great success in either role and most were put into storage. With the start of World War I Mle 1909s were also produced by Enfield in .303 caliber for service in the British Army as the .303, gun, machine, Hotchkiss in an attempt to make good the shortage of machine guns at that time. In British hands they fared little better than in French, the fragile strip feed system proving far too vulnerable to the mud and dirt of trench warfare—although the weapon did prove successful when fitted as armament in the early tanks. Indeed, a special version was produced, the Mk. II, that was fitted with a belt feed. Some of these weapons were still in service with the British Army in 1939, and more were taken from reserves at a time when, for Britain, any weapon was better than none.

RIGHT AND ABOVE RIGHT The .303 Hotchkiss, a veteran of World War I that was to see action again in World War II—albeit briefly.

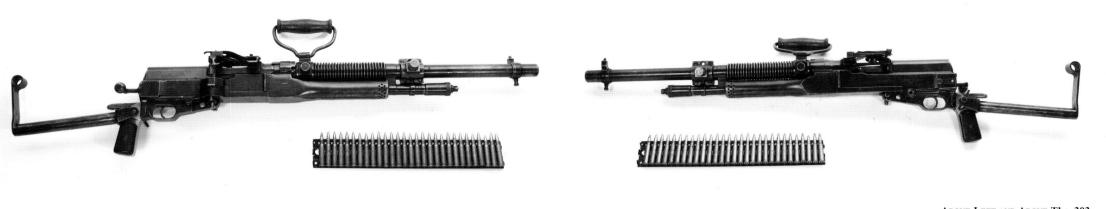

ABOVE LEFT AND ABOVE The .303
Hotchkiss with shoulder stock
attached and loaded ammunition
strip.

LEFT Top view of the weapon
showing the ammunition strip
loaded into the receiver. These
strips were very fragile and proved
to be one of the weak points of the
design.

Italian Machine guns

Breda Model 1930 light machine gun

Caliber: 6.5mm
Length: 48.4in (1.23m)
Weight: 22lb 8oz (10.21kg)
Barrel: 20.5in (520mm) long, four grooves, right–hand twist
Feed system: 20–round attached box

System of operation: Delayed blowback
Rate of fire: Cyclic, 475rpm
Manufacturer: Societa Anonima Ernesto Breda, Turin, Italy
Values: $8,000–$9,500 (Class III)

The Breda company was a heavy engineering firm specializing in railway locomotives, and first entered the weapons business as a subcontractor for FIAT machine guns during World War I. After the war Breda decided to retain its foothold in this new business and set about designing a light machine gun. The first design was the M1924, of which the Italian Army bought 2,000. It was then replaced by the slightly modified M1930, and this became the standard Italian light machine gun. Unfortunately the M1930 was a poor design that suffered from several defects. First, it relied on the blowback system to recock the weapon. This was totally unsuitable for such a high-velocity weapon. For while the 6.5mm ammunition used was relatively weak in machine-gun terms, the charge was still sufficient to distort the cartridge causing it to fail to extract. Breda's solution to this was to incorporate an oil reservoir that lubricated each round as it was fed in. This turned out to be as big a problem as the one it was intended to solve because the oil-covered rounds became coated in dirt and grit that was then transferred into the chamber of the gun causing wear and carbon build up.

The magazine was a permanent fixture on the right side and could be hinged forward to allow it to be reloaded by either pushing in a 20-round clip or reloading from rifle chargers. In theory this is a good idea, because it means that the magazine lips, which are critical for correct feeding, are machined within the gun body and thus are less liable to accidental damage. But what it really meant was a low rate of fire because of the need to reload instead of simply changing magazines. In addition the 20-round charger was flimsy and gave frequent trouble, and the hinges were not as robust as they should have been and when they broke the weapon was rendered useless.

The barrel change process was also difficult: there was no handle on the barrel, and hence no carrying handle for the gun, This meant that the gunner had to wear gloves to remove a hot barrel. Anyone carrying the weapon was also hindered by the awkward shape and many projections which snagged on clothing and equipment. The final drawback was that the quick-change barrel lay on a recoil slide, because it had to move about 4mm to

Right and Far Right The Breda Model 1937 was the best heavy machine gun to see service with the Italians but still left a lot to be desired.

the rear before the breech opened. As a result the sights were on the gun body and not on the barrel; this, plus the fact that the barrel support bearings soon showed signs of wear, led to considerable inaccuracy. In spite of all its faults, the Italian Army was forced to use the Breda 30 throughout the war as its standard light machine gun, because there was no alternative.

VARIANTS

Model 1938

In 1938 the Italian Army began to introduce a 7.35mm cartridge, and a small number of Model 1930 machine guns were rechambered for the new round. Such conversions were known as the Model 1938, but few were issued.

Breda Model 1937 heavy machine gun

Caliber: 8 mm

Length: 50.06in (1.27m)

Weight: 43lb (19.5kg)

Barrel: 26.75in (680mm) long, four grooves, right-hand twist

Feed system: 20-round strip

System of operation: Gas, vertical sliding lock

Rate of fire: Cyclic, 450rpm

Manufacturer: Societa Anonima Ernesto Breda, Turin, Italy

Values: $20,000–$25,000 (Class III)

This Breda design was to become the standard heavy machine gun of the Italian Army in World War II. The mechanism was a simple gas piston that, unfortunately, had the same violent action and extraction problems as Breda's light machine gun designs. It was also provided with the same solution: a mechanism for oiling each round as it was fed into the weapon.

This led to the same problems of fouling, as dirt and dust clung to the oiled rounds and was transferred to the mechanism of the gun.

The design of the rest of the gun was straightforward enough, and it was mounted on a simple and robust tripod, but was hampered by an unnecessarily complicated and rather pointless feed system. It was based on the already outdated Hotchkiss system, in which a light-metal strip holding 20 rounds is fed into one side of the gun. As the gun fires, the rounds are pulled from the strip and the strip moved across, until eventually the empty strip falls from the other side of the gun. These strips were already prone to fragility, and the design of this weapon added further pointless complication by arranging the machinery so that when the empty case was extracted from the chamber, it was replaced in the strip before the strip was moved across.

Whatever advantage this system may have it possessed the grave disadvantage was that, unless the gunner had a supply of loaded strips handy, his unfortunate assistant had to spend time

BELOW The Breda Model 1937 maker's marks.

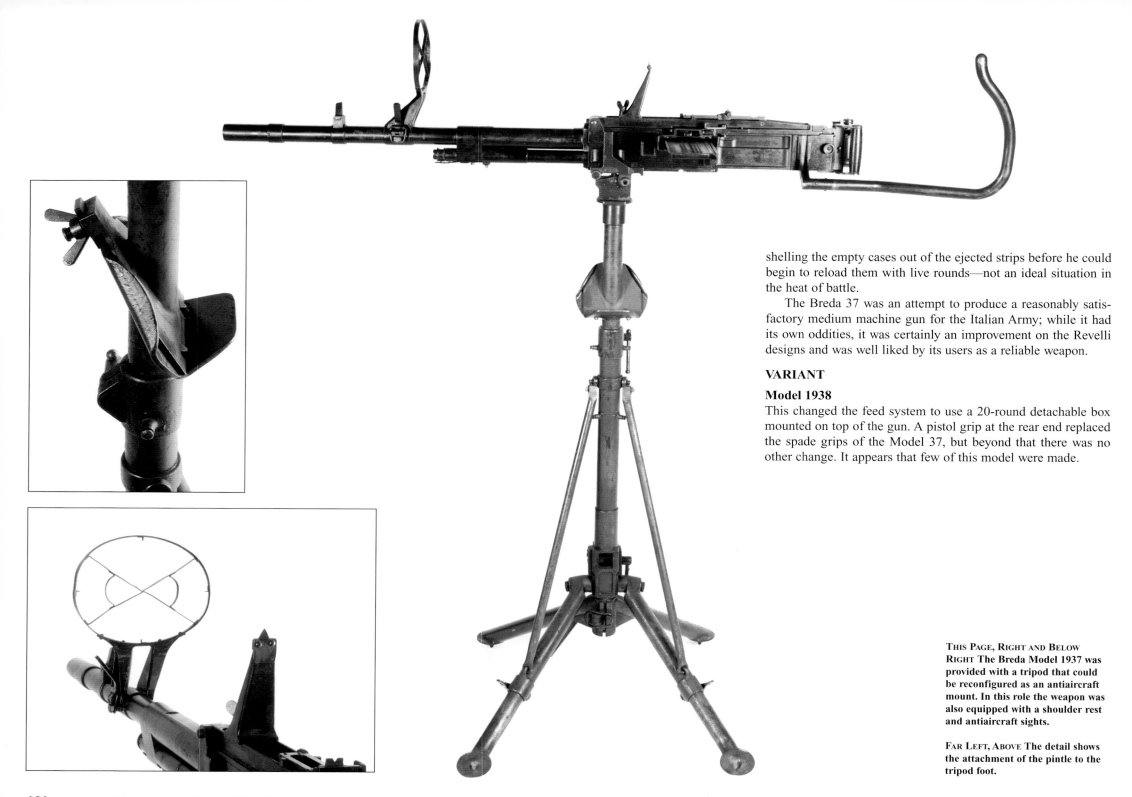

shelling the empty cases out of the ejected strips before he could begin to reload them with live rounds—not an ideal situation in the heat of battle.

The Breda 37 was an attempt to produce a reasonably satisfactory medium machine gun for the Italian Army; while it had its own oddities, it was certainly an improvement on the Revelli designs and was well liked by its users as a reliable weapon.

VARIANT

Model 1938

This changed the feed system to use a 20-round detachable box mounted on top of the gun. A pistol grip at the rear end replaced the spade grips of the Model 37, but beyond that there was no other change. It appears that few of this model were made.

THIS PAGE, RIGHT AND BELOW RIGHT The Breda Model 1937 was provided with a tripod that could be reconfigured as an antiaircraft mount. In this role the weapon was also equipped with a shoulder rest and antiaircraft sights.

FAR LEFT, ABOVE The detail shows the attachment of the pintle to the tripod foot.

Fiat-Revelli Model 1914 heavy MG

Caliber: 6.5mm
Length: 46.5in (1.18m)
Weight: 37lb 8oz (17kg)
Barrel: 25.75in (654mm) long, four grooves, right-hand twist
Feed system: 50-round strips
System of operation: Blowback
Rate of fire: Cyclic, 400rpm
Manufacturer: FIAT SpA, Turin, Italy
Values: $6,500-$7,500 (Class III)

The Model 1914 bears some resemblance to its contemporaries the Maxim, Vickers, and water-cooled Browning, but this is entirely superficial and the weapon is not in the same class. In spite of its manifold defects, however, it remained a part of the Italian Army's equipment from its introduction in 1914 until the close of World War II. The weapon was a delayed blowback using a mechanism long perpetuated in Italian gun designs. The barrel and bolt recoiled a short distance, held together by a swinging wedge; as this swung out of engagement the bolt was freed to be blown back by the recoil of the spent case. Like most blowback designs this led to extraction difficulties and an oil reservoir and pump were installed to lubricate the cartridges before being loaded. The feed mechanism was also unusual. A magazine of ten columns of five rounds was entered into the left side of the gun. As each column was emptied, the magazine was indexed across to bring the next column into line, until finally the empty magazine was ejected from the right side of the gun. As may be imagined, the mechanism required for this operation was rather complex and its functioning was not improved by the oil and dust coating it acquired during firing; it was notoriously prone to jamming.

Finally, an operating rod forming part of the bolt structure protruded from the rear of the topmost portion of the receiver and recoiled with the bolt, passing across the top of the gun and striking a buffer unit placed just in front of the operating handles. Oscillating back and forth at 400 times a minute, it was a constant hazard to the gunner's fingers as well as being a highly effective device for pumping grit and dirt into the mechanism. Taking one thing with another, the Revelli (FIAT came into it only as manufacturers) was not a particularly outstanding design, not unlike many Italian models.

Fiat-Revelli, Model 1935 heavy MG

Caliber: 8mm
Length: 50in (1.27m)
Weight: 40lb (18.14kg)
Barrel: 25.75in (654mm) long, four grooves, right-hand twist
Feed system: Belt
System of operation: Blowback
Rate of fire: 500rpm
Manufacturer: FIAT SpA, Turin, Italy
Values: $4,500-$6,000 (Class III)

The Italian Army, feeling the need of an improvement on the 1914 model, developed this Model 1935. The principal changes from the 1914 were: first, adoption of a new 8mm cartridge to improve its hitting power; second, getting rid of the water-cooling arrangements and making it air-cooled; and third, removing the magazine feed of the 1914 and replacing it with a more conventional belt feed. At the same time the barrel was arranged for rapid changing, doubtless because it was rather underweight for sustained fire.

In spite of these very laudable improvements, there was still enough of the 1914 model left to damn the design. The oil pump was discarded, but since the mechanism was still the same delayed blowback, extraction was still a problem. This time it was overcome by fluting the interior surface of the chamber to float the case out on gas, but this rarely seemed to work the way it was intended, and a large number of guns actually had the oil pump of the M1914 replaced as a modification. For the rest, the cartridges were greased as they were put into the belts, which was an even worse solution.

Probably the worst feature of the design was that the mechanism had been altered to make the weapon fire from a closed bolt, presumably in the interests of improved accuracy. As a result, when firing stopped a cartridge was chambered but not fired. Since the chamber of the thin barrel was invariably hot, this led to frequent cook-offs, with all the attendant hazards. To sum up; it seems fair to say that the 1935 was actually a worse design than the weapon it was intended to replace.

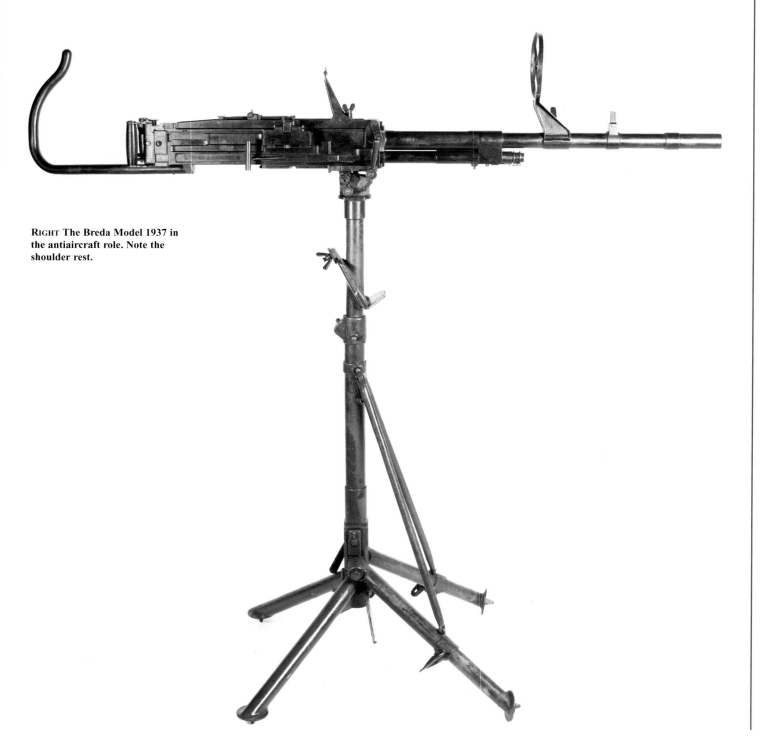

RIGHT The Breda Model 1937 in the antiaircraft role. Note the shoulder rest.

Japanese MGs

Taisho 11 light machine gun

Caliber: 6.5mm	System of operation; Gas
Length: 43.5in (1.11m)	Rate of fire: Cyclic, 500rpm
Weight: 22lb 8oz (10.21kg)	Manufacturers: Japanese State Arsenals
Barrel: 19in (483mm) long, four grooves, right-hand twist	
Feed system: 30-round hopper	Values: $4,500–$6,000 (Class III)

The Japanese Army was one of the first to appreciate the potential of the machine gun and by 1902 had purchased manufacturing rights to the French Hotchkiss Mle 1897 and was issuing it to the army. It was used with considerable success in the Russo-Japanese War, and as a result, the Hotchkiss design was retained as the basis of further developments.

After World War I the Japanese military was keen to develop an indigenous range of modern weapons to reduce reliance on foreign suppliers. One of the fruits of this policy was the Taisho 11 gun of 1922, the 11th year of the Taisho Era, and was designed by Colonel Kirijo Nambu, the noted Japanese firearms expert. The basic Hotchkiss gas-operated system was retained, but a unique feed system was introduced: a square hopper on the left of the gun accepted six standard five-round rifle chargers lying on their sides. As the gun fired, so the rounds were stripped from the bottom charger, the empty charger being discarded and the next full one falling into place. In theory this system allowed any rifleman to provide ammunition for the squad weapon; in practice the standard rifle round was too powerful for the smooth working of the gun, and led to the rate of fire being too fast for the rather complicated feed mechanism. As a result, a special cartridge, loaded with a slightly less powerful charge, had to be provided for the machine gun, which rather negated the benefits of the hopper feed.

Another fault of the weapon was that the action was so built that the bolt opened suddenly and jerked the empty case out of the breech; there was no period of slow opening with powerful leverage to give what is called "primary extraction." This led to separated and split cases. The solution to this was to add an oil reservoir arrangement which lubricated every round as it entered the chamber. Like every other lubricated-feed design this gave good results under ideal conditions but in the dust of battle it simply meant that the round was coated with grit and dirt as it entered the breech leading to rapid wear of the chamber. The sights and butt on the Taisho 11 were offset to the right, giving the weapon a peculiar appearance, and the barrel was extensively finned in order to assist cooling. The gun was widely used during the Manchuria and China campaigns of the 1930s, but by the time of World War II it was about to be replaced by improved models. However, the manufacturing capacity of Japan was never capable of producing the new weapons in sufficient quantity and so the Taisho 11 remained in service until 1945.

Type 92 medium machine gun

Caliber: 7.7mm
Length: 45.5in (1.15m)
Weight: 122lb 8oz (55.3kg)
Barrel: 27.5in (698mm) long, four grooves, right-hand twist
Feed system: 30-round strip

System of operation: Gas
Rate of fire: Cyclic, 500rpm
Manufacturers: Japanese State Arsenals
Values: $13,000–$15,000 (Class III)

As a newly emerged industrial nation at the turn of the century Japan had little experience in the design and manufacture of modern weapons. As a result development of new weapons was often based on western designs. The resultant weapons were often hampered by basic design flaws resulting form the inexperience of the designers, and when a successful weapon was produced there was a reluctance to change or develop it. Partly due to the lack of technical expertise and partly because Japan's fledgling heavy industries could not keep pace with existing demand let alone cope with the disruption caused by design changes. As a result, most of their machine guns were Hotchkiss guns. The Model 92 was developed from the Taisho 3 Model of 1914, which in its turn was a copy of the French Model 1914 Hotchkiss. The Taisho 3 barrel was more prominently finned, and two spade grips placed at the rear, but the principal difference was a slight change in the connection between the gas piston and the breechblock. This was made to give efficient operation with the lower-powered Japanese 6.5mm cartridge, and because of this alteration the extraction was violent and, as usual, the cartridges had to be oiled before loading.

In 1932 the army began changing to 7.7mm caliber and the machine gun was again redesigned by General Nambu to suit the characteristics of the new cartridge. The main external change was the addition of a flash hider to the muzzle and a new pattern of firing grip at the rear, which resembled two pistol grips hanging beneath the gun. The internal mechanism was basically unchanged and oiling remained a necessity. Perhaps the most unfortunate feature was its weight, 122lb (55.34kg) when on its tripod. As a result the tripod, like that of the earlier Taisho 3, had two sleeves on the front legs into which carrying poles could be slipped for two men,

while the third member of the gun team attached a yoke, resembling overgrown bicycle handlebars, to the rear tripod leg. In this way three men could carry the whole equipment fairly rapidly about the battlefield without dismantling it. The Type 92 was the most common medium machine gun of the Japanese Army throughout the war, and its slow and distinctive rate of fire earned it the nickname "Woodpecker" among Allied troops.

Type 96 light machine gun

Caliber: 6.5mm
Length: 41.5in (1.05m)
Weight: 20lb (9.07kg)
Barrel: 21.7in (55.12kg) long, four grooves, right-hand twist
Feed system: 30-round detachable box

System of operation: Gas, rising lock
Rate of fire: Cyclic, 550rpm
Manufacturers: Japanese State Arsenals
Values: $4,500–$6,000 (Class III)

This weapon was introduced in 1936 (year 2596 in the Japanese calendar, hence Type 96) with the intention of replacing the Taisho 11. In the end, production did not keep up with demand so it never completely ousted the earlier gun from general use. Although still based on the same action as the Taisho 11, it is obvious that a number of ideas had been taken from the Czechoslovak ZB designs, probably from guns captured from the Chinese. The most important feature was that the complicated hopper feed of the Taisho 11 was replaced by a more usual form of top-mounted detachable box magazine; unfortunately this did not do away with the troubles because of the full-power rifle round, and the reduced charge cartridge was still necessary.

The offset butt and sights were abandoned in favor of a more conventional form of butt and a drum-set rear sight copied from the ZB design. The quick-change barrel was heavily ribbed throughout its length and a bayonet boss on the gas cylinder allowed a large sword bayonet to be attached. One of the approved doctrines with this weapon was to sling it from the shoulder so that it could be fired from the hip during the assault, and in this role the bayonet was usually fixed. It was probably quite useless as an offensive weapon, but it may have served to hold the muzzle down and thus make the gun easier to control. Another change from the Taisho 11 was the removal of the cartridge oiling system. But because the action was the same, the rounds still required lubrication and this was now done by a combination oiler and magazine loading tool; if anything, this led to a worse state of affairs, because the gun team now ran around with magazines full of oily cartridges that attracted dust and grit like magnets. It comes as no surprise to find that the gun hand-

book lists 26 different types of stoppage or malfunction as being likely. One unusual feature of the Type 96 is that it was often found fitted with a low-power sighting telescope. Sighting telescopes are extremely uncommon on light (or any other) machine guns, and there is no satisfactory explanation for it since the degree of accuracy of this class of gun did not warrant the fitting of such a sight.

Type 99 light machine gun

Caliber: 7.7mm
Length: 42in (1.07m)
Weight: 20lb (9.07kg)
Barrel: 21.66in (550mm) long, four grooves, right-hand twist
Feed system: 30-round detachable box

System of operation: Gas; rising lock
Rate of fire: Cyclic, 800rpm
Manufacturers: Japanese State Arsenals
Values: $6,500–$8,000 (Class III)

After using 6.5mm ammunition since 1897, the Japanese Army decided in 1932, as part of the program to expand the Japanese East Asian empire in China and Manchuria, to change to something more powerful. After studying various types they developed a 7.7mm round more or less copied from the British .303. Unfortunately, they also developed a rimless and a semi-rimmed round; having all three types in service at once lead to considerable logistics problems.

The Type 99 machine gun used the rimless 7. 7mm round and was introduced in 1939 with the new ammunition, the rimmed and semi-rimmed types having been put into service in 1932. It was intended to issue the weapon in place of the Models 11 and 96, but production never approached demand and all three guns remained in service, the Type 99 only appearing in relatively small numbers.

Its appearance is virtually the same as the Type 96, because it was little more than 96 in a new caliber. But one or two internal changes were made, the most important being that at last the need for adequate primary extraction had been appreciated. The breech was designed to give a slow initial opening movement, and at long last the Japanese Army had a machine gun that did not need to have its cartridges oiled. As a result it was one of the most reliable weapons they ever produced. Another addition, this one of doubtful utility, was the addition of a monopod beneath the butt in order to provide a firm base for firing on fixed lines at night.

Lewis light machine gun

Caliber: .303	**System of operation:** Gas
Length: 49.2in (1.25m)	**Rate of fire:** Cyclic, 450–500rpm
Weight: 27lb (12.25kg)	**Manufacturers:**
Barrel: 26in (661mm)	BSA Co. Ltd., Birmingham,
Feed: 47 or 97-round overhead	England
drum magazine	**Values:** $12,500–$15,000
	(Class III)

The Lewis machine gun, generally called just the Lewis Gun, was an international weapon, for though its origins were American, it was first produced and manufactured in Europe. Its inventor was an American, one Samuel McLean, but the basic concept was developed further and "sold" by Colonel Isaac Lewis, another American. The U.S. military authorities were unenthusiastic about the new gun, so Lewis took the design to Belgium, where it was put into production for the Belgian Army. That was in 1913, and in the following year production was switched to the UK, BSA (Birmingham Small Arms) taking over the program.

The Lewis Gun was put into production at BSA as the Lewis Gun Mk. I for the British Army for the simple reason that five or six Lewis guns could be produced in the time it took to produce a single Vickers machine gun. The fact that the Lewis was light and portable was secondary at that time, but once in service the Lewis proved to be a very popular front-line weapon with a host of mobile tactical uses. The Lewis Gun was one of the first of the true light machine guns, and with its distinctive overhead drum magazine it was soon a common sight on the British-manned sector of the Western Front.

The Lewis Gun was a gas-operated weapon, gas being tapped from the barrel on firing to push a piston to the rear; the piston pushed back the breechblock and mechanism and compressed the coil spring under the gun that then returned everything to the start position The mechanism was rather complex and took careful maintenance, but even then was still prone to jams and stoppages, some of them introduced by the overhead drum magazine, which was a constant cause of trouble, especially when only slightly damaged. The barrel was enclosed in a special air cooling jacket that was supposed to use a forced draught system of cooling, but experience showed that the jacket's efficiency had been overrated and the gun worked quite well without it. Aircraft-mounted Lewis guns had no jacket.

Only after large numbers of Lewis guns had been produced in Europe did the United States finally realize the weapon's potential and order it into production for the U.S. Army chambered in the American .30 (7.62mm) caliber. Some Lewis guns were used on the early tanks and more were used by naval vessels. A similar role cropped up again in World War II when stockpiled Lewis guns were distributed for the defense of merchant shipping and for home defense in the hands of the Home Guard and Royal Air Force airfield units.

TOP Lewis camera gun.

ABOVE The elderly Lewis Gun was brought out of storage in World War II for Home Guard use, and defense of airfields and merchant shipping.

Madsen machine gun

Caliber: 7.92mm

Length: 45in (1.14m)

Weight: 20lb (9.07kg)

Barrel: 23in (584mm) long, four grooves, right-hand twist

Feed system: 25, 30, or 40-round detachable box magazines

System of operation: Recoil, rising block

Rate of fire: Cyclic, 450rpm

Manufacturer: Dansk Rekylriffel Syndikat AS Madsen, Copenhagen, Denmark

Values: $8,000–$10,000 (Class III)

ABOVE AND TOP The Danish Madsen gun. This example has been equipped with a vehicle mounting.

The Madsen was a unique weapon, using an action totally unlike any other, produced in virtually the same model for 50 years, used in almost every war from the Russo-Japanese to Vietnam, and yet never officially adopted in quantity by any major power. It was designed by the Dane Jens Torring Schouboe, and was probably the only one of his many weapon designs that was a success. It was then adopted by the Danish cavalry and named Madsen, after the Danish Minister of War who had advocated its adoption. After that it was bought in small numbers by almost every nation and evaluated both in peace and war. It was the Norwegian Army's light machine gun in 1940, being used in the brief campaign against the German invasion.

The action of the Madsen is based on recoil of the barrel, which transmits movement to a pivoting breechblock similar in concept to that of a Martini rifle. Since the block is working in a vertical arc, a separate rammer is needed to insert the cartridge and a separate extractor to remove the fired case. In spite of its undoubted mechanical perfection, the action is open to criticism on the grounds that the cartridge is slightly distorted or bowed as

it is forced into the chamber. This appears to be borne out by the fact that jams frequently occur when the weapon is used with rimmed ammunition or with slightly over-size cases. It seems to work well enough with rimless cartridges, however, and the majority of Madsens have been built for this type. One major innovation of the Madsen design was the top-mounted curved magazine, widely copied after its introduction on this gun.

As well as being used in Norway, Madsens were found in Estonia, Lithuania, Latvia, Poland, and many other European

countries, many of which found their way into German service. As well as employing them as they stood, the Germans developed an ingenious conversion unit that allowed the use of the standard German Army machine-gun belts instead of the box magazines.

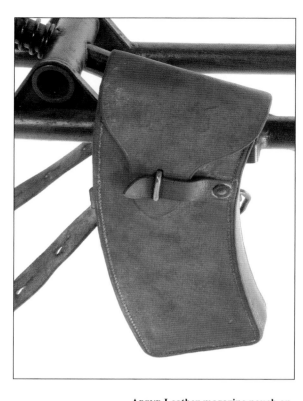

ABOVE Leather magazine pouch on tripod.

BELOW The front attachment point.

ABOVE AND PAGE 197 The Danish Madsen remained in production, largely unchanged from 1904 to 1956. This is an infantry model mounted on a tripod in the medium machine gun role.

LEFT Maker's mark and serial number.

RIGHT Detail of receiver showing trigger and cocking handle.

BELOW Rear mounting point and traversing gear.

Maxim M1910 heavy machine gun

Caliber: 7.62mm

Length: 43.6in (1.11m)

Weight: gun 52lb 8oz (23.81kg); mounting 110lb (72.58kg)

Barrel: 28.4in (721mm) long, four grooves, right-hand twist

Feed system: 250-round fabric belt

System of operation: Recoil; Maxim toggle lock

Rate of fire: 550rpm

Manufacturer: Russian State Arsenals

Values: $17,000–$20,000 (Class III)

The history of the Maxim machine gun dates back to 1887 when Hiram Maxim himself demonstrated the weapon at St. Petersburg, and eventually the Tsar's army was provided with British-made Maxims. In 1905 manufacture began at Tula Arsenal in Russia, and from then until 1945 the weapon was in more or less continuous production. The original model had a cast bronze water jacket, but in 1910 this was replaced by a steel jacket and slight improvements were made to the feed mechanism, and with that the design was settled for evermore. The only minor changes made subsequently were the fitting of a corrugated water jacket during World War I and the fitting of a much larger filler cap, reputed to be originally designed for a tractor petrol tank, during World War II.

The mechanism was, of course, the basic Maxim toggle lock operated by recoil; not the simplest mechanism ever made but certainly one of the most reliable. Where the Russian weapons were unique was in the matter of weight. The British Vickers, more or less the same gun, weighed 32.5lb (14.74kg), and the German Maxim 1908, which was virtually the same gun as the Russian 1910, only 40.5lb (18.37kg). Doubtless the massiveness of the Russian construction contributed to its reliability but it certainly made it a difficult proposition to move. As a result the

Russians developed their unique wheeled Sokolov mounting, a tubular steel trail into which the gun was mounted and which acted both as a carrying cart and a firing mounting. Early models had two extra legs that could be extended forward to raise the gun for firing over parapets, but this was abandoned during World War I. A more conventional tripod mounting was also provided but in smaller numbers than the Sokolov mount and it was rarely seen. The wheels of the Sokolov could be removed in the winter and replaced with a pair of sledge runners, when the whole affair could be towed by ski-troops. While ingenious, the result was an equipment weighing 162.5lb (73.71kg) without water or ammunition. The Maxim 1910 was widely used in both world wars, in the Revolution, in the Spanish Civil War, and after 1945—when replaced in Soviet first-line service, it was given to many satellite countries.

BELOW The Maxim was in production in Russia from 1905 to 1945. It was heavily built even by Russian standards and the wheeled, Sokolov mount was no luxury as the combined weight of the gun and mount was more than 160lb (72.58kg). In winter the wheels could be replaced with skis.

ABOVE The coolant filler cap. The Maxim M1910 was a rugged design even by Russian standards and virtually anything could be used as a coolant.

LEFT The Sokolov mounting provided a significant degree of traverse.

LEFT The maker's marks.

RIGHT The muzzle and fore sight of the M1910. Note also cooling jacket with filler cap open. The brass fitting by the muzzle is the drain plug.

BELOW The Maxim M1910 was virtually indestructible in normal use and could be fired continuously for hours on end.

MG15 heavy machine gun

Caliber: 7.92mm

Length: 52.5in (1.33m)

Weight: 28lb (12.7kg)

Barrel: 23.5in (597mm) long, four grooves, right–hand twist

Feed system: 75–round detachable saddle drum magazine

System of operation: Recoil, rotating bolt

Rate of fire: Cyclic, 850rpm

Manufacturer: Rheinmetall AG, Düsseldorf, Germany

Values: $11,000–$13,000 (Class III)

In 1929 the German Rheinmetall company established a subsidiary in Switzerland, Waffenfabrik Solothurn AG, which was to act as its developmental unit for designs that could not be produced in Germany. One of the first products was the original MG15—an aircraft machine gun that was redesigned in 1932 by Rheinmetall for the Luftwaffe.

The action is by short recoil and the mechanism is rather complicated; as the barrel and breechblock move back, the block is rotated by two rollers riding in tracks in the gun body. This rotation unlocks the breech lugs from the barrel and the last part of the recoil movement actuates an accelerator that throws the breechblock to the rear. Feed is from a double-drum magazine that fits saddle-wise across the body and is fed from both sides alternately, thus keeping the weight evenly balanced. The net result was a very sound gun for its purpose; the mass of the barrel tended to absorb a lot of recoil, but the lightweight breech-block and accelerator gear gave quite a high rate of fire. As an aircraft gun it was very successful.

As the war progressed, the MG15 was superseded in aircraft by heavier caliber weapons, and at the same time there was a continual demand from the Army for more machine guns. As a result the MG15 was taken into infantry service in 1944. It was fitted with a bipod, a simple butt stock, and a carrying handle. As a ground gun it had one good feature: that the stock was in line with the action. This meant very little tendency to rise, so the MG15 was a stable gun when firing. However, it was too cumbersome to be a successful infantry weapon. Numbers were used, because they had to be used, but they were never liked, although they were accurate and reliable.

BELOW The MG08/15 with bipod and stock folded.

ABOVE AND BELOW The MG15 with stock extended and bipod deployed. Developed from an aircraft gun, and while reliable and accurate, it was really too bulky to be a successful infantry weapon.

BOTTOM Detail of trigger and bolt.

MG34 general purpose machine gun

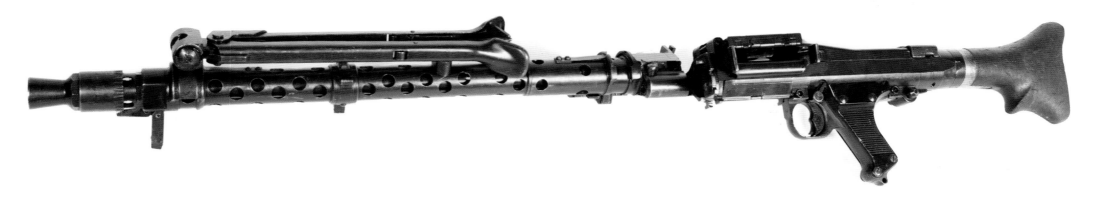

Caliber: 7.92mm	**Rate of fire:** 850rpm
Length: 48in (1.22m)	**Manufacturers:**
Weight: 26lb 11oz (12.1kg)	Mauserwerke AG, Berlin, Germany
Barrel: 24.75in (629mm) long, four grooves, right–hand twist	Steyr-Daimler-Puch AG, Austria
Feed system: Belt or 75-round saddle drum magazine	Waffenwerk Brunn (Brno), Czechoslovakia
System of operation: Recoil, revolving bolt head	**Values:** $15,000–$16,500 (Class III)

In 1930 the Solothurn produced a machine gun known as the MG30, which was offered to the German Army. Although many were bought by Austria and Hungary, and doubtless a number were used during the war, the German Army was less impressed and passed the gun across to Mauserwerke with the request that it be improved. This Mauserwerke did, with great efficiency. The box magazine was dispensed and operators were given the options of belt feed or, by substitution of a different feed unit, the 75-round saddle drum of the MG15. The bolt-locking system was changed so that only the bolt head revolved, locking by interrupted threads, and an additional recoil impulse was given to the barrel by adding a muzzle gas trap. Barrel changing was simplified by hinging the gun body to the rear end of the barrel casing. To change barrels the gun body was swung sideways and the barrel pulled straight out of its bearings. (See illustration on page 206.)

The most far-reaching feature of the MG34 was tactical rather than mechanical: it was the first example of what is known today as the general-purpose machine gun. Fitted with a bipod it functioned as the squad light automatic; on its tripod, which incorporated a sprung cradle to reduce the recoil and vibration and thus make continuous fire less fatiguing for the gunner, it functioned as a medium machine gun; and on a different pattern of light tripod and fitted with the saddle drum magazine, it made a good antiaircraft weapon. It was the first belt-fed weapon to be used as a light machine gun in quantity and it proved that the concept was valid; previously it had always been considered that the feed system of the light machine gun had to be one to which riflemen could contribute in an emergency, and this meant some form of easily filled box magazine. The MG34 showed that provided the supply organization was efficient, belt feed was perfectly acceptable in this role, and incidentally led to the familiar image of German gun crews going about the battlefield festooned with belts of ammunition.

The MG34 only had one real defect: it was not really suited to mass production. The design required a high level of workmanship, and long and extremely precise manufacturing processes, and eventually five factories were doing nothing but turn out MG34s as hard as they could, plus several others manufactured parts. By 1941 this was obviously impractical and a new design was sought, but in spite of this, the MG34 remained in production and use until the war ended.

ABOVE The MG34, the first true general purpose machine gun.

RIGHT Detail of the sight.

VARIANT

MG34s, MG34/41

These are virtually the same weapon, the 34s being the prototype of the 34/41. It was originally intended as a replacement for the MG34, and has various simplifications in order to speed up production. Only a handful were made before the advent of the MG42, which was both a better weapon and easier to produce.

**ABOVE AND BELOW The MG34 in
firing position on its bipod.**

ABOVE AND BELOW The MG34 could be belt or magazine-fed.

CENTER Detail of the 75-round, drum magazine. The magazine was identical to that used on the MG15 and MG42.

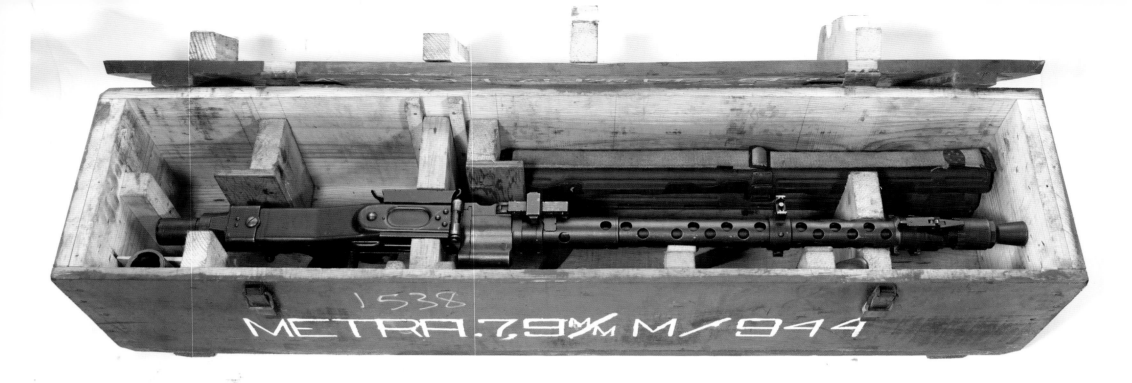

ABOVE The MG34 in its transit case. The markings on the outside of the case are evidence of its period of Portuguese army ownership.

BELOW The ingenious design of the weapon allowed for rapid barrel changes. The weapon was twisted open to allow the barrel to slide out of its sleeve.

BELOW AND RIGHT The MG34 on its antiaircraft mounting. The ammunition drums in their crate could be hung from the center of the tripod to act as ballast.

TOP LEFT AND RIGHT Details of the antiaircraft sighting system.

ABOVE LEFT Detail of drum magazine.

ABOVE RIGHT Close up of the mounting bracket.

MG42 general purpose machine gun

Caliber: 7.92mm

Length: 48in (1.22m)

Weight: 25lb 8oz (11.57kg)

Barrel: 21in (294mm) long, four grooves, right-hand twist

System of operation: Recoil, roller locking

Feed system: Belt or drum as MG34

Rate of fire: 1,200rpm

Manufacturer: Mauserwerke AG, Berlin, Germany

Values: $18,500-$22,500 (Class III)

When the production of MG34 models was obviously insufficient for the German Army's needs, a new design of weapon was begun, one which would be easier to mass produce. An expert in pressing and stamping metal, Dr. Grunow of the Johannes Grossfuss Metall und Lackierwarenfabrik of Dobeln, was involved from the start. As a result the final design was specifically laid out to suit stamping and pressing processes, with welding and riveting used for assembly.

The action of the MG42 was modified to use a non-rotating bolt locking into a barrel extension by two rollers cammed outward. Unless the rollers were out, thereby locking the breech, the firing pin could not pass through the center of the bolt. On recoil the barrel, bolt, and barrel extension locked together until cam tracks in the gun body moved the rollers inward to release the bolt. Movement of the bolt drove a feed arm mounted in the top cover of the gun which, in turn, operated pawls to feed the ammunition belt; the design was most ingenious and fed the belt smoothly and reliably and has been widely copied in other weapons since its original appearance in the MG42.

One of the results of the redesign was to raise the rate of fire to 1,200rpm, much higher than any other contemporary machine gun and a rate that has only rarely since been exceeded. As a result the barrel had to be designed for quick changing: every 250 rounds was the recommended figure. This was done by unlatching the breech end and swinging it out through a long slot in the right-hand side of the barrel casing; a fresh barrel could be fitted in five seconds.

As with the MG34, the MG42 was used on a bipod as a light machine gun or on a tripod as a medium gun, though the high rate of fire made it difficult to control on a bipod. It was extremely reliable, highly resistant to dust and cold conditions and was extremely popular with the Wehrmacht. It was first used in action by the Afrika Korps at Gazala in May 1942, and more than 750,000 MG42s were made before the war ended. At the cessa-

tion of hostilities many countries seized stocks of the guns, among them France and Yugoslavia. When the German Bundeswehr was reconstituted and required a machine gun, it simply put the MG42 back into production in 7.62mm NATO caliber as the MG1.

ABOVE The MG42 on its "Lafayette" mount, probably the best machine gun of the war.

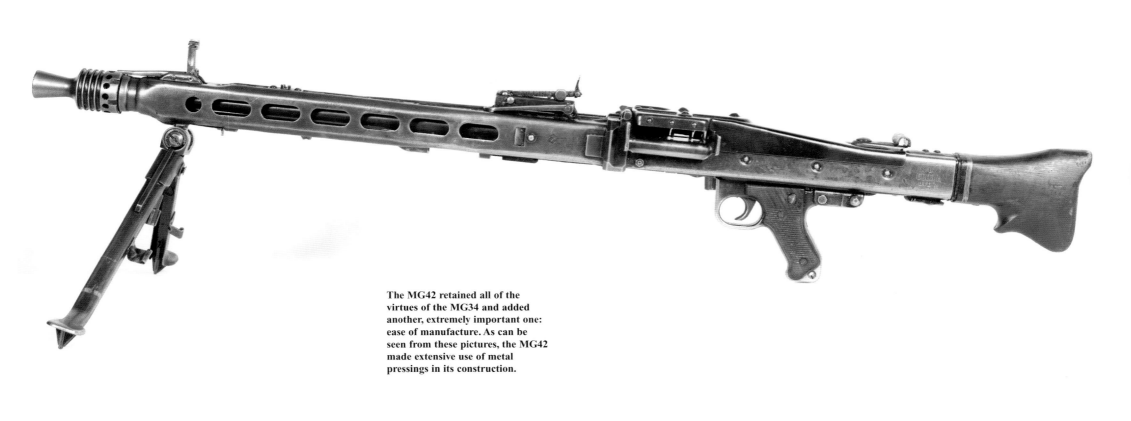

The MG42 retained all of the virtues of the MG34 and added another, extremely important one: ease of manufacture. As can be seen from these pictures, the MG42 made extensive use of metal pressings in its construction.

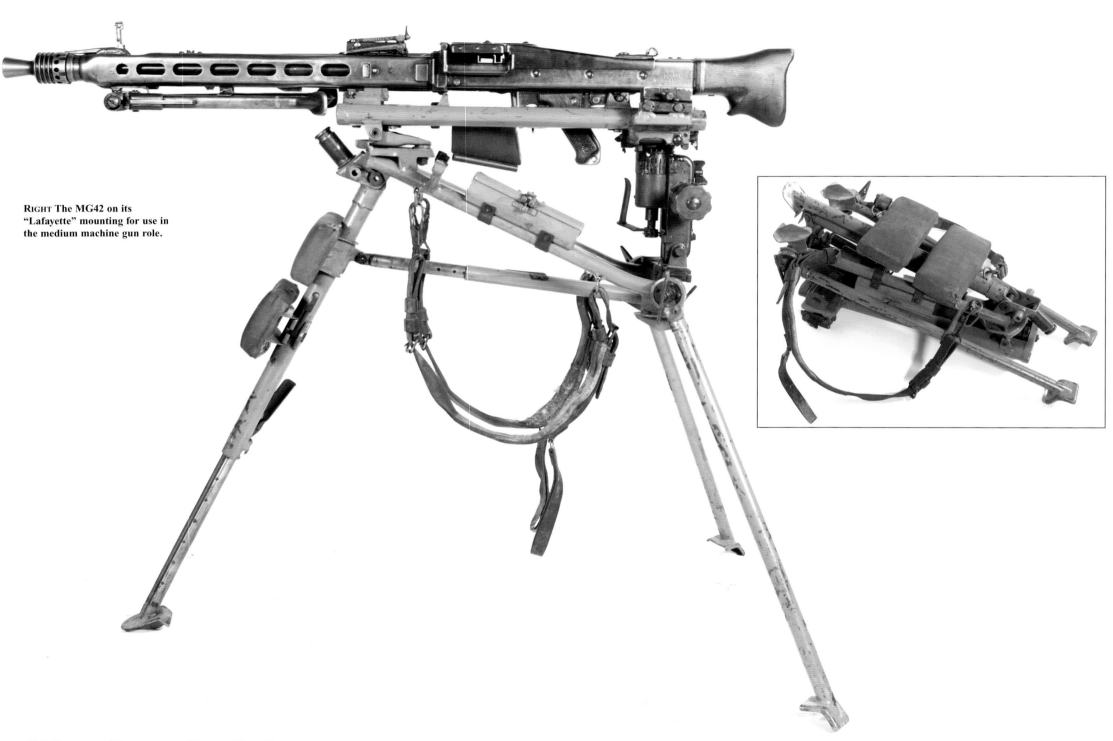

RIGHT The MG42 on its "Lafayette" mounting for use in the medium machine gun role.

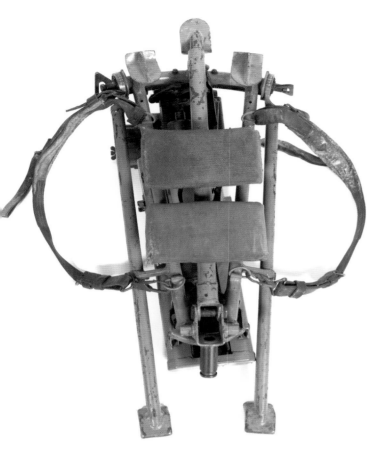

FAR LEFT AND LEFT The mounting was man-portable over short distances when collapsed. The rectangular pads are to protect the carrier's back.

BELOW LEFT AND BELOW, FAR LEFT Detail of attachment of the MG42 to the "Lafayette" mount.

BELOW Detail of the traverse and elevation gear. Note the metal plate bearing the data tables for the gun.

LEFT AND BELOW The MG42 could be belt or magazine fed. Detail of the drum magazine and body of the gun. The butt could be easily removed to reduce the length of the weapon in transit.

ABOVE AND OPPOSITE PAGE, BELOW RIGHT The MG42 could be belt or magazine-fed.

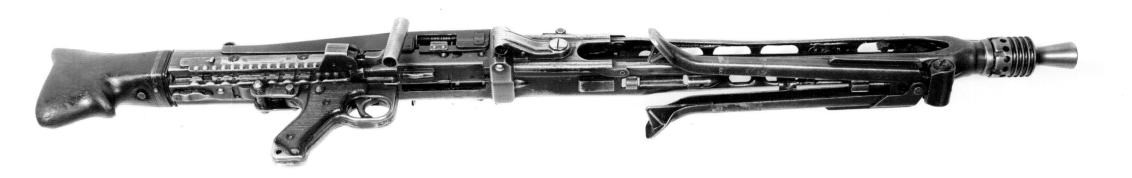

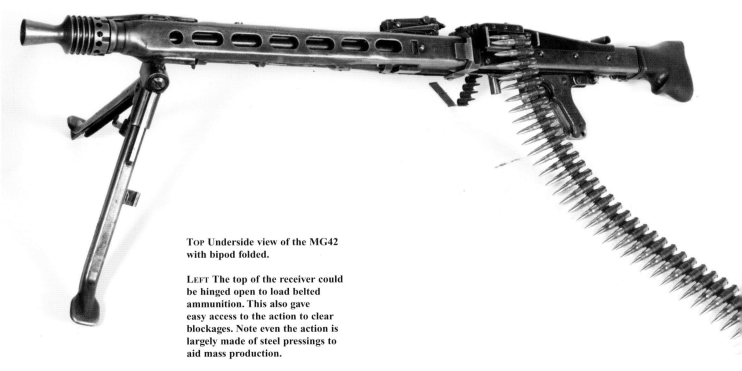

Top Underside view of the MG42 with bipod folded.

Left The top of the receiver could be hinged open to load belted ammunition. This also gave easy access to the action to clear blockages. Note even the action is largely made of steel pressings to aid mass production.

Vickers heavy machine guns

A late production Vickers .303, with the uncorrugated cooling jacket and late model flash hider on the muzzle. Note the ammunition box and cooling water can.

Vickers .303 Mk. I

Caliber: .303
Length: 45.5in (1.16m)
Weight: 40lb (18.14kg)
Barrel: 28.5in (724mm) long, four grooves, right-hand twist
Feed system: 250-round belt
System of operation: Recoil, Maxim toggle lock

Rate of fire: 450rpm
Manufacturer:
Vickers, Son & Maxim, Crayford, Kent, England
Royal Ordnance Factories, England
Values: $17,000–$20,000 (Class III)

The British Army originally adopted the Maxim as its standard medium machine gun, and this was produced by the Maxim Gun Company, the chairman of which was Albert Vickers. Later the company became Vickers, Son & Maxim, and it was in that company's Crayford factory that the Maxim design was reworked to produce the Vickers Gun. The principal change was to invert the Maxim lock mechanism so that the toggle broke upward. The gun was also lightened and various small modifications incorporated, making production a little easier. The Mk. I gun was introduced into service on November 26, 1912, and it was eventually followed by a further ten marks, though all of these were for either aircraft or tank use. The Mk. I remained the standard infantry gun until it was declared obsolete on April 24, 1968, having outlived all the others by a considerable margin.

The mechanism of the Vickers reflects the era in which it was designed; it was a complicated engineering solution to a difficult problem, that of feeding a rimmed cartridge from a fabric belt. Consequently it was built the hard way, with expensively machined and precisely fitted components made of critical materials. In spite of this, or possibly because of it, the Vickers Gun became synonymous with reliability. Failure in action was almost unheard of; it could and did jam sometimes, and there are some 25 different types of stoppage noted in the drill book as being possible, together with involved descriptions of the symptoms; if the gun stopped with the crank handle in such-and-such a position, then so-and-so was at fault, all of which demanded a good memory and a cool head in an emergency. But such stoppages were brief and did not affect the long-term reliability. During both world wars, though more so in the first due to the tactics, Vickers guns fired for phenomenal lengths of time, the most often-quoted case being that of ten guns on the Somme in 1916 which between them fired a million rounds in twelve hours, using up one hundred barrels and untold quantities of water in the process. One gun actually averaged 10,000 rounds an hour for twelve hours. There were no failures—enough said!

Right-side view of a late production Vickers .303. Note the heavy cast-steel construction of the tripod.

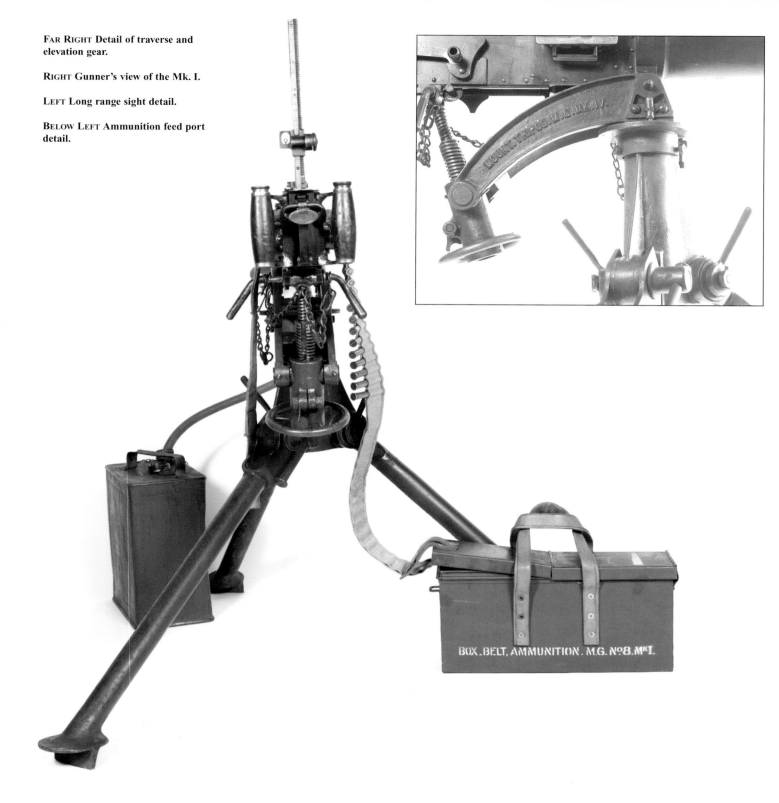

FAR RIGHT Detail of traverse and elevation gear.

RIGHT Gunner's view of the Mk. I.

LEFT Long range sight detail.

BELOW LEFT Ammunition feed port detail.

BOX. BELT. AMMUNITION. M.G. N°8. Mᴷ I.

ABOVE Ammunition feed mechanism.

RIGHT Mark I in its transit case.

BELOW, LEFT TO RIGHT
Three muzzle flash hiders: early production; mid-production; late production.

BELOW Side view of a early production Vickers .303, with the corrugated cooling jacket and mid-production flash hider on the muzzle. Note the ammunition box and cooling water can. The two metal posts with pronged feet are range markers for presighted fire zones.

BOX. BELT. AMMUNITION, No.8. MkI.

Vickers .50 Mk. I

Caliber: .50

Length: 54in (1.37m)

Weight: 52lb (23.6kg)

Barrel: 31.1in (790mm) long, seven grooves, left-hand twist

Feed system: 100-round metal link belt

System of operation: Recoil, Maxim toggle lock

Rate of fire: Cyclic, 450 or 675rpm

Manufacturers:
Vickers Ltd, Crayford, Kent, England
Royal Ordnance Factories, England

Values: $17,000-$20,000 (Class III)

The Gun, Vickers, .5in, Mk. I was simply a scaled up version of the famous Vickers .303in Mk. I. The design differed only in the provision of a flash hider and the fitting of a pawl mechanism that made it possible to select one of two rates of fire. It was issued in limited numbers as a ground gun in 1932 for trials, but did not enter general service in this role. Also produced in 1932 was the Mk. II. This was adapted to be used as a tank gun and was fitted with a pistol-grip trigger and selective fire control. It saw service in several British armored vehicles, especially in the early war years, such as the Matilda Mk. I and the Light Tank Mk. VI.

The Mk. III arrived in 1934. Produced for the Royal Navy as an air-defense weapon, it was fitted with a wire toggle cocking mechanism. A bronze guide block to support the wire was attached to the rear of the receiver. This version was available in left and right-hand feed versions to allow it to fit multiple mountings. The final model was the Mk. IV. This was similar to the Mk. I, but was fitted with a mounting plate to allow it to be substituted for the .303 in some vehicles.

LEFT Top view of of a Mk. III Vickers .50 produced as an air defense weapon for the Royal Navy.

BELOW Side view of the RN Mk. III. Note the wire toggle cocking mechanism.

ABOVE Detail of top of weapon showing serial number.

Vickers-Berthier light machine gun

BOTTOM RIGHT Note the magazine guard ahead of the rear sight.

LEFT Oblique view of gun body showing rear sight, magazine port and guard, and pistol grip.

BOTTOM LEFT Maker's marks identifying this weapon as Vickers-Berthier No. 5354.

FAR LEFT Top view of Vickers-Berthier Mk. II.

Caliber: .303

Length: 46.5in (1.18m)

Weight: 22lb (9.98kg)

Barrel: 23.5in (597mm) long, five grooves, right-hand twist

Feed system: 30-round detachable box magazine

System of operation: Gas, tipping bolt

Rate of fire: Cyclic, 600rpm

Manufacturer: Royal Ordnance Factory, Ishapore, India

Values: $30,000–$35,000 (Class III)

The Vickers-Berthier series of light machine guns evolved from the design of a Frenchman, Adolphe Berthier, who patented the essential details as early as 1909. The weapon was not adopted in any numbers by any of the combatants in World War I, but a prototype gun was completed in the early 1920s, and in 1925 the manufacturing rights were purchased by Vickers of England. The early models were purchased in small numbers by several countries, and in 1933, after a series of British Army trials, the Indian Government adopted it as its standard light machine gun. As a result of these same trials the British Army opted for the Bren (see page 156) Gun as its standard light machine gun. As a result, a production line was established for the Berthier at Ishapore in India, and the Indian Army was to remain the sole large-scale user of the gun.

Visually and mechanically there is very little difference between the Berthier and the Bren, but a closer examination shows small differences in contour of the barrel, barrel handle, pistol grip, and other components. The action is very similar, both weapons using a tilting bolt driven by a gas piston and feeding from a curved magazine mounted above the gun.

The VB was in service with Indian Army divisions throughout the war, although lost weapons were often replaced with the more readily available Bren. Because of the similarity between the two weapons there seems to have been little problem in retraining the troops. The Vickers Berthier is one of the least known machine guns of World War II, partly because it was overshadowed by the far more numerous Bren, and partly because actions that involved the Vickers Berthier were often attributed to the Bren in error. There was one derivative of the Berthier that certainly did attract its fare share of publicity, the Vickers G.O. or K gun (see page 222).

BELOW AND BOTTOM Side views of Vickers Berthier, the standard squad machine gun in the Indian Army. The Vickers Berthier bears a strong resemblance to the Bren Gun and was often misidentified as such in reports.

DETAIL Butt showing shoulder rest extended.

Vickers K light machine gun

Caliber: .303
Length: 40in (1.02m)
Weight: 21lb (9.52kg)
Barrel: 20in (508mm) long, five grooves, right–hand twist
Feed system: 100–round drum magazine

System of operation: Gas, tipping bolt
Rate of fire: Cyclic, 1,050rpm
Manufacturer: Vickers, Crayford, Kent, England
Values: n/a

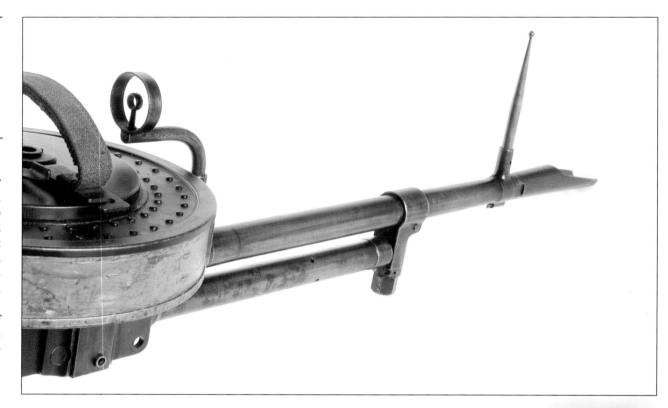

The Vickers K or GO was a derivative of the Vickers-Berthier machine gun (see page 220), developed by a French designer, Adolphe Berthier, in 1909. The Vickers-Berthier went on to become the standard light machine gun of the Indian Army and performed effectively throughout World War II. In Britain it lost out to the Bren Gun as the standard light machine gun and was not used in this role in the British Army. It was, however, produced in large numbers in modified form for the RAF, with whom it was known as the Vickers K or GO, for gas-operated.

The new model was designed to be mounted on the Scarff ring of open cockpit aircraft for use by the observer/gunner. It mounted a large, 100-round drum magazine above the receiver and had twin spade grips instead of the normal stock. Unfortunately the new weapon was introduced at time when the RAF were switching to the type of high speed, enclosed cockpit, monoplane aircraft for which the Vickers was simply not suitable. Although some did soldier on in some of Britain's more anachronistic aircraft such as the Fairy Swordfish, the majority were put in to store or allocated for airfield defense in North Africa.

It was here that the Vickers K finally came into it's own—not with the RAF, but the irregular forces that operated behind enemy lines in the desert, such as the Long Range Desert Group and the Special Air Service. Indeed twin K guns came to be a virtually standard weapons fit on the Jeeps of the SAS.

Right and Center Right Maker's marks.

Above Right Note how the sights are raised clear of the drum magazine.

Far Right Top view of the Vickers K gun with magazine removed.

Opposite Page Left and right-hand side views of the Vickers K gun, with magazine attached.

MORTARS

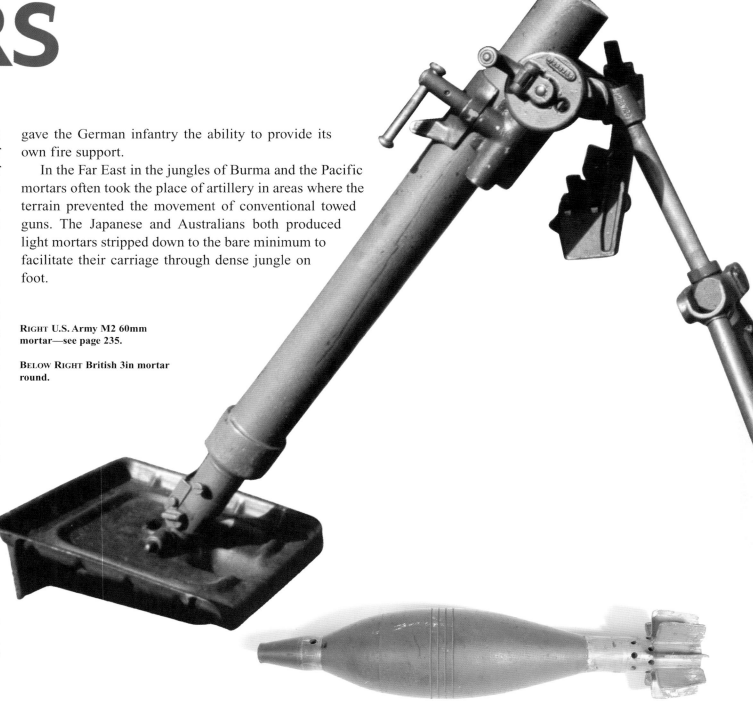

Mortars had been tried and tested in World War I and so were in the inventories of the armies of World War II A cost-effective and simple way of providing fire support for infantry, in World War II the majority of mortars were between 2in and 3in caliber. They were based on the original Stokes design as modified by Brandt—and most mortars of this caliber are virtually indistinguishable from each other.

Of the combatants only Russia and, to a lesser degree, Germany made widespread use of larger caliber mortars. The double benefits of easy production and ease of use suited the Russians. The Russians also used mortars to provided organic heavy-fire support for infantry units, a role that in other armies was generally fulfilled by artillery. The Russians made great use of artillery—indeed, some of the heaviest artillery barrages of the war took place on the Eastern Front—but their organization did not allow for support in the way the United States and her allies used artillery. Russia's vast artillery resources were generally employed en masse for maximum shock effect and were not available for smaller-scale fire missions.

The Germans did not, initially, make use of large-caliber mortars, but after facing the Russian 120mm mortars on the Eastern Front, they soon produced a virtual carbon copy of the Soviet design. In the difficult conditions of the Russian steppes, fighting a defensive war, the ability to bring down a heavy barrage to break up an attack at short notice was vital, especially in the "cauldron battles" in which the Wehrmacht found itself embroiled toward the end of the war. When retreating, under air attack and closely pressed by opposing forces, artillery could not always be counted on, and the mortars

gave the German infantry the ability to provide its own fire support.

In the Far East in the jungles of Burma and the Pacific mortars often took the place of artillery in areas where the terrain prevented the movement of conventional towed guns. The Japanese and Australians both produced light mortars stripped down to the bare minimum to facilitate their carriage through dense jungle on foot.

RIGHT U.S. Army M2 60mm mortar—see page 235.

BELOW RIGHT British 3in mortar round.

ABOVE Baseplate from a U.S. Army
M2 60mm mortar—see page 235.

RIGHT British tank 2in mortar
used for launching smoke.

British mortars

2in mortar

Caliber: 2in	**Elevation:** 45–90 degrees
Barrel: 21in (533mm), smooth-bore	**Traverse:** By hand
Weight: 19lb (8.62kg) with large baseplate; 10.5lb (4.76kg) with small baseplate	**Projectiles:** HE 2lb (910gm); Smoke 2lb (910gm); Illuminating 1lb 5oz (595gm)
Firing mechanism: Trip	**Max range:** 1,500ft (457m)
	Rate of fire: 8rpm

In common with most other armies, the early 1930s the British Army had investigated the use of hand and rifle grenades to provide close fire support. It soon became apparent that grenades alone would not suffice, and would need to be supplemented with a weapon of greater range and destructive power. The most likely candidate appeared to be a small mortar, and a variety of designs was acquired for trial. The best of these was the Spanish 5cm (1.97in) model made by Esperanza & Cie of Vizcaya. This weapon formed the basis for further development by the Armament Research Department of what was to become the 2in mortar. This completed its trials in 1938 and by the time war broke out in 1939 large numbers were already in service.

As originally issued the 2in mortar had a large baseplate, a trip-firing mechanism, and a collimating sight with elevating and cross-level bubbles. However, operational experience and the need to speed up production soon prompted the introduction of a greatly simplified design. The baseplate was reduced to a small curved plate and the sight was deleted, aiming being done by a white line painted on the barrel to give direction and the firer's experience in estimating the elevation.

The projectile was a simple high-explosive bomb with an impact fuse in the nose and a die-cast four-finned tail carrying a single primary cartridge. A smoke bomb was also provided, the smoke-producing chemical being ignited through a delay unit by the propellant flash. Later more types of ammunition were provided including a parachute illuminating bomb, white phosphorous smoke bombs, and a variety of colored smoke signals.

The 2in mortar formed part of the standard equipment of every infantry platoon throughout the war and was in constant use. In addition it was issued to antitank gun detachments to provide them with a way of illuminating their targets at night.

VARIANTS

There were many versions of 2in mortar with minor differences in their attachment points for vehicle transport. There were, however three main variations:

Marks II*, II** and VII Standard pattern with large baseplate.

Marks II***, VII* Standard pattern with small baseplate.

Mark VIII 14in barrel and small baseplate for Airborne troops. The short barrel restricted range to 1,050ft.

ABOVE AND BELOW The 2in mortar, a common sight in the British Army during the war. It was a simple weapon to begin with; later versions also did away with the sight when it was found a white line painted on the barrel was sufficient for aiming purposes. Elevation was by holding the tube at the required angle judged by eye and experience. The 2in mortar, therefore, did not have a bipod. Note also the abbreviated base-plate.

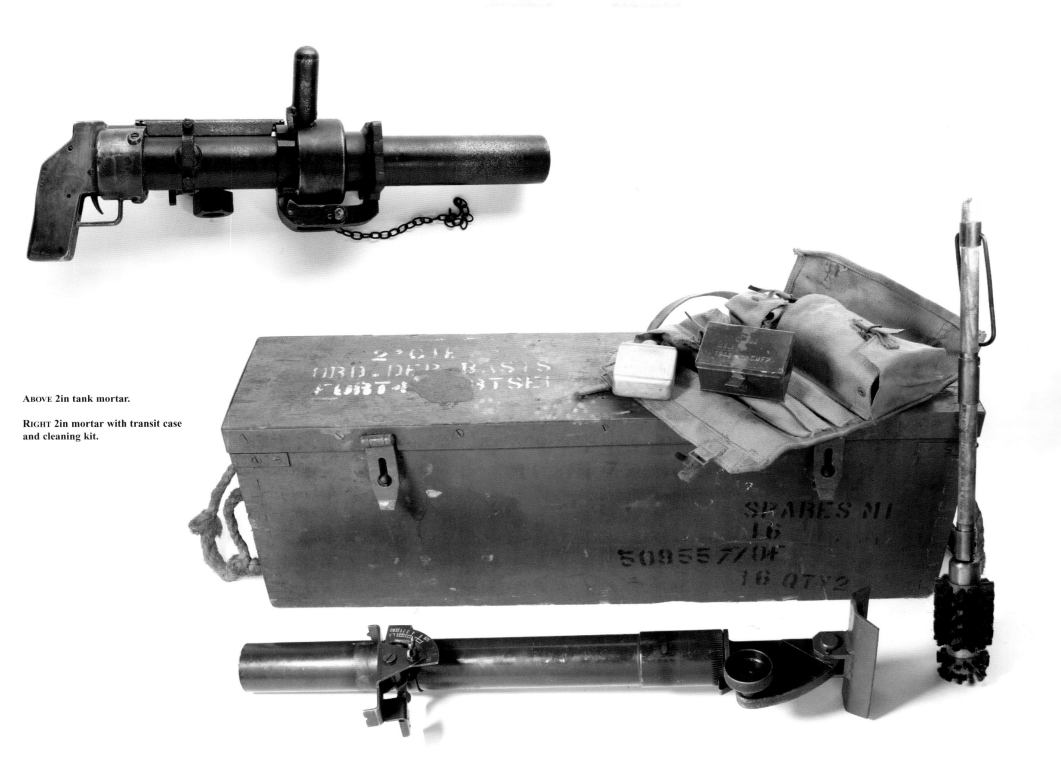

ABOVE 2in tank mortar.

RIGHT 2in mortar with transit case and cleaning kit.

3in mortar

Caliber: 3in	**Elevation:** 45–80 degrees
Barrel: 51in (1.3m), smoothbore	**Traverse:** 5.5 degrees right or left
Weight: 126lb (57.2kg)— barrel 44lb (19.96kg), bipod 45lb (20.14kg), baseplate: 37lb (16.78kg)	**Projectiles:** HE 10lb (4.54kg); smoke 10lb (4.54kg)
	Max range: Mk. I—4,800ft (1,463m); Mk. II—8,400ft (2,560m)
Firing mechanism: Drop, fixed striker	**Rate of fire:** 10rpm

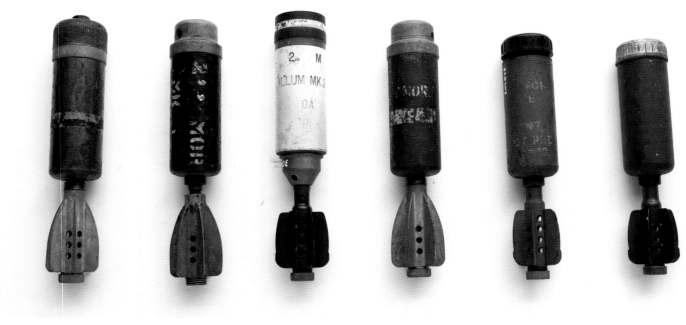

BELOW A variety of 3in mortar rounds and transit cases—bottom left, two-round man-portable sling; bottom right, eight-projectile box.

Developed from the World War I Stokes mortar, the British 3in was much the same as its foreign contemporaries. The breech end of the mortar rested on a baseplate and the muzzle end was supported by a bipod with a screw elevating and traversing gear. To reduce the effect of firing shock on the mounting, the barrel was free to slide in the yoke of the bipod and was controlled by two tension springs clipped to a barrel band. It fired fin-stabilized bombs by means of a charge consisting of a primary cartridge in the tail unit and four secondary cartridges, celluloid tubes containing smokeless powder, located between the tail fins and retained by a wire spring As originally developed the mortar had a maximum range of 4,800ft (1,463m) but, inevitably, the army soon asked for more range. By adopting a slightly heavier barrel of stronger steel and a stronger baseplate it was found possible to adopt a six-charge secondary propelling charge which sent the bomb to 8,400ft (2,560m), and this Mk. II model became standard.

VARIANTS

As with the 2in mortar, there were a number of subtypes of the 3in that were largely concerned with minor variations in mounting points for various methods of transportation.

The Australians produced a short-barreled model to reduce weight and improve portability in the jungle. With extreme range of less importance in dense jungle, it was provided with a barrel only 30in (762mm) long. This led to some difficulty in obtaining accuracy, and eventually special fast-burning cartridges had to be produced to suit this short mortar. It was only made in small numbers and was never adopted outside the Australian Army.

RIGHT The 3in mortar was a common sight in the British army during the war.

FAR RIGHT The baseplate with its ball and socket joint.

BELOW To offset the effects of recoil the barrel was free to slide through the bipod clamp. The spring dampened the recoil.

LEFT AND BELOW LEFT Details of the British 3in mortar sight.

BELOW British 3in mortar bipod detail.

BOTTOM British 3in mortar traverse and elevation gear detail.

German mortars

Granatwerfer (mortar) 34

Caliber: 81.4mm	**Firing mechanism:** Drop
Barrel: 45in (1.14m), smooth-bore	**Elevation:** 40-90 degrees
Weight: 124lb 5oz (56.38kg)— barrel 40lb 5oz (18.28kg), bipod 40lb (18.14kg), baseplate: 44lb (19.96kg)	**Traverse:** 9 to 15 degrees, varying with elevation
	Projectiles: HE 7lb 8oz (3.4kg)
	Max range: 7,875ft (2,400m)
	Rate of fire: 8rpm

The *8cm Schwere Granatwerfer 34* (GrW34) was a conventionally designed mortar, based on the Stokes pattern but with some modifications. It was standard equipment in all rifle companies, two mortars being held in the *Granatwerfergruppe* (mortar unit). On the march the mortar was usually carried in a light horse-drawn cart, one member of the detachment being described in the establishment as the *Pferdführer* (horse leader). In action the three basic sections were carried by the members of the detachment, together with 21 rounds of ammunition.

The GrW34 was provided with a range of ammunition which included two unusal bombs, the *Wurfgranaten* 38 and 39. These were "bouncing bombs" which were intended to produce an air-burst effect at the target. The normal method of obtaining air bursts is, to provide the bombs with a time fuse, but this means calculation of the necessary time of flight and the setting of each fuse before firing, a time-consuming and impractical process in infantry mortar operations.

The *Wurfgranaten* 38 and 39 resembled a normal bomb in appearance, but instead of the bomb body being a solid casting, the head was separate and pinned to the rest of the body. The body proper terminated in a flat head containing a channel filled with gunpowder, and the space within the head carried a charge of smokeless powder. An impact fuse was fitted in the nose. When the bomb landed at the target, this impact fuse ignited the smokeless powder, which exploded. The explosion sheared the pins holding the body and head together and blew the body back up into the air; at the same time the flash of the explosion ignited the channel of gunpowder. This filling burned through rapidly and detonated the body of the bomb when it was some 15 to 20ft (4.5–6m) above the ground, showering the area with fragments. The rebound action, of course, depended upon the nature of the ground at the target; if it were soft, the explosion might well blow the nose into the ground instead of sending the body into the air, but on any firm surface it was quite effective. A copy was later developed in Britain for the 3in mortar, but its erratic behavior on soft ground led to the idea being dropped.

VARIANTS

8cm Kurz GrW42 "Stummelwerfer"

This was a shortened, lightweight version; it used the same ammunition but had the barrel length reduced to 29.4in (747mm), and had the baseplate and bipod lightened and simplified. The total weight was reduced to 62lb (28.12kg) and the maximum range dropped to 3,600ft (1,097m). Originally developed for airborne troops, it was later taken into use by all infantry and largely replaced the standard model. Easier handling compensated for loss of range.

Granatwerfer (mortar) 36

Caliber: 50mm	**Traverse:** 17 degrees right or left
Barrel: 19.3in (490mm), smoothbore	**Projectiles:** HE 1lb 15.5oz (893gm)
Weight: 30lb 9oz (14kg)	**Max range:** 1,640ft (500m)
Firing mechanism: Trip	**Rate of fire:** 40rpm
Elevation: 42–90 degrees	

The 5cm mortar was part of the equipment of every German rifle platoon at the outbreak of war; it was handled by a three-man squad who carried the mortar and 45 rounds of ammunition between them. The GrW36 was typical of the equipment of the prewar Wehrmacht; a well-designed weapon, well-made of the best materials, and immaculately finished. The barrel was attached to the baseplate by a locking pin and could be leveled independently of the baseplate's orientation. A quick-release gear allowed elevation to be set rapidly and even a cleaning rod formed part of the basic equipment, clipped to the baseplate. For long-distance carriage the locking pin was removed and the elevating gear disconnected, so that the barrel and elevating screw became one load and the baseplate and leveling base a second. For short moves in action the whole assembly could be lifted and carried by a handle provided on the barrel.

The first issues were provided with a collimating sight, but as with the British 2in, this was dispensed with in due course, aiming being a matter of the firer's experience. Mortars issued after mid-1938 were never provided with sights.

The 5cm mortar appears to have declined in importance in the German Army much as it did with the Soviets, and it became less used as the war continued, being largely superseded by the GrW34.

It is interesting to note that a trial of a captured 5cm mortar was conducted in Britain in 1941, and the report observed that it was, "well constructed and easy to operate, but the degree of accuracy is unnecessarily high."

Granatwerfer (mortar) 42

Caliber: 120mm	**Firing mechanism:** Selective drop or trip
Barrel: 73.5in (1.87m), smoothbore	**Elevation:** 45–84 degrees
Weight: 628lb (284.9kg)— barrel 231lb (104.8kg), bipod 154lb (69.9kg), baseplate 243lb (110.2kg)	**Traverse:** 8 to 16 degrees, varying with elevation
	Projectiles: HE 34lb 11oz (15.8kg)
	Max range: 19,845ft (6,049m)
	Rate of fire: 15rpm

In the early days of their advance against Russia in 1941, the German Army captured vast quantities of artillery material, much of which was put to use against its former owners. Among this booty were large numbers of the 12cm Soviet Mortar Model 1938; in Soviet hands this was an artillery weapon, but the German Army issued it as an infantry mortar under the nomenclature GrW378(r). It was successful and well-liked by its new operators, and as a result it was decided to manufacture a German copy, which was issued late in 1942 as the GrW42. There were some small differences in the German design, both to improve the weapon and to facilitate manufacture by German methods. Thus the maximum elevation of the Russian weapon was only 80 degrees and the traverse 8–14 degrees; these were increased. The baseplate, bipod, and transporter were made more robust and thus somewhat heavier; a total increase in weight of about 100lb (45.36kg) in the transit mode.

The design of the mortar was quite conventional. A smoothbore barrel was locked into a circular baseplate and supported by a bipod with a two-spring shock absorber unit connecting the barrel and bipod together. For movement, a transporter was provided; this was a framework of steel tubing carrying two short axles on which were mounted pressed-steel wheels (perforated in the German model, plain in the Russian) with pneumatic tires. A towing eye at the front end allowed it to be pulled by any con- venient vehicle. At the front end of the framework was a circular clamp to hold the mortar barrel, and the rear end was formed into a U-shape which fitted into two brackets on the baseplate of the mortar. To bring the mortar out of action, all that was necessary was to lift the bipod out of the ground, bring the mortar barrel vertical and swing the bipod around it so that it lay, folded, at the rear of the barrel, and, then push the transporter into position with its frame vertical so that the U-brackets locked into the baseplate. The barrel was then pushed forward until it lay in the barrel clamp, where it was secured, and the bipod feet were strapped to a bracket on the frame. By pulling the towing eye downward, leverage was applied which would lift the baseplate from the ground and the unit was ready to travel. Bringing the mortar into action was simply the reverse process.

Italian mortars

Model 35

Caliber: 81.1mm	Elevation: 45–85 degrees
Barrel: 45.3in (1.15m), smoothbore	Traverse: 5 degrees right and left
Weight: 130lb 13oz (59.34kg)— barrel 47lb (21.32kg); bipod 39lb 11oz (18kg); baseplate: 44lb 2oz(20kg)	Projectiles: HE (light) 7.2lb (3.27kg), HE (heavy) 15.13lb (6.86)
	Max range: light—13,290ft (4,050m), heavy—4,920ft (1,500m)
Firing mechanism: Drop	Rate of fire: 8rpm

The Italian 81mm Model 1935 is virtually the same weapon as the U.S. Army's 81mm M1 (see page 238), because both were derived from the same Brandt design. The U.S. model differed slightly from the original, because of changes for manufacturing convenience, but the Italian weapon was substantially Brandt's design. As such, the data above exhibits some differences from the U.S. model: the American barrel was lighter and elevated from 40 degrees; the U.S. bipod and baseplate were heavier; but the Italian model outranged the U.S. by some 1,800ft (550m) with its light bomb, while the American outranged the Italian by 2,700ft (823m) with its heavy bomb. The bombs are virtually the same, differences in weight being accounted for by different grades of metal and types of explosive in use by the different countries, and the range difference stems from different composition of the propelling charges and probably, in the case of the light bomb, indicates a somewhat lower factor of safety in the Italian design.

Brixia 35

Caliber: 45mm	Elevation: 45–85 degrees
Barrel: 10.2in (259mm), smoothbore	Traverse: None
Weight: 34lb (15.42kg)	Projectiles: HE 1lb 5oz (595gm)
	Max range: 1,755ft (535m)
Firing mechanism: Trip	Rate of fire: 25rpm

Italy produced some peculiar weapons during the war, and among them was this mortar, probably the most complicated machine

ever devised for throwing one pound of explosive less than 600 yards. To start with the weapon is a breech-loader; it consisted of two concentric tubes, the inner one being the barrel and the outer forming the breech cover, both tubes having a slot in their sides through which, when they were aligned, a bomb could be placed into the barrel. A magazine of propelling cartridges was also attached to the breech assembly, and operation was done by a large "actuating lever," which lay alongside the barrel. The operator pulled this to the rear, which slid the breech cover rearward and aligned the two loading ports. The second member of the team dropped a bomb through the port into the breech end of the barrel, whereupon the operator pushed the lever forward, closing the breech and loading a cartridge into a small-firing chamber. He then fired by squeezing a trigger with his other hand.

In order to have room for all this mechanical performance, it was necessary to have the mortar suspended on a tripod, leaving room beneath for the breech mechanism and firing trigger and for the movement of the breech cover. Elevation was achieved by a hand wheel operating a toothed arc attached to the barrel, and the sights were simply a barleycorn front and aperture rear similar to those of a rifle. To traverse, the operator simply moved the whole weapon.

To add to the complication and the weight a padded pack board was provided, to which the weapon could be attached and then folded up so that it could be carried on a man's back, the padded section easing the burden on his spine. It could be unfolded, still attached to the carrier, whereupon the firer sat on the padded section and operated the mortar rather like a man on a rowing machine. As well as altering the range by changing the mortar's elevation, a gas port was also used; by opening or closing this, gas could be vented and the propelling force altered. With the port fully open the maximum range was reduced to 1,050ft (320m).

The projectile was a streamlined finned bomb with a filling of 21oz (595gm) of a TNT-dinitronaphthalene mixture, a winding of steel wire to increase fragments, and a wind vane-armed fuse that is probably the most complicated design ever seen on a mortar projectile.

All in all the Brixia 35 was one of the less successful mortars. It rarely figures in wartime reports and it is believed that, except for the early part of the Libyan campaign, it was rarely used.

Japanese mortars

Type 89

Caliber: 50mm	Traverse: Nil
Barrel: 10in (254mm), rifled, eight grooves, right–hand twist	Projectile: Grenade, 1lb 7oz (652gm); HE shell 1lb 12oz (794gm)
Weight: 10lb 1oz (73kg)	Max range: 2,100ft (640m)
Firing mechanism: Trip	Rate of fire: 25rpm
Elevation: 45 degrees	

The Mortar Type 89 was more properly known as a "Grenade Discharger," and was known to the Allies as the "Knee Mortar" which led to considerable misfortune. The weapon was extremely simple but ingenious, and was an inseparable part of every Japanese platoon, being much preferred to the other available designs of 50mm mortar. Range control was by screwing the support rod up into the barrel. This rod carried the firing pin inside, so that when the bomb or grenade was loaded into the muzzle it only dropped as far as the screwed-in rod allowed, being fired from that point. Thus there was a variable chamber space for the propelling gas to expand in; the greater the space to be filled, the less pressure was available to drive the projectile.

The support rod terminated in a very small curved spade, and it was this that led to trouble among Allied troops. During the early part of the war against Japan, the British 2in mortar had a large baseplate, and the small spade of the Model 89 was unusual. It was the habit of the Japanese troops to carry the mortar strapped to the leg of the mortar-man, and from this it appears to have been called the "Leg Mortar." An unfortunate translation by an Allied intelligence unit turned this into "Knee Mortar," and the belief arose that the approved method of operation was to kneel on one knee, place the curved spade on the other thigh, and thus fire the mortar; there appeared to be no other justification for the small spade, and it had just the right curvature. Unfortunately a number of Allied soldiers tried this and suffered broken thighs as a result.

The projectiles were either a shell designed for the weapon or the standard Type 91 hand grenade. It will be noted from the data given above that the weapon was also unusual in being rifled; the shell was provided with a copper driving band surrounding a propellant container that was perforated at the rear to allow gas to escape for propulsion, and was also perforated radially, beneath the driving band. When dropped into the muzzle the band was of small enough diameter not to engage the rifling, but when the firing pin was released, it struck a percussion cap in the base of the shell which ignited the propelling charge. This blew gas through the radial holes and expanded the driving band into the rifling. At the same time the gas escaping from the rear holes filled the chamber area and expelled the bomb. The hand grenade had no driving band. A small propellant container with percussion cap was screwed on to the base of the grenade to convert it for this role. Because of the lack of efficient sealing, the maximum range when firing the grenade was much less than that obtained when firing the shell.

Type 94

Caliber: 90mm	Firing mechanism: Drop
Barrel: 47.8in (1.21m), smoothbore	Elevation: 45–70 degrees
	Traverse: 10 degrees
Weight: 340lb (154.22kg)— barrel 74lb 8oz (33.8kg), baseplate 88lb 8oz (40.1kg), bipod 73lb (33.1kg), recoil system 104lb (47.2kg)	Projectile: HE 11lb 8oz (5.22kg)
	Max range: 12,150ft (3,700m)
	Rate of fire: 15rpm

The Type 94 was a heavy and complex weapon, a surprising piece of equipment to find in the Japanese Army where simplicity and lightness were the usual keynotes. But because of its massiveness, and particularly to its very effective recoil system, it was an outstandingly successful and effective weapon. However, it was relatively uncommon, and there do not appear to have been very large numbers manufactured.

The general design of the weapon was conventional, except for the inclusion of two hydro-pneumatic recoil cylinders. These were attached to a U-shaped yoke that rested on the baseplate. The lower end of the barrel was attached to a cross-piece that in turn was attached to the lower end of the recoil cylinders. The piston rods of the recoil system were attached to the barrel band and also to two spring shock-absorbers at the top of the bipod.

On firing, the barrel recoiled inside the barrel band, forcing the cross-piece down and thus pulling on the recoil cylinders. The cylinders moved rearward relative to the piston rods, displacing liquid and compressing air

which, after absorbing the recoil thrust, returned the barrel to the firing position. The total length of the recoil stroke was 5.75in (146mm). Although on the face of it this is an unnecessary complication to add to a mortar, it has the advantage of reducing the blow on the baseplate, which meant the plate was not driven so deeply into the ground when firing and was thus easier to remove.

In addition to the customary high explosive bomb, this weapon fired an unusual incendiary bomb containing white phosphorus, carbon disulphide and about 40 pellets impregnated with the incendiary composition. A small explosive charge in the nose served to burst the shell and scatter the contents. This projectile appears to have rarely been used during the war, and was apparently developed for use in China in the 1930s where its effect on Chinese villages would have been marked.

Type 98

Caliber: 50mm	Firing mechanism: Friction primer
Barrel: 25.6in (650mm), smoothbore	Elevation: 40 degrees, fixed
	Traverse: 10 degrees right or left
Weight: 49lb 5oz (22.36kg)— barrel 16lb 5oz (7.4kg), baseplate 33lb (15kg)	Projectile: HE 14lb 1.6oz (6.4kg)
	Max range: 1,200ft (366m)
	Rate of fire: 5rpm (estimate)

The Type 98 is a surprisingly primitive weapon when one considers it was introduced in 1938; it would have been more at home in 1915, firing jam tins. It seems to have been designed with the intention of providing the most simple and foolproof weapon possible, and yet one with a most devastating effect at the target. The mortar is a simple construction of barrel, baseplate and bipod; the bipod feet ride in a traversing arc at the front of the baseplate and there is no means of adjusting the elevation, which

is fixed at 40 degrees. There is a vent hole at the rear end of the barrel, reminiscent of a smoothbore cannon, and two hooks protrude at the sides of the barrel-bipod clamp. Around the muzzle is clamped an adjustable range scale in the form of a graduated rod that protrudes beyond the muzzle.

The projectile is most peculiar; a square box holding about 7lb (3.2kg) of Shimose (picric acid) explosive, attached to a stick. In the base of the explosive container are two holes, and into these screwed two friction igniters with pull-cords. The propelling charge was supplied in the form of small silk bags of gunpowder, and one or more of these, depending on the range required, was dropped down the barrel. Then the range scale was set, according to the charge in use, which caused a greater or lesser amount of the scale rod to extend past the muzzle. The stick of the projectile was now entered into the muzzle; because of the projecting range scale, the entry of the stick was stopped when the range scale touched the base of the explosive container. This determined the chamber volume and thus the range was controlled.

The strings of the two friction igniters were now looped around the hooks on the barrel clamp. Another friction igniter was inserted into the vent in the breech end, and its string pulled to fire the igniter and ignite the propelling charge, launching the bomb. As the bomb left the mortar, so the two strings on the friction igniters in the explosive charge were pulled free, igniting delay trains in the explosive unit that burned for seven seconds before detonating the charge. This form of fusing meant that for the best results one should adjust one's position and range so that the bomb landed just as the fuses burned through, and this is probably the reason why the Model 89 grenade launcher was more often used. While the charge gave a very effective result at the target, particularly against defensive works, the weapon was too inflexible.

BELOW The Type 89 50mm mortar was a common sight in the Japanese army during the war. It was known as the "Knee Mortar" to Allied troops.

Type 99

Caliber: 81mm	**Firing mechanism:** Selective drop or trip
Barrel: 25.25in (641mm), smoothbore	**Elevation:** 45–70 degrees
Weight: 52lb (23.6kg)— barrel 17lb 8oz (7.9kg), bipod 16lb 8oz (7.5kg), baseplate 18lb (8.2kg	**Traverse:** 16 degrees
	Projectile: HE 6lb 15oz (3.14kg)
	Max range: 6,600ft (2,012m)
	Rate of fire: 15rpm

The Japanese Army adopted an 81mm Mortar, the Type 97, in 1937, though it seems that few were used. It was adapted from the familiar Stokes-Brandt model, and except for one or two minor changes it was the same as that used by the United States and Italian armies. It was known, somewhat confusingly, as the Type 97 High Angle Infantry Gun, but due to its size it was not popular, and in 1939 a shortened version, known as the Model 99 Small Trench Mortar, was introduced. It is remarkably similar to the German "*Stummelwerfer*," and it may well be that the Germans adopted the idea after seeing the Japanese weapon.

The 81mm barrel was shortened and a new baseplate and bipod produced to suit the new dimensions. The result was efficient and produced a handy weapon with good performance. The original Type 97, like the other Brandt designs, was provided with two bombs, light and heavy; documentary evidence suggests that both were made available for the Model 99, but no report can be found which confirms the use of the heavy bomb in service, and it is believed that only the light bomb was ever used with the short model mortar.

The firing mechanism is of interest. The firing pin could be locked in position, protruding from its housing; in this mode the bomb could be drop-fired. As an alternative, the firing pin could be retracted into the housing until its base rested on a conical shaft which passed across the base cap and protruded from the breech end of the mortar at right-angles to the barrel axis. The bomb was now dropped down the barrel until it came to rest with its cartridge cap poised above the firing pin housing. To fire, the end of the cross-shaft was struck with a wooden mallet; this drove the shaft in and, due to its conical section, forced the firing pin up to strike the cartridge cap.

As well as high-explosive bombs, the Type 99 could fire a white phosphorous smoke bomb, a green signal flare, and a parachute smoke signaling bomb.

Russian mortars

M1940

Caliber: 50mm	**Elevation:** Fixed 45 or 75 degrees
Barrel: 21in (533mm), smoothbore	**Traverse:** 9° at 45°, 16° at 75°
Weight: 21lb 5oz (9.66kg)	**Projectile:** HE 1lb 8oz (0.68kg)
Firing mechanism: Drop	**Max range:** 800m
	Rate of fire: 30rpm

The Soviet infantry in the immediate prewar years were confronted with a bewildering variety of small mortars, largely the result of designers trying to tell the army what it ought to have, rather than the army telling the designers what it needed. The first 5cm mortar was issued in 1938 but was rapidly withdrawn and replaced by the Model 1939, which in turn was soon discarded in favor of the M1940. This latter model was rather more successful, having been designed with an ear to the army's complaints about the earlier versions, and it was a much simpler and more effective weapon.

The M1940 was fairly conventional in appearance, using a small baseplate, barrel, and pressed-steel bipod with elevating and traversing screws, but in addition it had a small recoil buffer between the barrel and the bipod yoke, a refinement hardly necessary in such a small weapon. The most interesting technical feature was the system of controlling range. Although the elevation gear allowed setting of any elevation between 45 and 75 degrees, the sights were arranged so that the mortar could only be fired at these two angles, and control of range at each elevation was achieved by venting a proportion of the propellant gas to the atmosphere, thus reducing the amount available to propel the bomb. The firing-pin holder was constructed to act as a spring-loaded poppet valve, the amount of opening of which could be governed by a setting sleeve.

While the M1940 was quite efficient, it was still capable of simplification in the interests of faster production and easier handling, and it was replaced in the following year by the M1941. This dispensed with the bipod and buffer and hinged the barrel to the baseplate. The sights were simplified and the gas system changed to vent through an exhaust pipe below the barrel. The same method of firing at fixed elevations was retained.

Although serviceable enough, and comparable with the British 2in and German 5cm models, the Soviet 5cm did not see

the war through. Its range and effect were satisfactory in a defensive role, but when the Red Army took the offensive its performance was insufficient. In 1941 the infantry division had 84 of these mortars, but by December 1944 there were none, their place having been taken by an increased allocation of 82mm models.

M1941 and M1943

Data: M1941	**Firing mechanism:** Drop
Caliber: 50mm	**Elevation:** Fixed 45 or 75 degrees
Barrel: 22in (559mm), smoothbore	**Traverse:** 9° at 45°, 16° at 75°
Weight: 22lb (10kg)	**Projectile:** HE 1lb 8oz (0.68kg)
	Max range: 800m
	Rate of fire: 30rpm

Data: M1943	**Firing mechanism:** Drop
Caliber: 82mm	**Elevation:** 45–80 degrees
Barrel: 48in (1.22m), smoothbore	**Traverse:** 3 degrees right or left
Weight: 99lb 3oz (45kg) in action— barrel 42lb 14oz (20.4kg), bipod and wheels 45lb 3oz (20.5kg), baseplate 41lb 14oz (19kg)	**Projectile and weight:** HE 7lb 6oz (3.4kg)
	Max range: 10,170ft (3,100m)
	Rate of fire: 15–20rpm

As with the 5cm model, the Soviet infantry was presented with a rapid succession of 82mm mortars: the models 1936, 1937, and 1941. The first two were quite orthodox, using the usual baseplate and bipod configuration, and although precise information is unobtainable it seems that their faults lay not so much in their performance as in their design; certainly the M1937 exhibited a baseplate made up from steel stampings welded together and other components showing an eye to mass-production techniques, and it may well be that the successive models merely showed improved constructional methods without changing the performance very much.

The 1941 model replaced all the others and carried the mass-production theme even further. The baseplate was a circular steel stamping, and the twin spring buffers of the 1937 model were replaced by a much simpler single-spring pattern contained in a tube beneath the barrel. But the greatest change was in the bipod assembly. Previous designs—indeed all designs based on the normal barrel-bipod-baseplate layout—required that either the three components be carried individually by manpower or that they be carried in some form of vehicle: for example the British 3in was usually carried piecemeal on a tracked Universal Carrier. Neither of these solutions satisfied the Russians; transport was in short supply, and while the soldiers were capable of carrying the component parts, once so loaded they could carry little else, such as their own personal equipment, arms, and ammunition. The designers of this mortar, therefore, adopted a novel solution and formed small stub axles on the lower ends of the bipod legs. Onto these axles fitted small pressed-steel wheels, so that the mortar could be trundled along with the barrel and baseplate clamped to the bipod, and brought into action very rapidly without having to reassemble the whole thing. Once in action the wheels were removed to allow the bipod feet to dig into the ground.

This design was eventually refined by designing the lower section of the bipod so that the wheels remained permanently attached, being so located that they were clear of the ground when the mortar was in action. As well as saving time, this also placed more weight on the bipod and made the mortar more stable when firing. This version became known as the M1943.

The 82mm mortars were the standard rifle division mortars of the Red Army. Originally the division was furnished with 84, but as the 5cm model declined in importance, holdings of the 82mm were increased and by the end of the war the divisional strength was up to 98 mortars.

United States mortars

M2 60mm mortar

Caliber: 60mm	**Firing mechanism:** Drop, fixed striker
Barrel: 28.6in (726mm), smoothbore	**Elevation:** 40–85 degrees
Weight: 42lb (19kg)— barrel 12lb 13oz (5.8kg), bipod 16lb 6oz (7.44kg), baseplate 12lb 13oz (5.8kg)	**Traverse:** 31 degrees right or left
	Projectile: HE 2lb 15oz (1.34kg)
	Max range: 5,955ft (1,815m)
	Rate of fire: 18rpm

During the course of World War I the U.S. Army adopted a variety of British and French mortars and rifle grenades, none of which proved satisfactory. In the 1920s research began to find some form of light mortar or grenade thrower. The 60mm mortar was a French design by the Edgar Brandt company, and to all intents and purposes it was no more than a scaled-down model of its 81mm model. After evaluation of a number supplied by Brandt, a license to manufacture was obtained and the drawings modified to U.S. standards, after which manufacture began in the United States.

The weapon, while similar in tactical use to the British 2in, is heavier and somewhat more complex. It consists of barrel, breech cap, and fixed firing pin, while the Mount M2 comprises baseplate and bipod with traversing and elevating mechanisms. Sighting was by the "Sight, Collimator M4," which carried deflection and elevation scales and was mounted on a special bracket on the mount traversing head.

The ammunition provided included the high explosive shell M49A2 of 2lb 15oz (1.34kg), a practice shell M50A2 similar to the HE shell but containing only a small charge of gunpowder to give a smoke puff on impact, and an illuminating shell M83. This carried a 100,000 candlepower star unit suspended from a parachute, and gave illumination for 25 seconds while falling to the ground. This shell was used in considerable numbers to provide battlefield illumination at night so that machine guns and other squad weapons could see their targets. The mortar was also issued to antitank gun detachments for the same purpose.

VARIANTS

Mortar M1 on Mount M1

The original French-manufactured model, purchased in small numbers for evaluation and later issued for service. It was almost identical with the M2, the only changes in the latter being for manufacturing convenience, ie, the adoption of standard American threads and tolerances.

The U.S. 60mm M2 Mortar

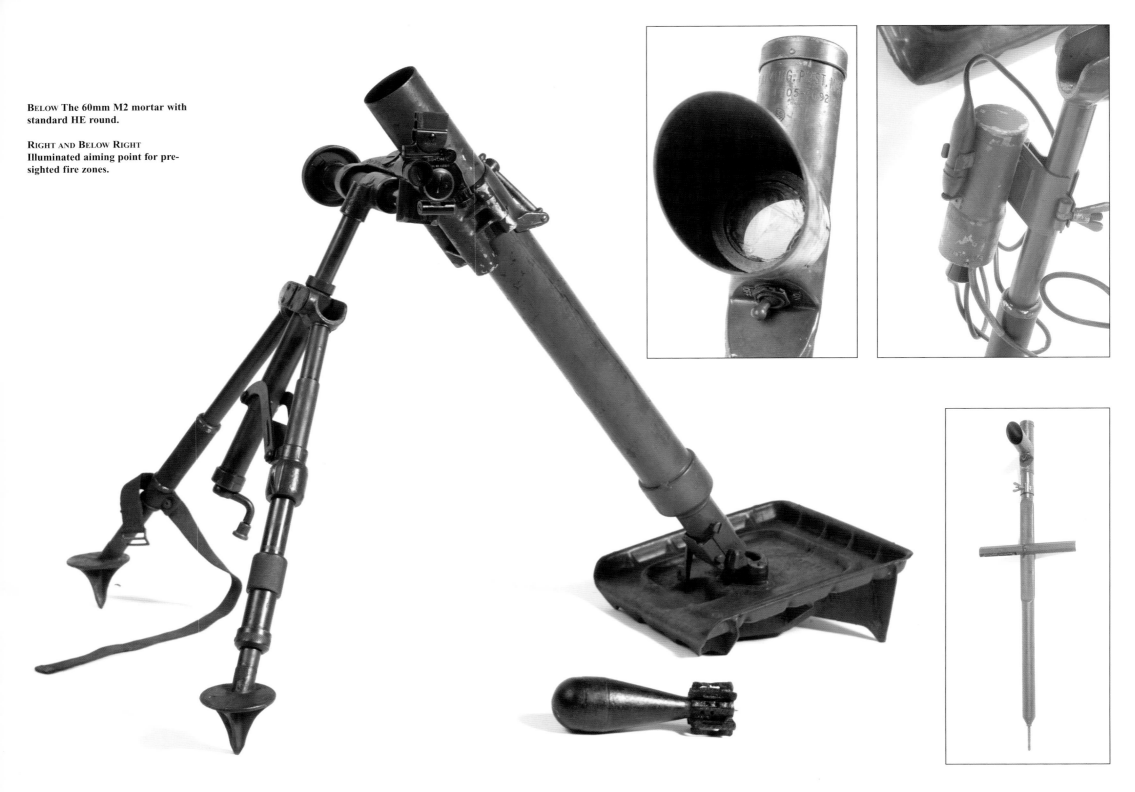

BELOW The 60mm M2 mortar with standard HE round.

RIGHT AND BELOW RIGHT Illuminated aiming point for pre-sighted fire zones.

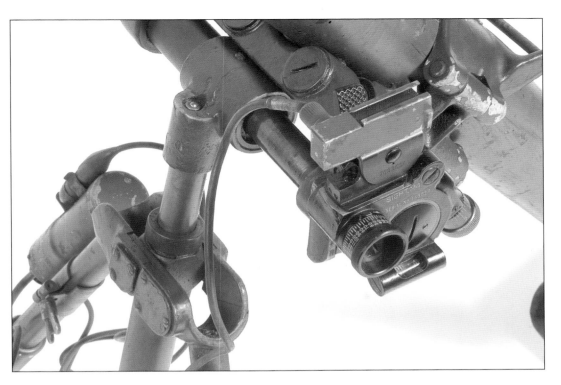

LEFT AND FAR LEFT In these views the battery pack for the illumination kit can be seen on the bipod leg. To this is clamped a small torch, powered from the same batteries.

RIGHT Data plate.

BELOW LEFT AND INSET Detail of the Sight M4 with illumination kit fitted.

BELOW AND BOTTOM RIGHT Two details of the traversing and elevating equipment.

MOUNT, MORTAR. 60 MM. M5 NO.
ORD. DEPT. U.S.A.
VIMALERT Co. 1944
INSP.

SIGHT, M4
SERIAL NO. 133627

M1 81mm mortar

Caliber: 81mm

Barrel: 49.5in (1.26m), smoothbore

Weight: 136lb (61.7kg)—
barrel 44lb 8oz (20.19kg),
bipod 46lb 8oz (21.1kg),
baseplate 45lb (20.4kg)

Firing mechanism: Drop, fixed striker

Elevation: 40–85 degrees

Traverse: 5 degrees right or left

Projectile:
HE M43 6lb 14oz (3kg),
HE M36 10lb 10oz (4.82kg),
smoke M57 10lb 12oz (4.9kg)

Max range:
HE M43 9,870ft (3,008m),
HE M36 7,674ft (2,339m),
smoke 7,410ft (2,259m)

Rate of fire: 18rpm

The U.S. Army adopted the Stokes 3in mortar in 1918 and retained numbers of them after the war ended. As the Stokes, in its 1918 guise, was a trifle primitive, work began in 1920 to improve it, with particular emphasis on improving the accuracy of the finned bomb. While this work was in progress the French company of Edgar Brandt had developed an 81mm mortar based on Stokes's design, and they offered this model to the U.S. War Department for test. As it appeared to meet the specifications stated by the army, a number were purchased for evaluation. Subsequent tests proving successful, the manufacturing rights were purchased from Brandt and the weapon entered U.S. service in the early 1930s.

It was originally provided with two high-explosive bombs, a "light" and a "heavy." The latter had an unusual type of fin assembly consisting of four fins, each with a pair of spring loaded fins at its outer edge. These spring units were folded up and secured by soft rivets until fired, when the force of the explosion drove a shearing ring forward and cut the rivets, allowing the fins to open out under spring pressure once the bomb had left the muzzle. Once unfolded, the fins were of greater caliber than the bomb, thus they were well out into the air stream to give the bomb excellent stability. While theoretically very sound indeed, Brandt was some years ahead of anyone else in appreciating the value of super-caliber fins. It was found in practice that the springs tended to lose their tension in storage and the cartridge explosion often bent or warped the fins, leading to unstable or inaccurate flight. As a result this bomb, the M45, was declared obsolete in March 1940 and replaced by the M56 model of the same weight and general appearance but with a cluster of conventional fins.

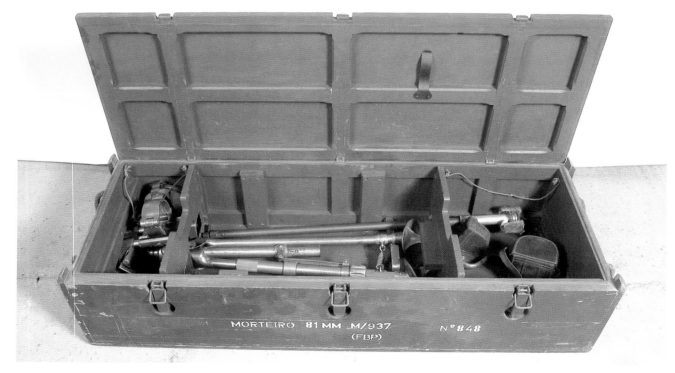

VARIANTS

There were no variant models of either mortar or mount. However there were a variety of self-propelled carriages provided or proposed that are summarized here:

Mortar Carrier M4 or M4A1
The 81mm mortar installed in the bed of a half-track weapons carrier, firing to the rear.

Mortar Carrier M21 (ex T19)
Similar to M4 but firing to the front, over the cab.

Mortar Carrier T27
Project believed to involve a tank chassis; initiated in April 1944 it was closed down shortly afterwards.

Mortar Carrier T27E1
Spin-off from the T27, this was intended to use redundant light tank chassis without turrets. Begun in April 1944 it was closed down about a year later without having shown any results.

RIGHT **The 81mm M1 mortar.**

LEFT **Unpacking the 81mm M1 mortar—this one a Venezuelan version—from its case.**

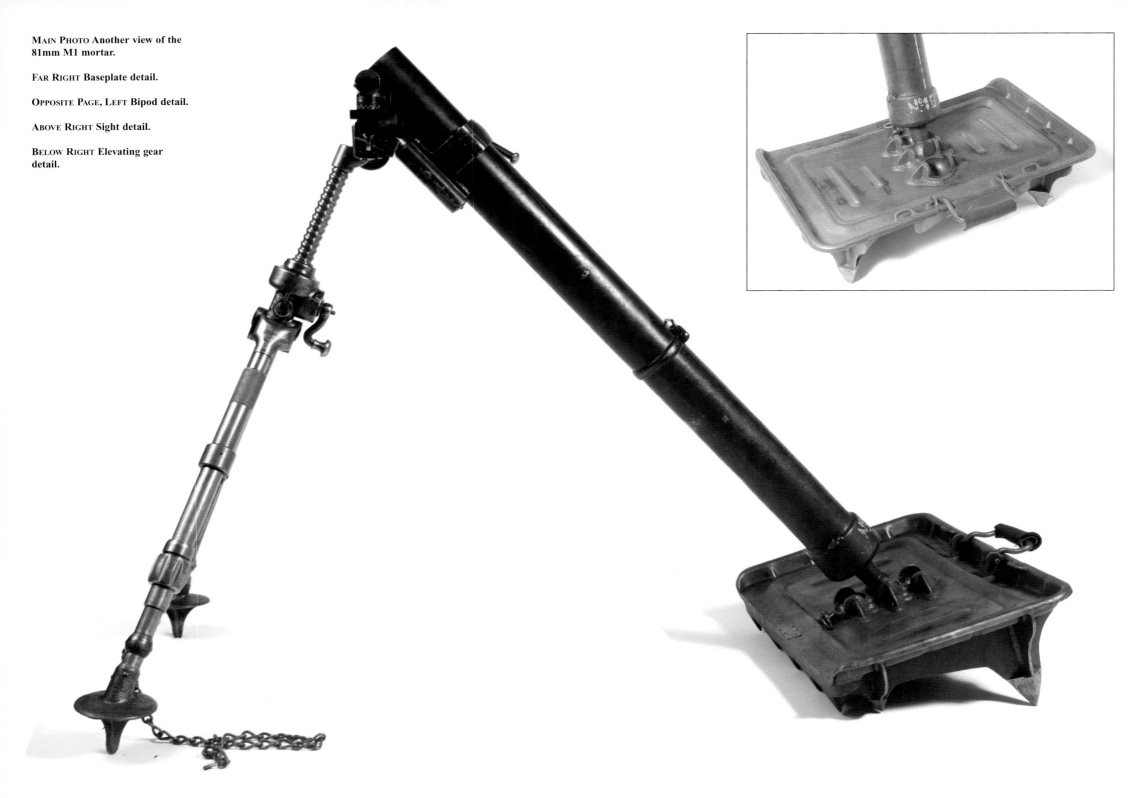

MAIN PHOTO Another view of the 81mm M1 mortar.

FAR RIGHT Baseplate detail.

OPPOSITE PAGE, LEFT Bipod detail.

ABOVE RIGHT Sight detail.

BELOW RIGHT Elevating gear detail.

ANTITANK WEAPONS

Of all the weapons in the infantryman's armory the antitank weapon most clearly illustrates the changing face of war in the 1930s and 1940s. The earliest infantry antitank weapon was the German T Gewehr of World War I an emergency counter to the appearance of British tanks. This was basically an oversized rifle and the principal persisted into the interwar years with Poland, Germany, Russia, Britain, and Japan all producing antitank rifles.

With the start of the war the thickness of armor protection applied to new generations of AFVs rapidly increased, and inevitably a stage was reached where a weapon that relied solely on the kinetic energy of a bullet to penetrate armor was too large to be man-portable. The antitank rifle was largely rendered obsolete by 1940, although some ingenious devices permitting the firing of overcaliber warheads served to extend the usefulness of German antitank rifles.

The solution was the development of the shaped charge warhead, which depended on focusing explosive energy to burn a hole through the armor. There were a variety of means employed to get the warhead to the target, ranging from the suicidal placement by hand of magnetic mines or "sticky bombs;" the hand-thrown *Panzerwurfmine* or RPG1943; and even the use of trained dogs. But the most successful infantry-borne antitank weapons were the British PIAT, the U.S. Bazooka, and the German *Panzerfaust* and *Panzerschreck*. The rocket-propelled weapons were a sign of things to come: today rocket propelled infantry weapons are common in all modern armies.

ABOVE The German T Gewehr, the first infantry antitank weapon.

RIGHT The Boys antitank rifle—see page 244.

CENTER RIGHT The U.S. Army's Bazooka—see page 248.

FAR RIGHT Two views of the German Bazooka—the *Panzerschreck*—see page 247.

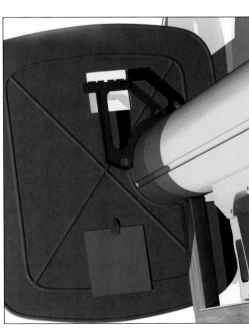

Boys antitank rifle

BELOW Right-hand side view of the Boys antitank rifle.

BOTTOM RIGHT Ammunition box.

BOTTOM LEFT Montage of ammunition clip, ammunition pouches, and manual.

Caliber: .55

Length: 63.5in (1.61m)

Weight: 36lb (16.33kg)

Barrel: 36in (914mm), seven grooves, right-hand twist

Feed system: Five-round, top-mounted, detachable box magazine

System of operation: Bolt action

Muzzle velocity: 3,250ft (991m)/sec

Penetration: >0.1in (20mm) of armor at 1,640ft (500m), 0 degrees slope

Manufacturer: Royal Small Arms Factory, Enfield Lock, England

Values: $2,500–$3,700

The Boys antitank rifle was developed in 1936 and entered service on November 24, 1937. It was probably the best of its class at the time. Firing a steel-cored bullet it could penetrate any current tank at 750ft (230m). In 1937 the average tank armor was 15mm (0.06in) thick, so the Boys Rifle stood a good chance of making its presence felt. The recoil of the heavy cartridge was vicious, and the gun was fitted with a muzzle brake and allowed to recoil in a cradle mounting against a powerful buffer spring. A monopod acted as front support, and the butt was thickly padded with rubber.

The Boys saw action in France, Norway, and the Far East, but it was rarely successful. When used from a prepared ambush position, it was marginally effective. But it was ineffective in the face of wide-ranging Blitzkrieg tactics. It was rarely seen after 1941, being replaced by less conventional but more effective weapons.

VARIANT

Rifle, Boys, Mark II

Approved on July 4, 1942, this version had a barrel 4.5in (114mm) shorter than the Mk. I, with certain unstressed components of aluminum and the butt pad stuffed with feathers, all in an endeavor to produce a lighter model for use by airborne troops. Although approved, it was never taken into action; shortening the barrel had reduced the velocity and penetration, and by the time the airborne troops went into action they had been provided with the PIAT (see page 250).

German antitank weapons

Panzerfaust

	30K	30	60	100	150		30K	30	60	100	150
Tube:	31.5in	31.5in	31.5in	31.5in	31.5in	Tube:	800mm	800mm	800mm	800mm	800mm
Bomb length:	14.25in	19.5in	19.5in	19.25in	21.85in	Bomb length:	362mm	495mm	495mm	489mm	555mm
Diameter, bomb:	3.95in	5.9in	5.9in	5.95in	4.13in	Diameter, bomb:	100mm	150mm	150mm	151mm	105mm
Velocity ft/sec:	98	98	148	200	270	Velocity m/sec:	30	30	45	61	82
Penetration at 11°:	5.5in	7.9in	7.9in	7.9in	7.9in	Penetration at 11°:	140mm	200mm	200mm	200mm	200mm
Weight complete:	7.5lb	11.5lb	15lb	15lb	14.75lb	Weight complete:	3.4kg	5.2kg	6.8kg	6.8kg	6.7kg

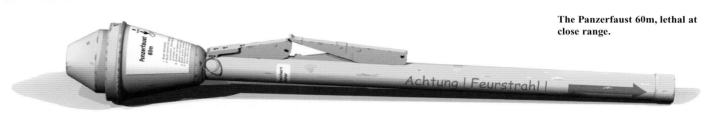

The Panzerfaust 60m, lethal at close range.

The appearance of the new T-34 and KV-1 Russian tanks in 1942 led to a demand for a light but potent antitank weapon for infantry use, and Dr. Langweiler of the Hugo Schneider Aktien Gesellschaft (HASAG) was given the task of developing a suitable weapon during the summer of that year. Langweiler produced a simple recoilless device with a hollow-charge warhead, which, while mechanically successful, was difficult to aim. This was modified, with a longer tube so that the flash was directed behind the holder. The warhead was fitted with thin spring steel fins which wrapped around the tail shaft until the weapon was fired. The warhead was of much greater diameter than the tube. A simple sight was fitted and this device was named *Panzerfaust 30*, the figure indicating the fighting range in meters. After a variety of tests it was put into production in October 1943 at a rate of 200,000 per month. Another version, the *Panzerfaust 30 Klein*, using a small diameter bomb, was also put into production, its target production being 100,000 per month.

The next model featured an increased propellant charge, a thicker-walled launch tube, raising the velocity and increasing the range. The design was completed early in 1944 and during the summer production was switched from the *Panzerfaust 30* to the *Panzerfaust 60*. Further development to increase range led to the *Panzerfaust 100*, in which the propelling charge was designed in two units separated by an air gap in order to achieve staggered ignition and a more sustained thrust. This went into production in November 1944 in addition to the 60.

All the Panzerfaust models so far had been one-shot weapons, the firing tube being thrown away after use. In an attempt to economize, as well as improve performance, the *Panzerfaust 150* was developed, in which the propellant charge was attached to the tail of the bomb and the firing mechanism used a strip of ignition caps. In this way the tube could be rapidly reloaded by the user up to ten times before it became unserviceable. The bomb was also redesigned to economize in explosive while still retaining the same penetrative performance and, as an antipersonnel device, a fragmentation sleeve of notched cast iron could be slipped over the warhead. Production of this model began in January 1945 and continued until April, during which time about 100,000 were made, but very few of them reached the hands of troops.

The design of all the models to see service was very similar. The launch tube was a mild-steel tube with a slight restriction in the rear end to serve as a venturi nozzle, and a simple trigger mechanism and rear sight unit on top. The warhead was of thin sheet metal on a wooden tail rod that carried the flexible fins. The propelling charge was in a paper tube behind the bomb and beneath the trigger unit. The fore sight was a pin on the edge of the bomb warhead. To fire, the safety pin locking the trigger was withdrawn and the rear sight leaf erected. This had three apertures for 30, 60, and 80 meters. Lifting the sight leaf also freed the trigger. The user tucked the tube beneath his arm and took aim at the target, squeezing the trigger downward to fire. This lifted and released a leaf spring carrying a small firing pin, allowing it to snap down on to a percussion cap which ignited the propellent charge and launched the warhead.

The Panzerfaust was a simple, easily produced and highly effective antitank weapon and it was widely used by the German Army on both the Eastern and Western fronts. In the hands of determined troops it could stop any tank then in existence.

Panzerbuchse S18-1000

Caliber: 20mm

Length: 85in (2.16m)

Weight: 120lb (54.4kg)

Barrel: 57in (1.45m) long, eight grooves, right-hand twist

Feed system: 5 or 10-round detachable box magazine

System of operation: Recoil, semi-automatic rotating bolt

Muzzle velocity: 3,000ft (914m)/sec

Penetration: 1.4in (35mm) at 984ft (300m) at 0 degrees slope

Manufacturer: Rheinmetall-Borsig/Solothurn AG, Germany

During the 1920s Rheinmetall obtained control of the Swiss firm, Solothurn AG, and through Solothurn a controlling interest in the Austrian Steyr company. This enabled enabling Rheinmetall to produce and sell weapons—something that the Versailles Treay had banned. One of the weapons so developed was a 20mm anti-tank rifle known as the S18-100, which was sold to a number countries either for trials (as, for example, Britain) or for adoption into service (as, for example, Hungary). It was later improved by lengthening the barrel and providing a more powerful cartridge. This model was known as the S18-1000, and was adopted by Switzerland, Holland, Italy, and Germany.

It would appear that the number bought by Germany was relatively small and the weapon was adopted largely on an extended trial basis; it did not receive a model number and it was rarely seen in action. While the 20mm, armor-piercing shell, with explosive filling and base fuse, was efficient, the weapon itself was too heavy and cumbersome to show much advantage over the PzB38 and 39 rifles.

Operation was semi-automatic; the barrel recoiled within a support sleeve and the rotating bolt, then unlocked, moved rearward to extract and eject the fired case, and then returned to chamber a fresh cartridge. The magazine was mounted on the left side of the gun and the weapon was supported by a bipod and butt monopod. As well as the usual type of open sight, a telescope sight was issued with some models, and there was also a two-wheeled mounting provided for movement, pulled by the two-man team.

Panzerbuchse 38

Caliber: 7.92mm

Length: 51in (1.3m)

Weight: 35lb (15.9kg)

Barrel: 43in (1.09m) long, four grooves, right-hand twist

Feed system: Single shot

System of operation: Vertical sliding block, semi-automatic

Muzzle velocity: 3,975ft (1,212m)/sec

Penetration: 1in (25mm) at 984ft (300m) at 30 degrees slope

Manufacturer: Rheinmetall-Borsig AG, Düsseldorf, Germany

The German PzB38 antitank rifle was an elegant design with a good performance obtained by using a 7.92mm bullet allied to a 13mm cartridge to give an extremely powerful propelling charge. The mechanism was unusual in that the breech closure was by a vertical sliding block on the lines of an artillery weapon. To operate the weapon the breech was opened by swinging the pistol grip forward and down, whereupon the block was held open by the extractors and the pistol grip could be returned to its normal place. A cartridge was then loaded by hand, releasing the extractors and allowing the breechblock to close by spring pressure. On firing, the weapon recoiled in its stock and a cam opened the block to eject the empty case on the return movement of the barrel, coming to rest with the block held open ready for the next round to be loaded.

The ammunition was unusual in that the bullet contained a steel core and a small capsule of lachrymatory (tear) gas, the intention being to penetrate the tank and there liberate the gas to contaminate the atmosphere inside and force the crew to evacuate the vehicle. In this it seems to have been quite unsuccessful. The chemical agent was only 0.4 grains in weight, and because it was next to the tracer element, it seems probable that the chemical had been destroyed by the heat of the tracer before it ever reached the target. In any event no one ever appears to have noticed the lachrymatory effect and it was not known by the Allies until specimens of ammunition were captured and examined. The legality of such a cartridge seems to sail rather close to the Geneva Convention on gas, though it probably escapes the letter of the law by being primarily a piercing projectile and not a chemical projectile. So far as is known the PzB38 seems to have been little used in combat. The only likely theater for its use would have been the Polish campaign, because it was largely replaced in service by the PzB39 before the 1940 campaign in France. Moreover the rapid movements of the German Army did not invite the use of antitank rifles.

BELOW The Panzerfaust 60m projectile—note fins.

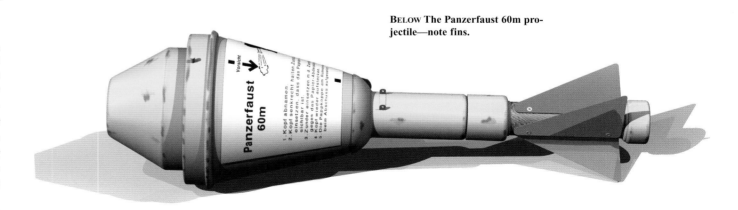

Panzerbuchse 39

Caliber: 7.92mm

Length: 62.25in (1.58m)

Weight: 27.25lb (12.36kg)

Barrel: 42.75in (1.09m) long, four grooves, right-hand twist

Feed system: Single shot

System of operation: Vertical sliding block, hand-operated

Muzzle velocity: 3,975ft (1,212m)/sec

Penetration: 1in (25mm) at 984ft (300m) at 30 degrees slope

Manufacturers: Rheinmetall-Borsig, Düsseldorf, Germany Steyr-Daimler-Puch AG, Vienna, Austria

The PzB38 was a satisfactory weapon, but like much of the German Army's early equipment, it was too luxurious a solution and ill-suited to manufacture in quantity. It was, therefore, decided to develop a simplified version, and the PzB39 was the result. The vertical sliding breechblock was retained but the semi-automatic feature was discarded, the block being entirely hand-operated by swinging the pistol grip back and forth. The recoiling barrel was also dropped, but by way of recompense, it was now fitted with a muzzle brake, so that the recoil felt by the firer was about the same as before. A minor addition was the fitting of two ready-use magazines, small boxes each containing ten rounds clipped to brackets at each side of the breech where they could be reached easily by the firer. This was an interesting reversion to the "quick-loader" that was common on Continental single-shot military rifles in the 1880s.

Because the barrel was almost the same length and the ammunition was the same, the performance of the PzB39 was equal to that of the PzB38, but apart from very limited use in the 1940 campaign in France, the PzB saw practically no action. An interesting comment was made in a British report on the examination of a captured specimen in October 1941: "This weapon appears to be as cheap as a Sten gun; it would be difficult to better it."

VARIANTS

Granatbuchse 39

Once the antitank rifle's usefulness was put to an end by the increasing thickness of tank armor, the German Army very ingeniously converted numbers of the PzB39 rifles into grenade dischargers. The barrel was cut down to 24in (610mm) length and fitted with the usual 3cm rifled discharger cup. A special discharger cartridge, using the 13mm case with a special propelling charge and wooden bullet, was provided to launch the grenades. Its effective range in this role was 1,640ft (500m).

Raketenwerfer 43 (Puppchen)

Caliber: 8.8cm

Barrel length: 63in (1.6m)

Weight: 315lb (142.9kg)

Barrel: Smoothbore

Feed system: Single shot

System of operation: Closed-breech rocket launcher

Elevation: -14 to +23 degrees

Max range: 2,461ft (750m)

Muzzle velocity: 460ft (140m)/sec

Penetration: 4in (100mm) at 2,461ft (750m) range at 0 degrees slope

Manufacturer: Westfalische Anhaltische Sprengstoff AG, Reinsdorf, Germany

In 1944 the German Army requested designs of a light antitank gun for infantry use. One of the designs put forward was this weapon, developed by Dr. Erich von Holt of the Westfalische Anhaltische Sprengstoff AG of Reinsdorf (known as WASAG). In effect it was the 8.8cm *Panzerschreck* rocket launcher mounted on the carriage of the *2.8cm schweres Panzerbuchse 41* taper-bore gun (which by that time was obsolete), and with the rear end of the launcher closed by a breech mechanism of simple sliding-block pattern. The projectile was the same rocket-propelled hollow charge bomb as used with the *Panzerschreck*, but with the addition of a sealing unit on the tail drum which resembled a short cartridge case.

The exact number of RW43s that saw use is in some doubt; some reports speak of several, others refer to it as a prototype. Obviously it did not meet the requirements of the army in one respect in that it still used a rocket, and the demand was for a weapon using less propellant than a rocket solution. But it seems likely that upward of a hundred were actually in the hands of troops when the war ended, and what few accounts there are seem to indicate that the design was successful.

Raketenwerfer 54 (Ofenrohr or Panzerschreck)

Caliber: 88.9mm

Length: 64.5in (1.64m)

Weight: 20.25lb (9,19kg)

Barrel: 62.5in (1.59m), smoothbore

System of operation: Single-shot rocket launcher

Projectile: Hollow-charge, 7.25lb (3.29kg)

Max range: 492ft (150m)

Penetration: 4in (100mm) at 492ft (150m) at 0 degrees

Manufacturer: HASAG, Meuselwitz, Germany

Ofenrohr (Stovepipe) or *Panzerschreck* (Tank Terror) was a shoulder-fired rocket launcher inspired by the U.S. Army's 2.36in Bazooka after specimens had been captured by the Germans. The German Army had been looking for a suitable weapon to use against Soviet tanks. After trials of the Bazooka it was decided to produce a German equivalent. The opportunity was taken of making improvements which, it is interesting to note, were incorporated by the U.S. in later models of the weapon. The caliber was increased to 88mm in order to provide a better and more effective warhead; a drum tail was used, and the electric firing current was derived from an impulse magneto driven by squeezing the firing gap. As with most first-generation launchers, the motor was still burning when it left the launcher and so a shield, which incorporated the rear sight, was provided. The weapon became notorious for the flame and smoke that came when it was fired, leading to the nickname *Ofenrohr*. The *Panzerschreck* was widely used; first issued in 1943, it remained on issue throughout the war, although when propellant became difficult to come by, other weapons were developed to replace it. It was highly effective against the tanks of the time, and appears to have been well liked by the soldiers.

The Raketenwerfer 54 with shaped-charge rocket projectile.

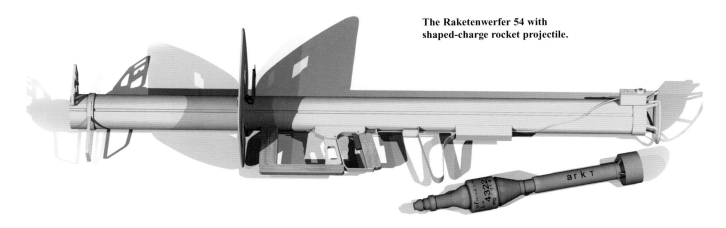

M1 Bazooka

Caliber: 2.36in	**Max range:** 1,200ft (366m)
Length: 54in (1.37m)	**Muzzle velocity:** 300ft (92m)/sec
Weight: 13.25lb (6.01kg)	**Penetration:** ca 80mm
Barrel: Smoothbore	**Manufacturer:**
Firing system: Electric; two dry batteries in pistol grip	Rockets by Edward G. Budd Co., Philadelphia, Pa., U.S. Launchers by General Electric, Bridgeport, Conn., U.S.
Projectile and weight: HEAT 3.4lb (1.54kg) rocket	

The Bazooka was a result of rocket research that had been carried out at Aberdeen Proving Ground since 1933. Service development of the weapon began in early 1942 and the Launcher, Rocket, 2.36 inch, antitank, M1 came into service in 1942 in time to be used by the U.S. troops in North Africa. At that time one of America's favorite comedians was Bob Burns, and one of his props was a wind instrument of his own invention which he called his "Bazooka." The similarity between this and the long pipe of the 2.36in launcher led to the adoption of the unofficial name Bazooka, though strictly speaking only this one is entitled to the name. A larger version, of 3.45in caliber, was developed towards the end of the war, but since the 2.36in appeared to be capable of doing all that was needed, the Super Bazooka was shelved, and it was not put into production until 1951, when the appearance of the Russian T-34 tank in Korea rendered the 2.36in model obsolete over night.

VARIANTS

Launcher M9
Improved design with the barrel in two pieces, joined by a bayonet catch, so that it could be dismantled and carried more easily. The firing gear was changed to an impulse magneto in the pistol grip. The shoulder stock and other fittings were improved, and the weight became 16lb (7.26kg).

Rockets M6, M6A1,2,3, etc.
A number of differing models of rocket were issued, with changes being made in various details such as electrical contacts, fin assembly.

Early models had a pointed nose; the M6A3 and subsequent models had a hemispherical nose.

Rocket M10
This rocket carried a warhead loaded with white phosphorus for producing smoke screens and also for anti-personnel use.

THIS PAGE AND OPPOSITE Photographs of the 60mm M9 Bazooka with an M6A1 shaped charge round. The M9 launcher was designed to be broken down into two halves to ease transport.

PIAT (Projectile Infantry Antitank)

Caliber: Not applicable
Length: 39in (991mm)
Weight: 32lb (14.5kg)
Barrel: None
Feed system: Single-shot
System of operation: Spigot discharger

Muzzle velocity: 350ft (107m)/sec
Penetration: ca 75mm
Projectile: Hollow-charge, 3lb (1.4kg)
Manufacturer: ICI Limited, England

The Projector, Infantry, Antitank (or PIAT, by which name it inevitably became known) was the result of several years of trial and experiment by Lt-Col Blacker, RA with various types of spigot mortars. In 1940 Blacker became involved with MD1 (Ministry of Defence 1) a military establishment concerned with the development of unorthodox weapons. There he produced a 29mm spigot mortar known as the Blacker Bombard in 1941, which was used extensively by Home Guard and airfield defense units.

Lt-Col Blacker then developed a smaller, man-portable, version that he called the Baby Bombard, but before he could do much with it he left MD1 for another post. The prototype Baby Bombard was left with MD1 where it was worked on by Major Jefferis and in June 1941 the Bombard, Baby, 0.625 inch No. 1 was given its first trials before the Ordnance Board. It was not until some months later, when Jefferis had developed an effective hollow-charge warhead, that the weapon was deemed workable. By mid-March pilot models of the PIAT were being made and the possibility of producing high explosive, smoke, flare, and signal projectiles was being explored. Trials of the new bomb were successful and the weapon went into production, final approval being given on August 31, 1942.

The mechanism of the PIAT was very simple; an enormous spring was compressed by unlatching the shoulder pad, standing on it, and lifting the weapon so that the spring and spigot were withdrawn into the body and held by a simple sear mechanism. The body was then returned to the shoulder pad and the weapon was ready to fire. A round was placed in guideways at the front and on pressing the trigger the spigot was released, entering the tail unit of the bomb and exploding the propelling cartridge. This explosion launched the warhead, and at the same time blew the spigot back into the body of the weapon, recocking it ready for the next shot. The maximum engagement range was about 300ft (91m), although the bomb could reach to 2,250ft (686m). The proposed anti-personnel and signal bombs never materialized.

Within its limitations the PIAT was a startlingly effective weapon, but it was never popular. It was heavy, awkward to cock, and violent to fire, but in spite of all that it was grudgingly respected as a weapon that did what it set out to do and could effectively stop a tank when used by a resolute man.

THIS PAGE AND OPPOSITE The Projector Infantry Antitank or PIAT with practice projectile. Note the firing "trough" and spigot (details below left) that fits inside the hollow tail of the projectile.

PTRS antitank rifle

Caliber: 14.5mm
Length: 84in (2.13m)
Weight: 46lb (20.87kg)
Barrel: 48in (1.22m) long, eight grooves, right-hand twist
Feed: 5-round box magazine

System of operation: Gas; semi-automatic; tipping bolt
Muzzle velocity: 3,320ft (1,012m)/sec
Penetration: 25mm (1in) at 1,640ft (500m) at 0 degrees slope
Manufacturer: State arsenals

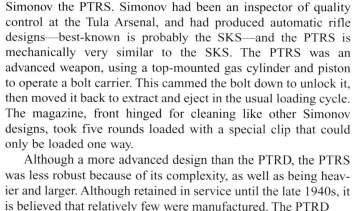

LEFT Cleaning kit and clip of cartridge cases.

The Russians realized before World War II started that it did not have an efficient infantry antitank capability. Two well-known designers projected 14.5mm antitank rifles: Vasily Degtyarev proposed the PTRD (D for Degtyarev) and Sergei Gavrilovich Simonov the PTRS. Simonov had been an inspector of quality control at the Tula Arsenal, and had produced automatic rifle designs—best-known is probably the SKS—and the PTRS is mechanically very similar to the SKS. The PTRS was an advanced weapon, using a top-mounted gas cylinder and piston to operate a bolt carrier. This cammed the bolt down to unlock it, then moved it back to extract and eject in the usual loading cycle. The magazine, front hinged for cleaning like other Simonov designs, took five rounds loaded with a special clip that could only be loaded one way.

Although a more advanced design than the PTRD, the PTRS was less robust because of its complexity, as well as being heavier and larger. Although retained in service until the late 1940s, it is believed that relatively few were manufactured. The PTRD had the same performance, because it used the same ammunition, and was easier to use and produce. Both weapons were retained in front-line use long after antitank rifles had disappeared from the inventories of other armies. Soviet soldiers used them against soft-skinned vehicles and even as a type of close support weapon in house-to-house fighting.

ABOVE AND BELOW Left and right-hand sides of the PTRS antitank rifle

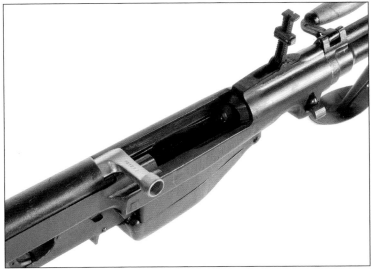

FAR RIGHT Detail of the open breach.

RIGHT Detail of the muzzle brake.

Bibliography

Adam, R.: *Modern Handguns*; Grange Books.

Badsey, Dr. S.: *D-Day*; Tiger Press.

Chant, C.: *Small Arms*; Silverdale Books.

Flack, J.: *Rifles and Pistols*; Select Editions.

Ford, R.: *The World's Great Handguns*; Brown Books.

Forty, G.: *Japanese Army Handbook 1939–1945*; Sutton Publishing.

Foss, C. & Gander, T.: *Infantry Weapons of the World*; Ian Allan Ltd.

Gander, T.: *The Bazooka*; Parkgate Books

Gregory, B. & Batchelor, J.: *Airborne Warfare 1918–1945*; Pheobus.

Hogg, I.: *Infantry Weapons of WW2*; Arms & Armour Press.

Hogg, I.: *Jane's Guns Recognition Guide*; Harper Collins.

Hogg, I.: *Military Small Arms Data Book*; Greenhill Books.

Hogg, I.: *Military Small Arms of the Twentieth Century*; John Weekes Purnell Book Services Ltd.

Mouret, J-N.: *Hand Guns of the World*; Bramley Books.

Myatt, Maj. F.: *Illustrated Encyclopedia of Pistols and Revolvers*; Blitz editions.

Norris, J.: *Infantry Mortars of WW2*; Osprey.

Schwing, N.: *Standard Catalog of Military Firearms, 2nd Ed.*; Krause Publications.

Walter, J.: *Military Rifles of Two World Wars*; Greenhill Books.

Walter, J.: *Rifles of the World*; Arms & Armour Press.

Zaloga, Z. & Grandsen, J.: *Soviet Tanks & Combat Vehicles of WW2*; Arms & Armour Press.

Index of weapons